Crisis Cultures

Crisis Cultures

Narratives of Western Modernity in the Digital Age

Nicholas Manganas

LEXINGTON BOOKS
Lanham • Boulder • New York • London

Published by Lexington Books
An imprint of The Rowman & Littlefield Publishing Group, Inc.
4501 Forbes Boulevard, Suite 200, Lanham, Maryland 20706
www.rowman.com

86-90 Paul Street, London EC2A 4NE

Copyright © 2025 by The Rowman & Littlefield Publishing Group, Inc.

All rights reserved. No part of this book may be reproduced in any form or by any electronic or mechanical means, including information storage and retrieval systems, without written permission from the publisher, except by a reviewer who may quote passages in a review.

British Library Cataloguing in Publication Information Available

Library of Congress Cataloging-in-Publication Data

Library of Congress Control Number: 2024945893

ISBN 978-1-66693-521-9 (cloth)
ISBN 978-1-66693-522-6 (electronic)

Dedication
Nuestro guía, Federico García Lorca nos dice "El más terrible de todos los sentimientos es el sentimiento de tener la esperanza muerta." Gracias, Ramón, por revivir mi esperanza cada día. Te dedico estas páginas con todo mi amor.

Contents

Acknowledgments		ix
Introduction		1
1	The Exper*i*ence *is* Out of Jo*i*nt	23
2	Crisis Ambientality	53
3	Confabulations	91
4	Queering Crisis	143
Conclusion		183
Bibliography		191
Index		211
About the Author		225

Acknowledgments

Writing a book on crisis cultures was always a challenging task. This project has encapsulated nearly every aspect of my being—every experience, conversation, hardship, and observation has shaped its pages. For this reason, my reading of our crisis-ridden culture cannot but be subjective. This subjectivity stems from the roots of my upbringing in a working-class neighborhood, my life straddling two cultures—the immigrant and the imposter—and the unwavering support of parents who always prioritized our family's well-being. Yet, this journey is not mine alone; it has been influenced and enriched by many remarkable individuals.

My deepest gratitude goes to Paul Allatson, Murray Pratt, and Alfredo Martínez-Expósito, who provided invaluable feedback on extensive portions of the manuscript. The lively and insightful conversations with Nicole Yade, Penda Gandega, Ibra Yade, and Sanou Yade at Bar Italia have continually prompted me to reevaluate my view of the world. I am also immensely thankful to my friends including Kiran Grewal, Julie Robert, Artemis Theodoris Papoutsis, Mariana Rodriguez, Ral García, Ruth Garreta, Beatriz Gándara, Elaine Millar, Ana Perić, Arantxa Lestón, Nick Hicks, Gary Quayle, Antonella Biscaro, George Tillianakis, and Adrián "Fos" Cendrero Brown—we will never forget you—for constantly keeping me thinking and challenging me to explore new intellectual terrains.

A special acknowledgment to my colleagues at the University of Technology Sydney, who have been a constant source of inspiration. Alice Loda, Kristine Aquino, Ilaria Vanni, Angela Giovanangeli, Macarena Gordillo de Paz, Elena Sheldon, Don Carter, Sita Chopra, and Carolyn Cartier, in particular, deserve mention; their engaging dialogues have subconsciously woven into the pages of this book. I extend a heartfelt thank you to Andrew Hurley and Alan Davison for their invaluable support and for granting me the time to fully commit to completing this work.

Finally, my deep appreciation is reserved for Ramon Fernández Díaz, who has been my steadfast supporter from the inception to the conclusion of this project. The lessons I've learned from you are innumerable, and your encouragement was indispensable in the creation of these pages.

In Crisis Cultures we live and breathe; in love and friendship we exhale and persevere. And as the celebrated Greek poet Constantine P. Cavafy reminds us, *Και αν δεν μπορείς να κάνεις τη ζωή σου όπως τη θέλεις, τούτο προσπάθησε όσο μπορείς: μην την εξευτελίζεις* ("And if you can't shape your life the way you want, at least try as much as you can not to degrade it"). As this book goes out into the world, it carries with it a piece of everyone who has touched its creation; my deepest thanks to each of you for being part of this story.

Introduction

We are living in a crisis culture. Living in a crisis culture refers to that uncanny feeling that something fundamental about the world has changed. We might not be sure what that change is, when it occurred, nor whether it is permanent. Deep down, though, we know that it is happening. Living in a crisis culture is living in an endless and uncertain present. A key characteristic of these crisis cultures is their ability to disrupt the usual flow of time, unsettling our understanding of past, present, and future. Although it is possible to refer to a crisis culture in the singular, it is more precise to refer to crisis cultures in the plural. We are immersed in *crisis cultures*.

In this book, I reflect on the processes whereby crisis as an epistemological category comes to be seen as characteristic of our historical moment. Rather than ask what is a crisis, I am more interested in asking what do crises *do*? What does it mean to call something a "crisis" or to claim that we are living *in* a crisis? What happens when crisis is everywhere, and we begin to experience crisis not as an event but as an ongoing process, without a beginning or an end? Inspired by Sara Ahmed's exploration of what emotions "do" (2004), I similarly interrogate what crises do within the framework of Western modernity. One of the book's central claims is that competing narratives of crisis circulate in the public domain until they form what can be described as *crisis cultures*. I do not offer any singular theory about what these complex crisis cultures do. Instead, my aim is to critically read the crisis narratives that circulate in crisis cultures and attempt to untangle the discursive knot they embody (Carpentier 2017). I, therefore, seek to expand the concerns of current scholarship on crisis by drawing on historical and transnational case studies and extending them to the current historical moment. My analysis will show that crisis cultures are generative. Crisis cultures beckon us to imagine a communal becoming when the horizons of past and future are blurred, our state of forgetfulness an anchor (Berger 2016, 139–140). Crisis cultures not only provoke temporal dislocation in that the past and the future overload one's ability to make sense of the present, but they also stimulate creative and communal responses to that sense of dislocation. This book tells the stories of some of those creative and communal responses.

While the epistemological concept of "crisis" is often discursively positioned as universal, crisis cultures are complex and culture specific. The way crisis cultures materialize varies according to time and place. I first began thinking about crisis as an epistemological category when I moved to Spain in the mid-2000s to pursue my doctoral research on the polarization of Spanish politics. By late 2007, there were faint whisperings that the economic system was unstable. The Socialist government at the time denied there was a "crisis" and insisted that the underlying foundations of the Spanish economy were sound. By 2008, the Global Financial Crisis (GFC), also known as the Great Recession, arrived and within months economies around the world began to implode. Financial crises are usually framed as historical events that emerge when there is a sharp downturn in economic conditions after a sustained period of expansion (Kindleberger & Aliber 2005, 1). Economies are somehow externally "shocked" at the peak of the business cycle and the system quickly learns to regenerate itself. Yet although I could *perceive* the crisis unfold in Southern Europe, I was not personally touched by it. Who experiences a crisis? Why was I, to paraphrase Lauren Berlant (2011, 222), *spared*?

In July 2011, I was visiting Athens with a Spanish friend. We traversed the old streets of Plaka, circling the ancient agora. When we arrived at the flea market in Monastiraki, we were suddenly caught in the middle of a tumultuous street protest, the smell of tear gas unnerving us. Caught in the middle of a narrow laneway, there were protesters throwing rocks and random objects on one side, a sea of policemen on scooters on the other. From ancient ruins that gave birth to Western democracy, we were witnessing something akin to a catastrophic turn, with little indication if the end result would be renewal or paralysis (Eliassen 2012, 56). We maneuvered ourselves out of the confrontation and followed the crowd to Syntagma Square at the foot of the Greek parliament. Just as we were approaching the square, the crowd stopped. Riot police wielding batons and shields suddenly appeared from around the corner and charged toward us. We followed the protesters' lead and ran for our lives. Unlike the young Greeks who were dressed in the middle of the Mediterranean summer in dark jeans, gas masks, and padded jackets, I was wearing the tourist uniform: shorts, t-shirt, flip flops, and a backpack. As we ran for our lives, somebody stepped on one of my flip flops, and I tumbled onto the hard asphalt, headfirst. To protect my fall, I fell on my hands and shoulder, spraining my wrist and chest, blood pouring out of my knees and elbow. I turned my head and saw the line of riot police just a few feet behind me, readying to fire off another round of tear gas. Pause. Evidently discerning that an unheeding tourist was caught in the local scuffle, they waited for me to clear out of the area before letting off more gas. Two local protesters approached and carried me away. They spoke to me in English as my tourist uniform demanded. Would the riot police have been so forgiving, I thought, had I not been wearing the tourist uniform?

I relate these anecdotes to underline how imbricated social bodies are within the crisis cultures that circulate around us, how personal they feel, and how inequitably their affective capacity is distributed. Yet in both the stories I tell above, I was a mere spectator. Crisis was something that was happening to *others*, not to me. I was a witness, an observer, training my academic eye on bodies that were not mine. These were not my stories to tell. If I would have to choose one pivotal event that spurred my thinking on the crisis cultures that I am discussing in this book, then the Global Financial Crisis would be it. Perhaps that is because of the deep impression that crisis made on me; what I witnessed was ongoing, immeasurable and—there is no better word for it—*knotty*. The crisis amassed an assemblage of intricate knots that were impossible to untie. Many of those knots are still entangled today.

Crisis as a concept has become ubiquitous in published output in recent years, both academic and journalistic. But this book is not about any one particular crisis. My analysis thus differs from much other scholarship on crisis as it does not follow the familiar pattern: crisis as a concept is defined, a particular crisis event or phenomenon is diagnosed, the workings of the crisis are laid bare, and its cultural impact named. Hence, we might hear that we now live in an Age of Anxiety (Wachs & Schaff 2020) or an Age of Anger (Mishra 2017), and some of the world's most important thinkers typically refer to axioms such as a New World Disorder (Žižek 2018), a Burnout Society (Han 2015), or Surplus Rage (Appadurai 2006).

Further contributing to this discourse is the concept of "polycrisis," articulated by Edgar Morin and Anne Brigitte Kern in *Homeland Earth: A Manifesto for the New Millennium* (1999). They argue that the world does not face a singular vital problem but a complex intersolidarity of multiple crises and uncontrolled processes (Morin & Kern 1999, 74). Unlike these authors, however, I am not particularly interested in naming our present historical moment, and *Crisis Cultures* is not an attempt to supersede any of the scholarship that does posit a critical diagnosis of society's troubles. Instead, it seeks to contextualize this wide-ranging published output within its very framework. In other words, the increasing prevalence of scholarship and mediated discussions on crisis is evidence of the very materiality of the crisis cultures I am critically reading. This observation aligns with Nico Carpentier's (2017) discussion on the intricate knot between discourse and materiality, suggesting that these two aspects are deeply entangled in the context of crisis cultures. Hence, by writing, reading, and discussing crises, we inevitably perpetuate *crisis cultures*. My focus is on critically reading the contested histories of crisis narratives, sketching out how they circulate, and ultimately how the productive tensions they engender build mass to form part of what I call *crisis cultures*. Although I do not proffer my own axiom for our current historical moment beyond advancing a framework that encompasses the multitude of crisis narratives that circulate in societies, my analysis of crisis cultures frames them as both affective and communal projects of becoming.

It is important first to distinguish between understanding crisis as an event and understanding crisis as an ongoing and protracted phenomenon. It is the latter that interests me in this book. The German historian Reinhart Koselleck's (2006) genealogy of the concept of crisis in the *Journal of the History of Ideas* remains the most noteworthy scholarly intervention with the concept, outlining its Greek origins and tracing its evolution to its more modern manifestations. The original Greek meaning of crisis is often recalled by scholars because it underlines how profoundly the concept evolved over the centuries. The etymology of crisis (κρίσις) traces to the Greek verb κρίνω—to separate—that could also refer to a decision or judgment (hence where the word criticism also has its roots) (Koselleck 2006, 358). For the Greeks, κρίσις was delimited to the specific subfields of medicine, law, and theology, and a crisis therefore typically referred to a critical moment between life or death, right or wrong, salvation or damnation (Koselleck 2006, 358). Since those early Greek origins, the concept was adopted into Latin and rapidly gained much metaphorical mutability, particularly in political language, and can now be found in almost all aspects of contemporary life (Koselleck 2006, 361).

Koselleck, however, is focused on how different permutations of the concept of crisis pertain to history itself; that is, how it has become the basic lens through which we interpret historical time (2006, 371). He identifies four interpretative possibilities in which the concept of crisis becomes a fundamental mode of interpreting history: (a) crisis is a decisive point requiring action after a particular chain of events; (b) crisis is an end point that will change the quality of history forever; (c) crisis is a permanent condition that may encompass a recurring critical situation or require decisions that have significant consequences; and (d) crisis is a historically immanent transitional phase that may lead to better or worse conditions depending on the proposed diagnosis (2006, 371–372). All of these interpretive possibilities indicate for Koselleck a new historical era in which crisis becomes the "structural signature of modernity" (2006, 372). And all of these possibilities, I might add, can still be utilized as lenses to interpret the array of crises that are continually unfolding around the globe.

One of my main claims in this book aligns with Koselleck's third interpretative possibility; that is, that crisis cultures are distinguished by the experience of crisis as an ongoing and protracted phenomenon. This is distinctly different from traditional understandings of crisis that generally conceptualized a crisis as a decisive and historically contingent event. But it does align with other recent theorists such as the anthropologists Henrik Vigh (2008) and Janet Roitman (2014), who suggest that crisis can be conceptualized as chronic, denoting it as a greater or lesser permanent state. Vigh suggests that crisis has now become a "pervasive context" instead of a rupture in the "order of things" (2008, 8), and Roitman posits that crisis is now presumed as "a protracted and potentially persistent state of ailment and demise" (2014, 16). The cultural theorist Lauren Berlant also interpreted our current moment as one of ongoing crisis or, in her words, a "crisis ordinary" where multiple histories converge (2011, 9). But since the publication of Koselleck's exhaustive account of crisis, there has been, I propose, a fifth and *new* interpretative possibility through which we may situate our current historical moment. Apart from crisis being experienced as chronic and all-pervasive, the fifth interpretative possibility I am proposing we add to Koselleck's list and which I utilize in my reading of the case studies in the ensuing chapters, positions crisis as *a constitutive state defined by a lack of meaningful events leading to the intensification of underlying tensions.* Below, I sketch out the parameters of this new interpretative possibility and its import in understanding both crisis and crisis cultures and their present manifestations.

A NEW INTERPRETATIVE POSSIBILITY OF CRISIS

Crisis cultures materialize when multiple crises emerge, overlap, foment, and build mass in any given society. I am seeking, then, to speculate on what crisis *does* when our current moment is defined by the very lack of meaningful events; events that have the power to shape us, propel us forward, and motivate our senses. Of course, events of some kind or another are constantly occurring. One need only switch on the evening news to watch an array of catastrophes both natural and manmade, political gaffes, sporting triumphs, and technological achievements. What I am suggesting, rather, is that such events fail to connect with us and provide us with meaning. Or, more simply, the oversaturation of events in our lives makes it difficult to ascribe those events with meaning. Hence, I am aligning my argument here with the Italian philosopher Giorgio Agamben in his *Infancy and History* (2007) who questions why it is that we have prodigious events in our lives but no longer have experience of them. Agamben draws on the work of Walter Benjamin who had already diagnosed a "poverty of experience" as early as 1933, pinpointing its origins to World War I (Agamben 2007, 15). The immensity of the violence of the Great War, Benjamin posited, was a "catastrophe" that annihilated the possibility of communicating experience. Four decades later, Agamben argued that a catastrophe was no longer a prerequisite for the destruction of experience (2007, 15). Instead, he suggested, the fact that events will not be translated into experience is now part of our unexceptional, everyday lives. He writes: "Modern man makes his way home in the evening wearied by a jumble of events, but however entertaining or tedious, unusual or commonplace, harrowing or pleasurable they are, none of them will become experience" (Agamben 2007, 16). Agamben is referring here to a specific type of experience. Aligned with Benjamin who distinguished between the two German words for experience, *Erlebnis* (an experience you live through) and *Erfahrung* (a lived experience that profoundly affects you), it is the latter definition of experience that he argues has been lost (see chapter 1 for a more detailed examination of this distinction) (De la Durantaye 2009, 86–87).

There are two key points about Agamben's argument about experience that need mentioning here. First, his idea of experience is intimately connected to language. Experience, for Agamben, is about the power of words and narration, and in his view almost nobody in our current historical moment has the necessary authority to wield that power and guarantee the truth of experiences (2007, 16). In a world traumatized by mass-scale crises, the ability of cultures to tell stories about themselves and to share and transmit those stories is thus undermined. Second, he is not suggesting that there are no more experiences, but rather that they are "enacted outside the individual" and that we "merely observe them, with relief" (2007, 17). Tellingly, he points to how most visitors to the Alhambra would prefer their camera to experience the astounding majesty of the building instead of taking in its beauty for themselves (2007, 17). With the advent of social media and selfie culture, he was thus quite prescient about how experience understood as *Erfahrung* (a lived experience that profoundly affects you) may increasingly elude us. In a comparable manner, I propose that although we are constantly bombarded by one crisis after another, and oftentimes impacted by overlapping crises, we have lost the capacity to *experience* crisis in Benjamin's and Agamben's sense; that is, although we have a lived experience of crisis, we cannot assimilate it into any "real" experience. Or put another way, there is no sufficient authority that can translate for us our experience of crisis into language—language here referring to words and narrations that have the capability of transmitting to us some kind of guaranteed truth about ourselves, our world, and our position within it. Crisis cultures are therefore the manifestation of that lack of real experience. Although we are barraged by endless interpretations of specific crises, whether it be in the news media or narrativized in film and novels and television series, and even symbolized in poetry, we have no sense of its overarching meaning. Instead, we remain disoriented by the sheer multitude of crisis-related talk, texts, and interpretations. This disorientation is further exacerbated by the nature of discourse itself, which, while attempting to grapple with these crises, is mired in continuous contestation. Such contestation is marked not by clarity but by its own lack of coherence, mirroring the fragmented and elusive nature of crisis in our contemporary understanding. Therefore, crisis cultures can be seen as not merely a lack of real experience, but also as a reflection of our collective struggle to construct meaning amid this pervasive disorientation.

It is probably a futile task to collate an exhaustive list of the crises that have impacted large parts of the world in recent decades. On one hand, almost any significant issue can be framed as a crisis: energy, care for the elderly, obesity, lack of sleep, food, housing, mental health, opioids, and so on. On the other hand, some issues like climate change are so big that to call it a crisis might seem a misnomer. It is no wonder, then, that Timothy Morton refers to such large-scale existential crises as *hyperobjects* (Morton 2013). And then there are crises that have the power to reshape the geopolitical system and reorient political discourses, such as Russia's invasion of Ukraine in 2022, the COVID-19 pandemic, and the Capitol Hill attack in the United States on January 6, 2021. Yet crisis cultures are not necessarily about any particular crisis, no matter how large or small, protracted or finite. They are neither lived through in the same way nor is their affective capacity equally distributed. As the political sociologist Dimitra Kotouza (2019) argues, when talking about crisis on a national scale, there is a tendency to universalize the experience of crisis. In her study on the economic crisis in Greece, she highlights that in political discourse about the crisis, "Greek" citizens are branded the "victims" of a neoliberal crisis (2019, 3). Yet it is problematic to assume that the crisis affects all Greeks in the same way. Crises can impact citizens (and non-citizens) differentially based on race, class, gender, and so on and certain groups such as the LGBT+ community can become renewed targets in the context of a return to identification(s) with the nation (see chapter 4) (Kotouza 2019, 6). Similarly, we must not universalize the lived experience of crisis on a global scale. It is impossible to compare living through crisis cultures in Western Europe and North America with West Africa, South Asia, Pacific Island states, Central America, and so on. For this reason, the case studies I discuss are predominantly focused on Western societies, as this book seeks to explore crisis cultures specifically through the lens of Western modernity. Despite the long-term trend since the Industrial Revolution that has contributed to much of the world becoming richer and safer, recent decades have witnessed in many Western societies decreasing levels of economic security, slower overall economic growth, widening income inequality, declining or stagnant wages, and the curtailment of the welfare state

(Inglehart 2018, 29). The political scientist Ronald F. Inglehart argues that such fundamental changes to economic equality have led to an "authoritarian reflex" in many Western nation-states, contributing to democratic principles currently being in retreat (2018, 138). The crisis cultures that have emerged in Western societies in the last few decades, I argue, can partly be traced to this underlying and prevailing context. This transition has been accompanied by the rise of neoliberal governance, which prioritizes market mechanisms over traditional state functions, affecting how crises are managed and perceived (Harvey 2005). Moreover, Western societies provide a unique context where the promises of modernity—progress, prosperity, and stability—are increasingly questioned, reflecting a deeper existential crisis about the future of modernity itself (Bauman 2000). Zygmunt Bauman's analysis of "liquid modernity" underscores the fluid and unstable conditions of contemporary life, where traditional structures and certainties have dissolved, leaving individuals in a state of perpetual insecurity. This fluidity creates fertile ground for the "liquid fear" that permeates society, characterized by diffuse and indeterminate anxieties that lack clear sources but profoundly affect social behavior and attitudes (Bauman 2006). In parallel, Frank Furedi's critique of the "culture of fear" reveals how contemporary society's preoccupation with risk and safety has normalized fear, influencing public perception and policy. Furedi (2002) argues that this culture amplifies the sense of vulnerability and erodes public trust, contributing to a pessimistic outlook and low expectations for the future. These perspectives align with the broader critiques of Western modernity by scholars such as Ulrich Beck (1992), who identified the "risk society" as a defining feature of our times, where global risks and uncertainties are interwoven into the fabric of everyday life. Additionally, theorists like Anthony Giddens have examined the reflexive nature of modernity, where constant questioning and self-examination further destabilize traditional norms and structures (Giddens 1991). This focus on Western modernity thus allows for a critical examination of how contemporary crisis cultures are interwoven with the narratives of progress and decline that are central to modern Western thought. By analyzing these significant shifts—from social democracy to neoliberal, market-driven reforms initiated in the 1980s—this book contributes to the broader discourse on modernity and its discontents, providing insights that resonate both within and outside Western contexts. This approach does not diminish the relevance of non-Western experiences but emphasizes the theoretical and practical implications of studying crisis cultures in a region where neoliberalism has profoundly altered the foundational structures of society.

Returning to Koselleck's interpretative possibilities in which the concept of crisis becomes a fundamental mode of interpreting history, it is precisely the decreasing levels of economic security in Western societies that have ushered in what I posit is a fifth interpretative possibility: crisis is *a constitutive state defined by a lack of meaningful events leading to the intensification of underlying tensions*. Until now, I have dealt with the first part of the formulation, that is, that in our historical moment, we cannot experience crisis events in Benjamin's and Agamben's sense, as *Erfahrung* (a lived experience that profoundly affects you). Here, I would like to turn to the second part of the formulation where I claim that the disorientation caused by a lack of meaningful events inevitably leads to the *intensification of underlying tensions*. By "tensions," I am referring to broad emotional responses, narratives, and conceptions of temporality that often clash, both sustaining and subverting social relations. Drawing from Hegel (1977), these "tensions" are not mere contradictions but tension-filled moments of a greater whole, a totality, that are now ongoing. This complexity relates to the potentially tense unity of the "I" and the "we." Therefore, in *Crisis Cultures*, I consciously mix the subjective "I" with the subjective "we" to underline the nature of these tension-filled moments. This reflective approach reveals the dialectical process in which individual subjectivities both shape and are shaped by the historical and social contexts they inhabit, providing a richer, more textured understanding of crises as phenomena that bridge the personal and the universal. My analysis contends that three key tensions underlie the perpetuation of crisis cultures. The first is the tension between hope and apprehension (emotion); the second, the tension between utopia and dystopia (narrative); and the third, the tension between history and futurity (temporality). The case studies I analyze aim to trace the conceptual shifts that these tensions embody, tensions with diverse genealogies; sometimes pronounced, other times existing as mere faint traces. While I attempt to detail these three tensions separately below, it is important to consider the possibility that all three are intimately connected and might be considered as smaller components of a larger whole.

Tension 1: Hope and Apprehension (Emotion)

The first tension between hope and apprehension is emotional and can be traced to the post-World War II era, when much of the post-war generation experienced unprecedented levels of economic growth, relative peace and prosperity, and the emergence of welfare safety nets, coinciding with the increasing significance of individual freedom and choice (Inglehart 2018, a) This period led to important cultural shifts such as the spread of democracy and rising levels of gender equality, leading to higher levels of happiness according to the World Values Survey (Inglehart 2018, 3). It is an era, I contend, that was marked by hope in the sense that many citizens increasingly had their material needs satisfied and could therefore shift to post-material values (though indeed it is important to acknowledge that not all citizens had access to this repertoire of hope; for example, many African Americans in the United States, Aboriginal peoples in Australia, the Roma in Europe, etc.). It was also a period when Western societies notably transitioned away from prosperity being linked to class and privilege and became increasingly associated with meritocracy; no longer would your class privilege determine your lot in life, but all citizens would have equal access to the post-war boom's spoils (Sandel 2020). According to the literary theorist Terry Eagleton, "for there to be genuine hope, the future must be anchored in the present" (2015, 52), and the post-war era provided the conditions for a sizable portion of citizens in Western nation-states to not only dare to hope but for their hopes to generally be realized, notwithstanding individual idiosyncrasies. Hope, of course, was never an absolute and never an emotional repertoire that reflected all citizens' circumstances—lest we forget the shadow of the Cold War and a string of conflicts from Vietnam to Korea. Yet hope was sufficiently abundant to allow for the general acceptance of the myth that historical progress was inevitable despite the advent of postmodern theories that suggested humanity had lost its faith in it.

The repertoire of hope that I am referring to was never extinguished altogether, and I am not suggesting that we are completely living in hope*less* times. I am arguing, rather, that a discourse of apprehension toward the future began to creep into many people's lived experiences. It is perhaps impossible to pinpoint when exactly the post-war repertoire of hope began to break down. Cracks in the post-war boom first emerged in the 1970s, consolidated in the 1980s with Reaganite and Thatcherite neoliberal reforms (TINA— There is No Alternative), and propagated by processes of late globalization in the 1990s. Even so, the 1990s in retrospect were rather hopeful times. The promise of a globalized world had its key supporters (notably *New York Times* columnist Thomas Friedman), and the end of the Cold War was even heralded as the End of History (Fukuyama 1992). Despite conflicts such as the Balkan wars, the 1990s were an era of geopolitical hope in how the European Union sought to expand eastward and how the West, more generally sought to integrate China and Russia into the global economy. In 2001, the terror attacks on the World Trade Center in New York and the Pentagon in Arlington ushered in a global "War on Terror" that included ongoing wars in Iraq and Afghanistan. Yet these geopolitical events can only partly explain the creeping apprehension that I contend has become a fundamental attribute of crisis cultures. A more convincing explanation, rather, is the increasing economic fragility that has fueled what I call the "repertoire of apprehension." That is, for large numbers of people in the West, life has become defined by economic insecurity. And even when economic security has been attained and maintained, the threat that it could be taken away has been amplified. Young people can no longer hope that their standard of living will exceed that of their parents and will most likely lead more economically insecure lives defined by large debts and higher housing costs (Kingman 2013; Siminski 2021). Today, political discourses, cultural texts, and events that could be said to promote a hopeful vision of the future are scant, and those that propagate more apprehensive views more commonly prevail. For example, even populist narratives such as "Make America Great Again" are essentially responses to an underlying apprehension, embodying a yearning for a past perceived as more secure. Our historical moment is therefore missing a Thomas Friedman-style champion. The emotional repertoires of hope and apprehension are, to use Sara Ahmed's term, "sticky" (2004, 4). They "stick" to the lenses through which we attempt to view and understand crises, and it is therefore nigh impossible to synthesize any meaning of crisis cultures outside of these emotional repertoires. The tension between hope and apprehension can be seen as dynamic elements within a broader historical and societal context, where each emotional state significantly influences the evolution of crisis cultures. Emotions are thereby viewed as integral components of a larger totality, shaping and being shaped by the social and historical conditions of their time. For this reason, I argue that the emotional tension between hope and apprehension is one of the key attributes of crisis cultures. For some people, the present conditions still allow for a genuine hope anchored in the present (Eagleton 2015, 52); for most others, the horizons of past and future are blurred, and I thus seek to trace how this emotional tension both informs and conditions our responses to crisis cultures.

Tension 2: Utopia and Dystopia (Narrative)

The second underlying tension between utopia and dystopia is a broader and more fundamental tension at a narrative level. Interpretations of crises are usually put into "story" form, fictionalized in order for people to make sense of them. As Janet Roitman points out, interpretations of crisis "all proceed from the question, what went wrong? All search for origins, sources, roots, causes, reasons" (2014, 11). As social beings, it is difficult for us to accept that events might be random and that a particular crisis might not necessarily be easily reduced to simple plot lines. The desire to answer that question—what went wrong?—is a means for us to put order where there is disorder and ensure that crisis events do not reoccur. The fact that a crisis can significantly impact our lives means that we need narratives to synthesize our experiences of it and translate the disordering power of a crisis into a story with a beginning, middle, and end. Studying historical events as narrative has been, and continues to be, controversial in scholarship. As M. C. Lemon points out, it is inherently "messy" for philosophical or scientific purposes (2003, 110), and postmodern scholarship, in particular, has been often attacked for promoting the idea that there are no valid truth-claims and instead each group of people, whether it be sexual minorities, national identities, or any other identity group, is free to narrate its version of the group story and that each of these narratives is equally valid (see Žižek 2006, 40). Yet there is no escaping the fact, as Somers and Gibson (1995) argue, that narrative is conceived as *the* principal and inescapable mode by which we experience the world. Even if we overcame the postmodern proclivity to narrativize group identities, the world would not suddenly revert to a narrative-*less* state of self-functioning individuals. Instead, the enduring narrative tension between the collective "we" and the individual "I" shapes our understanding and experience of crises, reflecting a broader sociopolitical conflict that juxtaposes personal autonomy against collective identity. Roitman's question—what went wrong?—will always require an answer in narrative form, and such an answer will always need to engage with identity, whether it be the identity of the nation, the individual, or the group.

But if it is the case that any interpretation of crisis can only be understood in narrative form, why am I suggesting, as I did above via Agamben, that the ability of cultures to tell stories about themselves and to share and transmit those stories has been undermined? My answer lies in the manifestation of crisis cultures that I am describing in this book. Although narrativization is both useful and necessary to make sense of individual crisis events, it is less capable of making sense of *crisis cultures* (when a number of crises amass and circulate) and when crisis is experienced as an ongoing and protracted phenomenon. That is not to say that narratives are not propagated to explain crisis cultures, but rather that they are less successful at ordering the disordering power of crisis cultures. Instead of neat stories that explain crises such as—*Crisis A was caused by B because of C. Due to reason D, E and F are suffering, unless we do G*—the narratives that circulate within crisis cultures are discursively knotty (Carpentier 2017), oftentimes ambiguous, and sometimes nonsensical. Such narratives, I contend, can generally be classified as either utopian or dystopian, and they often follow familiar tropes in their presentation of their utopic or dystopic visions of the world. In my reading of the creative and communal responses to crisis cultures in the following chapters, I identify their utopic and dystopic qualities and argue that the tension between competing utopian and dystopian narratives that are mobilized to explain crisis cultures only leads to less clarity and more polarization. It may seem odd, however, to suggest that an era defined by crisis cultures is one that promotes utopian narratives. But it is the very fact that crisis cultures engender narrative incoherence that utopias, as idealized objects, can act as a blind spot (Roitman 2014, 11). In other words, since crisis cultures perpetuate incoherence, utopias are necessary to promote some kind of end goal, and this end goal acts as an ontological object of hope; that is, it acts as an object in which people can displace their wish fulfillment for a better, and more secure, tomorrow. The utopian end goal could be anything from Brexit (a utopian vision of a United Kingdom free from the constraints of the European Union) and Catalan independence (a utopian vision of a Catalonia free from the constraints of the Spanish state) to the desire for a nation exercising greater control over immigration and a post-political society defined by progress, diversity, and inclusion. I am not suggesting here that people necessarily believe in utopias but rather that they cannot bear a world without them. But there is always an inherent risk at stake when big ideas such as the "purity of the nation" are set up as an ontological object of hope since it sets up an idea or end goal that can never be realized. It is, in Pankaj Mishra's words, a "demented utopianism" (2017, 24). Even so, within crisis cultures, utopian narratives are often articulated in the language of hope and tend to circulate in public discourses, typically serving as potential means to address the incoherence that crisis cultures perpetuate. This is where Ernst Bloch's (1995) "principle of hope" becomes relevant. Underpinned by a politics of emotion, this principle suggests that despite the chaotic and ambiguous nature of crisis narratives, there remains an intrinsic human drive toward hope. Bloch's concept underscores how utopian narratives within crisis cultures serve not just as a vision but also as a mechanism to reintroduce and sustain an emotional repertoire of hope in both public discourse and individual experiences.

With every narrative, however, there is always a counternarrative. Although utopian narratives are common in crisis cultures, so is their opposite: narratives of dystopia. On one hand, dystopic narratives are mere fantasies of what we do not desire, of a world that we do not want to live in. For a pro-Brexiter, the dystopic vision is living in the European Union; for a Remainer, the dystopia is a Britain outside of it. On the other, dystopic visions that are mobilized to make sense of crisis cultures are much more deep-rooted and abject. They, too, are an ontological object, but of apprehension instead of hope. Crises such as climate change and the COVID-19 pandemic fuel dystopic narratives since they directly impact people's bodies and are experienced as ongoing. Conspiracy theories such as those propagated by QAnon or revolts against current environmental policies by loose networks such as Extinction Rebellion are good examples of current dystopic narratives mobilized in our historical moment. Dystopic narratives, however, very rarely circulate independently. Instead, they tend to mirror utopic narratives, partly because the narratives of utopia propagated in crisis cultures are what Ernst Bloch calls "abstract utopias" and only have value insofar as they are able to offer a critique of the present (1995, 477). In my analysis of crisis cultures in the following chapters, "concrete utopias" are few and far between. It is the very lack of concrete utopias that mobilizes the propensity for the dystopic in crisis cultures. Yet overall crisis cultures are typically marked by the difficulty in distinguishing between the utopian and dystopian; they reinforce each other in a kind of push and pull between the emotional repertoires of hope and apprehension.

Tension 3: History and Futurity (Temporality)

The third tension between history and futurity also correlates with the two tensions above but underlines the temporal dimension of crisis cultures. Crisis cultures are defined by their overemphasis on the past and future and their tendency to either disregard the present or to destabilize understandings of the present. For this reason, the Polish sociologist and philosopher Zygmunt Bauman (2017) described the utopias that I identify as a defining trait of crisis cultures as actually "retrotopias," emphasizing a focus more on a return to the past rather than to the future. In turn, we could also say that the counternarratives of dystopia are *anterotopias* in how they perform and enact their dystopic visions in a forward direction. When multiple crises are experienced as ongoing, they can often blur the boundaries between pre-crisis, the lived experience of crisis, and the ability to imagine a post-crisis future, thus fragmenting the experience of linear time. When one is immersed in crisis cultures, the pre-crisis world is out of reach, or, in the writer John Berger's words: "The horizon of past and future are being blurred. We are being conditioned to live an endless and uncertain present, reduced to being citizens in a state of forgetfulness" (Berger 2016, 139–140).

In my reading of crisis cultures, I align my analysis with Muñoz's contention (via Bloch) that temporal dimensions are performative. According to Muñoz, the past *does things* to our present historical moment (2009, 28). Muñoz's presupposition that the past *does things* aligns with Janet Roitman's argument (via Koselleck) that crisis *is* history, that is, it is the means by which history is located, recognized, comprehended, and even posited" (2014, 7). For her, crisis has achieved the status of a "historico-philosophical concept" that defines both the past and the present (2014, 3). In my analysis, I not only accept this premise but also argue that the future also *does things;* that is, crisis is not only history, but *is* the future. I therefore extend Roitman's arguments by arguing that crisis is the means by which subjects may imagine a future, and locate, recognize, and comprehend themselves and their communities within that future. For this reason, I argue that crisis cultures beckon us to imagine a communal becoming. It is these processes of *doing* and *becoming* that I seek to unveil in my critical reading of the narratives that circulate in crisis cultures.

Yet there is tension between the temporal dimensions of history and futurity, particularly in how they impact people's sense of the present. This tension reflects the challenges in navigating the constant pull between historical determinism and the open possibilities of the future. Much of this tension is played out in the oft-repeated statement that we are now living in the "new normal." The new normal is, on the surface, an inoffensive phrase. It implies that *something* has disrupted the normal order of things; that *something* was supposed to be unchanging, yet somehow it has changed. Although we were comfortable with the *old normal*, we must now acclimatize ourselves to a *new normal* because, it seems, nothing stays the same.

Designating fundamental changes to working conditions, freedoms, cost of living, and so on, as the "new normal" that people must accept is a material component of crisis cultures. In her one-woman Netflix show *Not Normal* (2019), comedian Wanda Sykes builds her stand-up routine around the very premise that she does not accept the new normal as being normal ("this shit *ain't normal*" she repeats, referring to Donald Trump's antics during his presidency). In his *Discipline and Punish* (1979), Michel Foucault demonstrated that normalization was one of the key tactics that the state had at its disposal to maintain social control without the exertion of force. The French philosopher Jacques Rancière (2010) similarly suggests that processes of normalization have the power to create and maintain a politics of consensus. Normalization understood in this way refers to how behaviors and ideas that once lay outside of social norms have come to be considered "normal" over time. For example, in *The Politics of Fear*, Ruth Wodak argues that there is an intrinsic link between the normalization of nationalist, xenophobic, and racist discourse, and the politics of fear which can frame almost anything as a threat to the imagined community, including fear of changing gender roles and globalization (2015, 114). Moreover, calling the COVID-19 pandemic the "great equalizer" rested on understanding the crisis as a shared global event. The tendency to universalize the lived experience of the crisis and living in lockdown by asking people to adapt to the new normal of the pandemic by appealing to their sense of vulnerability and affective bonds only served to underscore that the pandemic did not, in fact, affect people equally. Indeed, the pandemic can be better understood as a phenomenon that amplified existing inequalities rather than equalizing them.

Let us first consider the power of designating fundamental changes to our lives within crisis cultures as the "new normal." According to Italian philosopher Franco Berardi, power is "the selection and enforcement of one possibility among many, and simultaneously it is the exclusion (and invisibilization) of many other possibilities" (2019, 2). Understood in this way, designating something the new normal delimits, excludes, silences, interrupts, and renders invisible any challenge to the existing order. As such, the narrative of the new normal acts as a tool to extinguish hope in its insistence that—*it is what it is*. Such a rationalization demonstrates the power of the past *doing things*. That is, past events are remobilized and reutilized as justifications for conditions in the present. This is a powerful mechanism that draws on the emotional repertoires of that past and sublimates it into a benign narrative that—*things are the way they are because that is how they are supposed to be*. Yet crisis cultures are neither a positive nor negative force, neither entirely past-oriented nor entirely future-oriented. In that sense, crisis cultures can act as an epistemological reinterpretation of the social terrain. Hence, in crisis cultures, the future also *does things*. Although the dominant narrative may claim that *it is what it is* there is also always a faint echo—*is it what it is?*

MAPPING CRISIS CULTURES

Crisis cultures materialize when multiple crises emerge, overlap, foment, and build mass in any given society. As crisis cultures are socially reproduced in a variety of contexts, they often remain elusive, as scholarly literature has yet to synthesize a number of disparate trends that crisis cultures articulate into a wider phenomenon. Although crisis cultures are made up of individuals whose bodies have been affected by crisis, they also allow for a space to reimagine the present moment as not conditioned by horizons of past and future, and a space that permits the possibility of transformation. My analysis of crisis cultures, therefore, proceeds by surveying key political, economic, and social events from the Global Financial Crisis until the present day and reading texts that circulate in the public domain that work to tighten the tensions that underlie crisis cultures. I draw on texts from the mass media, literature, television, film, and non-fiction books, examining with particular concern how these texts are mobilized to polarize political discourse and foment the crisis cultures we are living in. The overarching inquiry in each chapter is to explore what crisis cultures *do* to the individual, the nation, and group identities. Yet, my analysis does not cease at this *doing*. I argue that, although on the surface it may seem that crisis cultures can simply be read as an epistemological impasse (Roitman 2014, 4), I suggest that underneath, crisis cultures are defined by the *possibilities* that they open up. The aim, then, is to read crisis cultures not as a discursive impasse but as a potentiality that can reinterpret our position in the world—emotionally, narratively, and temporally. In *The Man Without Content,* Agamben praised the French writer Antonin Artaud's effort to "transform an *impasse* into an escape route and to seek salvation where the danger is greatest" (1999a, 68). Although I do not claim that my analysis in this book offers such an escape route, it is my sincere intention to avoid talking about historical impasses and instead read crisis cultures as being full of potentiality.

Crisis cultures are not hierarchical and do not have a specific origin or focal point, with no clear beginning or end. They are characterized by their fluid and ever-changing nature. This fluidity means that even if one element of a crisis culture disappears or becomes less prominent, it is likely to re-emerge, as the overall culture is constantly evolving and morphing. Crisis cultures understood as an assemblage in this way therefore allow for alternative cartographies to materialize; that is, the act of reading crisis cultures can be a tool to remap the public domain with the creative and communal responses that contest the new normal as being the new normal. It is this remapping that opens up possibilities even if they are not always actualized. Reading crisis cultures therefore has the potential to represent an alternative mapping of the world: a new map whose coastlines have been redrawn, oceans renamed.

The theoretical approach of this book draws selectively from history and modern philosophy, primarily influenced by writers and thinkers who have stimulated my own thinking. This selective approach has been instrumental in constructing an analytical framework that, while not exhaustive, offers a nuanced perspective on the complexities of crisis cultures in our contemporary world. Throughout this book, I explore a variety of case studies to examine the multifaceted nature of crisis cultures. However, I have intentionally chosen not to devote individual chapters exclusively to each case study. This decision stems from a recognition that isolating these crises in separate chapters could inadvertently suggest that they exist independently of one another. In reality, the essence of crisis cultures lies in their interconnectedness, where multiple crises overlap and intertwine, making them challenging to disentangle. The following chapters are thus not only an attempt to critically read what crisis cultures do to the individual, the nation, and group identities, but also to map out how these tensions are currently being played out. The organization of chapters follows a deliberate theoretical trajectory designed to gradually expand the reader's understanding from foundational theories to more complex interactions of crisis within various layers of human organization. This structured progression starts with a discussion of the philosophical and temporal theories that underpin the concept of crisis, establishing a critical framework essential for understanding the nuanced ways in which crises influence human perceptions and experiences. Moving from this broad theoretical base to a focused examination of individual subjectivity, the narrative explores how these theories manifest at a personal level, directly impacting individuals' lives and shaping their responses to crisis situations. This exploration underscores the inherent tension between individual agency (the "I") and the broader societal impacts (the "we"), as personal experiences of crisis are both influenced by and contribute to larger collective narratives. As the narrative progresses to the national dimension, it examines how individual and collective experiences converge, reflecting and reshaping national identities through the lens of crisis. This analysis highlights the phantasmatic relationship between personal narratives of crisis and national narratives, underlining the tension between personal identities and collective national identities. This tension is further explored in the discussion of group identities, particularly through a queering lens, focusing on how marginalized groups both influence and are influenced by crisis narratives, challenging traditional narratives and redefining the boundaries between the individual and the collective. By weaving through these scalar dimensions—from the individual to the national to the communal—the book maps out a complex terrain where the tensions between the "I" and the "we" are not only highlighted but are essential to understanding the full spectrum of crisis cultures.

In the opening chapter, "The Experience is Out of Joint," I establish a thematic framework for understanding crisis cultures, as opposed to a linear narrative approach. Drawing on a diverse range of philosophical thoughts from Rousseau to Walter Benjamin, the chapter undertakes a critical examination of the concept of crisis. This chapter commences with a focused analysis of temporality within modernity, emphasizing its crucial role in navigating crisis cultures. This segment highlights how our perceptions of past and future are integral in shaping responses to crises. The chapter then examines the fragmentation of experience, presenting it as both a lens and a concrete reality that frames our understanding of temporality and, consequently, crisis. This analysis elevates the role of experience as an indispensable epistemological tool in navigating the cultural and existential terrains of ongoing crises. Following this, the historical evolution of the concept of crisis is explored, tracing its etymological roots to provide context for its contemporary interpretations. Finally, the chapter culminates with an ontological positioning of crisis narratives, accentuating their role not merely in mirroring but in actively constructing our realities. This section advocates for a heightened level of critical scrutiny of the narratives that inform our perception of and response to crisis cultures. Overall, the chapter encourages readers to view crisis not simply as an event or a series of events, but as a dynamic, evolving concept deeply embedded in our cultural and existential comprehension of the world.

In the second chapter, "Crisis Ambientality," the narrative shifts to explore the intersection of individual subjectivity with the narratives emerging from crises. In this chapter, I introduce and elaborate on the term "crisis ambientality" to emphasize the influential role of smartphones and digital technologies in shaping our crisis experiences. Defined as the transformative impact of these technologies on our existential experiences, crisis ambientality signifies a shift in the role of digital devices from passive information channels to active agents in shaping perceptions and emotional responses to crises. The analysis of the Greek Economic Crisis, serving as the first case study, goes beyond mere analysis of disordered narratives. This section depicts the crisis as a multifaceted matrix of meanings, encompassing both the affective elements of crisis cultures and their impact on individual subjectivity. In the latter part of the chapter, the focus narrows to the COVID-19 pandemic, offering an analysis of its real-world impacts and the emotional responses it elicited. This analysis underscores the unique modalities in which crises are mediated and experienced in the digital era. The dual role of (digital) crisis ambientality is explored in this context, demonstrating how it functions both as a diversionary mechanism and as a tool for normalizing ongoing crises. This characteristic of crisis ambientality is pivotal in framing our understanding of these crises as the "new normal." The chapter concludes with a proposition to reconceptualize crisis topologies. This suggested remapping involves establishing new forms of relationality and emotional engagement that confront and challenge the existing normative frameworks of crisis narratives, thereby acknowledging and integrating the significant affective aspects of these narratives. By proposing this reconceptualization, the chapter aims to expand the scope of understanding and engaging with crises, motivating a departure from established narrative paradigms.

In the third chapter, "Confabulations," I turn the focus to crisis cultures within the framework of national identity. This expansive chapter is divided into three distinct sections, each examining different facets of national identity and its evolution, particularly in crisis contexts. The first section traces the historical development of the nation-state, starting from the significant Peace of Westphalia and extending to contemporary notions of nationhood. The aim is to underscore the dynamic, layered, and transformative nature of national identities across different eras. This approach brings to the forefront the inherent historical instability of nations as a vital element in comprehending their current complexities and manifestations. In the following section, the concept of national confabulations is introduced. Drawing upon clinical definitions, confabulation refers to a phenomenon where patients produce fabricated stories to fill gaps in their memories, without any intent to deceive and without consciousness of the falsehood (Hirstein 2005, 2–7). This chapter proposes the hypothesis that nations might experience a similar, yet broader, narrative evolution: a form of collective confabulation. Within such confabulatory narratives, national stories are subtly altered and perpetuated without collective awareness of the change. Analogous to clinical confabulations, these national narratives arise not from intentional deceit but from an unconscious process of filling narrative voids or reconciling inconsistencies in the national story. Thus, this section offers an analysis of how these unconsciously shaped narratives, influenced by historical events, cultural shifts, and political dynamics, are employed in crisis situations. The chapter culminates with an in-depth case study of the January 6, 2021, United States Capitol Hill insurrection. This event acts as a key case study to unravel the mechanics of national confabulations and their effect on real-world events. Through this analysis, the chapter draws out the dialectic relationship between nation-building and crisis. It reveals how national narratives, especially those crafted within crisis cultures, can unwittingly influence, dictate, and perpetuate the project of nation-building.

In "Queering Crisis," the concluding chapter, I employ the metaphor of the mirror as a rhetorical tool to critically examine the complex interactions within identity politics in the context of crisis cultures. This metaphor is instrumental in demonstrating how queer identities often function as mirrors, reflecting, refracting, and at times distorting broader political narratives. I reflect on how my own queer identity interacts with and redefines the concept of crisis, employing "queering" as a methodology to critically reassess traditional understandings of crisis. In the subsequent section, I engage with Jasbir K. Puar's (2007) concept of homonationalism, which is a quintessential example of the mirroring process. Homonationalism examines how LGBT+ identities are incorporated into nationalist frameworks, paralleling and sometimes contradicting dominant ideologies, and possibly diverging from the original aims of queer liberation movements. I propose that the rise of populist right-wing parties is precipitating a dissolution of what was once viewed as a homonational consensus, revealing inherent tensions and contradictions. This discussion aligns with Christopher Chitty's (2020) assertion that crisis serves as a fundamental element in the recognition and politicization of identities. The final section of the chapter presents a case study of contemporary Spain, particularly notable as an LGBT-friendly country. This case study offers a vantage point to observe the contours of this polarization as manifested in crisis cultures. The analysis focuses on how the Spanish context reveals a setting in which every element seems to mirror itself, leading to a critical reevaluation and recontextualization of established perceptions of marginalized identities, particularly queer identities. Through this dialectical analysis, the chapter aims to foster a space for reimagining identity boundaries and potentialities.

Taken together, the four chapters consider what crisis *does*; what happens when multiple crises overlap, foment, and build mass, forming a crisis culture. Some readers might question whether crisis cultures are indeed new. They might propose that societies and individuals have always faced multiple crises. While I acknowledge that the crisis cultures framework might be applicable to various historical eras or geographic contexts, my analysis is specifically anchored in our current historical moment. This moment is characterized by the instability of Western modernity, where the promises of progress, prosperity, and stability are increasingly questioned. While such questioning has always been a feature of modern philosophy, the digital era has brought Western modernity to an unprecedented level of polarization and instability. Hence, although the interpretative lenses that Koselleck identified are still valid and can still be utilized to interpret crisis and historical time, my argument is that something has indeed changed in our historical moment and that a new, additional, interpretative lens is required to make sense of these changes. I thus proffer a novel historical interpretation that not only posits that crisis is now experienced as an ongoing process, without a beginning and an end, but that crisis is a *constitutive state defined by a lack of meaningful events leading to the intensification of underlying tensions*. This state of perpetual crisis challenges traditional narratives of progression and resolution, suggesting that we exist in a liminal space where the usual markers of historical evolution are occluded. Within the context of Western modernity, crisis becomes an omnipresent backdrop to everyday life, a constant yet shifting presence that defies the conventional arc of cause and effect. It calls into question the linear perception of time and history, proposing instead a complex reality where past, present, and future coalesce. At the heart of this book lies an enduring hope, one that, even when momentarily veiled by the complexities of crisis cultures, steadfastly lingers on the horizon—a horizon rich with promise and possibility. This hope, enduring and ever-present on the horizon, steers the explorations and dialogues that unfold within these pages. In *Exterminate all the Brutes*, Sven Lindqvist wrote: "You already know enough. So do I. It is not knowledge we lack. What is missing is the courage to understand what we know and to draw conclusions" (2018, 2). In the interpretative possibility that follows, I draw my own conclusions, also in the hope that I do so in ways that invite readers to draw theirs.

Chapter 1

The Experience *is* Out of Joint

"How does this add to your personal brand?" she asks. "Well . . . um . . . it is hard to think of myself as a brand," I reply. "Sure. I know the terminology may be jarring. But what we are asking is how does this contribute to how people *perceive* you?"

Every aspect of this book—the cover, the title of this chapter, the syntactical choices on the page, the typography of the letters—all contribute to my personal brand, influencing how I am perceived by others. Each decision I make is a conscious (or not?) step in my entrepreneurial journey of self-crafting, or what might be termed the performative act of identity construction. Will my personal anecdotes hurt or build my brand? Will they help me connect with readers or disengage them? This ongoing project of identity crafting is an emergent trend that could be seen as a byproduct of our navigation through crisis cultures. Such cultures exert their influence not only on social structures and dynamics but also deeply permeate our individual lives and identities. This, in turn, affects the ways we connect with others and, ultimately, how we perceive and define ourselves.

The continuous process of negotiating one's identity is a fundamental aspect of how individuals react to the numerous tensions and instabilities that are characteristic of crisis cultures. In Anne Helen Petersen's *Can't Even: How Millennials Became the Burnout Generation* (2021), she underlines how systemic pressures—such as precarious labor markets, crippling student debt, and high costs of living—have resulted in a generation of millennials afflicted by chronic burn out and disillusionment. Compounding this is the ubiquity of an "always-on" digital culture, perpetuating the psychosocial burden of incessant self-surveillance and relentless self-comparison. The problem is not that we have a brand but that it consumes everything we do. "Is there a self left to excavate?" Petersen asks (2021, 205). Confronting that question proves daunting when multiple crises overlap, foment, and build mass, forming crisis cultures.

Byung-Chul Han's *The Burnout Society* (2015) offers a deeper examination of this question, positing burnout as an endemic condition of our current historical moment. Han contends that in our hyper-performative society, individuals become entrepreneurs of their own selves, perpetually engaged in acts of self-exploitation in the quest for productivity and self-optimization. For Han, the incessant drive toward achievement and success coupled with the self-imposed pressure to remain constantly active converge to produce states of mental and physical exhaustion, thereby cultivating what he identifies as the "burnout society." His assessment of modern society is trenchant: "It is not the imperative only to belong to oneself, but the *pressure to achieve* that causes exhaustive depression. Seen in this light, burnout syndrome does not express the exhausted self so much as the exhausted, burnt-out soul" (original emphasis) (2015, 10). He sketches a dystopian imaginary of Western societies, marked by what he calls an *"excess of positivity"* (original emphasis) (2015, 4). This burnout, as articulated by both Han and Petersen, represents a uniquely insidious form of psycho-emotional exhaustion that is a far cry from the bodily fatigue once experienced by working-class men like my father, laboring in factories for decades on end. This fatigue stems from a digital infosphere that inundates us with a constant barrage of choices, and what could be termed the affective labor involved in the relentless crafting of one's personal brand. In this neoliberal landscape, every decision—whether it be maintaining a facade of bodily fitness, navigating the politics of perpetual availability, or perhaps acquiescing to opportunities by affirming with a "yes"—may become a tactical maneuver in a never-ending competition for self-betterment. Choices deemed as negative, such as engaging in indulgences, asserting autonomy by establishing personal boundaries, or vocalizing a refusal by uttering "no," are often discursively framed as constraints that inhibit one's marketability, thereby narrowing the horizons of one's social survival. The burnout society that Han articulates—a society fatigued by the relentless logics of positivity and self-optimization—serves not merely as a crisis in itself but lays bare the complex intersection of modernity and crisis and their impact on individual subjectivity.

The exploration of crisis cultures cannot, then, be disentangled from an examination of the phenomenon that gives rise to it—modernity. Crisis cultures are the inexorable byproduct of modernity, a transformational force that has irrevocably reconstituted societies, reshaped our worldview, and precipitated an ongoing state of crisis. Jürgen Habermas, a key figure in interrogating the epistemological discourses around modernity, characterizes it as the epochal threshold separating the Middle Ages from the modern era. This transition was catalyzed by three pivotal events around the year 1500: the

Renaissance, the Reformation, and what he called the "discovery" of the new world (1985, 5). For Habermas, the essence of modernity lies in its orientation toward the future: "the modern world is distinguished from the old by the fact that it opens itself to the future, the epochal new beginning is rendered constant with each moment that gives birth to the new" (1985, 6). Yet for him, modernity is also an ongoing epistemological and ontological endeavor with theoretical tensions that contemporary thinkers continue to grapple with (1987, xix). This understanding of modernity as an ever-evolving, unfinished project provides the context for examining the proliferation of crisis cultures.

Philosophers of modernity such as Hegel, Nietzsche, Foucault, Horkheimer and Adorno, Derrida, among others, have launched rigorous critiques against the ideological substrates of modernity. They claim that the ideas rooted in the European Enlightenment have, to varying degrees, reached their saturation point. Arnold Gehlen argues that while the underlying principles of the Enlightenment may have reached their end, their lasting effects continue to influence and shape contemporary societies (see Habermas 1985, 3). One such persisting ontological imprint of modernity is the acceleration of historical time. In his seminal work *Futures Past: On the Semantics of Historical Time* (1985), Reinhart Koselleck, for example, argues that the modern world is characterized by an ever-growing temporal disjuncture between our anticipations for the future and the realities of the past. Such divergence arises from the rapid pace of social and technological transformations intrinsic to modernity, fostering expectations that the future will markedly differ from the past (Koselleck 1985, 47). As Michael Pickering underlines, this accelerated temporality erodes our connection with history in our everyday life, allowing for the projection of future plans, predictions and aspirations that bear no relation to our past experiences (2004, 283). Crisis cultures, I contend, exacerbate the innate tension inherent in modernity's unique focus on the future, leading to a state of hyper-futurism where, as Pickering puts it, society excessively dwells "too much in the future" (2004, 284). For example, the emergence of cryptocurrencies and decentralized finance, a particularly relevant and current illustration of the acceleration of time, reflecting the fast pace of innovation in today's financial landscape, illustrates how contemporary financial systems are rapidly evolving in directions that transgress traditional economic paradigms, often disconnected from historical precedent. This relentless pursuit of innovation, guided by an almost utopian futurism, can lead to both unforeseen opportunities and significant crises, as the past no longer serves as a heuristic guide for the future. Thus, the ongoing impact of this temporal divergence and the unrelenting pace of change in modernity creates a dynamic where the future takes precedence over the past and the present, ultimately leaving us in a state of perpetual flux, and hence, crisis. But as will be demonstrated below, the temporal dimensions of crisis cultures are anything but unidimensional.

Rather, they necessitate a nuanced understanding that accommodates the complex dialectics of past, present, and future as they coalesce to shape our individual and collective experience of crisis.

The continuous state of uncertainty that arises from the inherent conflicts and rapid pace of change in modernity requires careful examination. To this end, it is essential to consider its temporal and historiographical reverberations, particularly as described by Habermas. As he proposes, history is often viewed as replete with crises, with the present serving as a nodal juncture for critical decision-making, and the future as a vast expanse of unresolved challenges (1985, 58). This outlook heightens affective engagement with the potential outcomes that could occur if needed actions are not taken, leading to the perception of the current state as "the past of a future present" (1985, 58). Hence, in Habermas's formulation, our perception of history is influenced by a consciousness of crisis; the heightened sensitivity to potential crises renders the present moment feel as though it is already the past of a future present. That is, we are continuously conscious of how our current actions will impact our future outcomes, resulting in a constant responsibility and ontological burden to make decisions that will positively shape that future. Thus, the dialectical reverberation of Enlightenment ideals, in conjunction with the accelerated pace of life and an ever-present sense of impending crisis, compound to leave society grappling with chronic exhaustion and an ever-widening disconnect from its history, leading to the burnout society that Han (2015) elucidates.

My analysis in this chapter is thus anchored in the philosophical foundations of modern thought, drawing from the intellectual legacy mapped by figures ranging from Rousseau to Benjamin. In undertaking this exercise, my aim is not to present an exhaustive cartography of crisis but rather to focus on specific thematic clusters that best exemplify the varied entanglements of crisis cultures. While the reader might anticipate a more conventional, linear exposition, this first chapter takes on the role of a theoretical guide through the complex terrain of crisis cultures. I divide the chapter into four interlocking sections, each focused on a different dimension of crisis. This multifaceted approach allows me to cover extensive theoretical ground, positioning crisis cultures not as a fixed entity but as a "traveling concept" (Bal 2002)— one that evolves and adapts across different contexts and discourses and can be examined from various perspectives. In the first segment, I examine the philosophical nuances of temporality and modernity, exploring how seminal theories of modern philosophy are anchored in their understanding of time as a central axis in the discourse of crisis, highlighting its impact on shaping existential and historical narratives. It is from this foundation that I move into the second part, which centers on the conceptual domain of experience. This segment aims to broaden the aperture through which we understand the dynamic between the individual and the historical and how these shape our collective and personal understanding of crisis. The third part offers a brief genealogy of crisis, where I chart the evolution of the concept of crisis through its historical and contemporary permutations. This serves not only as a descriptive account but as an interpretive scaffold that enables me to examine the prevailing paradigms shaping our contemporary moment. The fourth and final part culminates in an exploration of narrative, particularly focusing on crisis narratives as they have come to be understood in contemporary discourse. My aim is to examine how narrative devices are employed, both to comprehend and to navigate the disjointed terrains we find ourselves traversing in these crisis-ridden times.

This chapter, therefore, aspires not merely to interpret crisis but to examine their operationality and ontological force. It questions and reimagines crisis, making them a lens through which we might view the world anew, acutely attuned to the realities and complexities of crisis cultures. Through this approach, I aim to redraw the conceptual map, identifying new pathways and possible routes of navigation. My analysis thus goes beyond merely understanding crises; it seeks to explore what crisis *does* by leading us to question, reconfigure, and reimagine the world in a way that is attuned to the complexities of crisis cultures and our individual subjectivities forged within them.

THE TEMPORAL DYNAMICS OF CRISIS CULTURES

In their introduction to *Thinking Catastrophes and Crises* (2012), Meiner and Veel embark on a detailed exploration into the language and meaning of catastrophes and crises, foregrounding their similarities and differences. Both phenomena, they argue, introduce stark dislocations to our sense of normality, yet they occupy different temporal domains—catastrophes are sudden ruptures, while crises unfold over a longer period, both shaking up the established order (2012, 1). These disruptions, they argue, are more than just anomalies; they are significant moments that force us to rethink our core beliefs and reevaluate historical contexts to understand the causes and effects of these events. However, their portrayal of catastrophe and crisis presents a crucial aspect of contention in my analysis. While they suggest a regenerative cycle following disruptions—implying a cyclical ontology of rupture and restoration—I posit that crisis cultures often manifest a protracted state of aporia, an ongoing state of crisis that defies simple resolution. Despite this disagreement, I share Meiner and Veel's interest in the "cultural life" of crises, which complements my own methodological imperative of affirming the agency of cultural narratives in shaping perceptions and interpretations of crisis cultures (2012, 1). This perspective underscores a deep connection between ongoing, omnipresent crises and the stories cultures tell about them, accentuating the interaction between lived experiences and collective sense-making processes.

As I attempt to read the cultural life of crises, it becomes clear that a genealogical exploration of temporality within modernity becomes not only an intellectual pursuit but also a heuristic imperative for navigating crisis cultures. These temporal dimensions, far from being static or linear, reveal themselves as fragmented and heterogeneous in their interaction with one another. In *Futures Past* (1985), Reinhart Koselleck maps the changing topographies of social perspectives on time, constructing a complex analysis of historical consciousness across different cultural and diachronic terrains. Koselleck's work is notable for its meticulous philological approach and sharp historical acumen in examining the relationship between past and future in any given present while questioning the erosion of history's role as a guiding tool for contemporary life (Pickering 2004, 272). Specifically, he questions how shifts, inspired by the Enlightenment's utopic imaginaries, have led to a pervasive crisis in our present times (Tribe 1985, xv). Koselleck's work poses an intriguing question: what type of experience opens up with the onset of Western modernity? To answer this, he introduces two conceptual dimensions, the "horizon of expectation" and the "space of experience," which emerge as indispensable tools for problematizing historical time due to their embodied dialectics of the past and future, respectively (1985, 271–276).

Koselleck's theory of social acceleration demonstrates that as the pace of societal changes quickens in the modern era, it intensifies the dynamic interaction between our perceptions of space and experience. This results in a heightened tension between our hopes for future possibilities and our grounding in the lessons of the past. According to Koselleck, this acceleration drives individuals to orient their goals toward a "horizon of expectation"—a metaphor he uses to describe a future shaped by present expectations (1985, 271–276). This "horizon" serves as the pinnacle of promise and potential, signaling the possibility of moving beyond our current limitations. However, Koselleck notes a growing divide in modernity between this aspirational "horizon of expectation" and the more ontologically grounded "space of experience." The latter concept refers to the collective knowledge accumulated from past events, both personal and historical, which forms the foundation of our understanding and interpretation of the world (1985, 272). While these categories maintain a certain hermeneutic fluidity—the "horizon of expectation" is future-oriented, the "space of experience" leans toward the past—they also harbor complexity. Expectation extends beyond mere hope, aiming toward a realm of potentialities (Koselleck 1985, 272). Experience, conversely, involves more than just memory; it represents the present past, including both conscious knowledge and subconscious behavior (Koselleck

1985, 272). Koselleck presents the idea of experience as a kind of "space" where different aspects of the past exist together, not necessarily in a sequential order. On the other hand, he describes expectation as a "horizon"—a limit that marks the edge of our current understanding, beyond which new experiences can occur but are not yet seen or understood (1985, 273). Despite these apparent contrasts, Koselleck underscores the essential interdependence between experience and expectation, asserting that one cannot exist without the other: there can be "no expectation without experience; no experience without expectation" (1985, 270). Thus, the concepts of the "horizon of expectation" and "space of experience" provide a critical framework for understanding the tension between our future aspirations and our anchoring in past experiences.

While the rapid pace of change in modern times poses its own set of challenges, an even more critical issue emerges from the widening disconnect between our lived experiences and future expectations. Prior to the Enlightenment era, the framework for understanding the world was primarily derived from immediate empirical encounters rather than historical narratives, using these experiences to draw connections across history's disparate timelines (Koselleck 1985, 56). The onset of modernity, marked by pivotal events like the French Revolution, disrupted this approach, transforming time and history into processes that extend beyond the scope of individual actors. As a result, a new modality of experiencing emerged, one in which progress was not a linear extension of the past, but a contested narrative shaped by technological growth, social evolution, and political transformations (Koselleck 1985, 57). This transition signified a crucial shift: the future became a complex blend of aspirations and anxieties rather than a direct outcome of past events. This change blurred the distinctions between past, present, and future, mirroring the complexities of modern life (Koselleck 1985, 272). Consequently, the concept of "progress," once a marginal concept, became fundamental in the modern worldview, defined by constant advancement and competition, and used as a means to project optimistic futures (Koselleck 1985, 279). In a parallel way, the contemporary climate crisis exemplifies this tension between experience and expectation. The historical "space of experience," once characterized by the optimistic narrative of technology taming nature, now confronts a "horizon of expectation" marked by a dystopian foreboding. We find ourselves grappling with the unsettling reality that our individual capacity to mitigate climate change may be severely constrained. Where once our interaction with nature was marked by control and success, our future expectations are now clouded by uncertainty and impotence, forming a grim counterpoint to past optimism. This incongruity between future expectations and the accumulated wisdom of past experiences, evident in the climate crisis, signifies more than a mere temporal dislocation; it indicates a seismic shift in our collective perception of progress and time.

David Harvey (1989) provides a unique yet complementary perspective to Koselleck's on the acceleration of social processes, focusing on the material aspects of spatial dynamics and capital flows. His approach aligns with Marx's view of social modernization, which ties it to the efficient exploitation of natural resources and the growth of a global network of commerce and communication (Habermas 1985, 63). Harvey introduced the term "time–space compression" to describe how technological advances in communication and transportation have made the world feel smaller, effectively shortening the distance between places (1989, 240). This phenomenon has not only sped up the movement of goods, information, and people but has also fundamentally altered our perception of time and space. But Harvey is not just talking about faster trains or internet speeds; he argues that these changes in our experience of time and space are intimately linked to broader social changes. With the world at our fingertips, there is a feeling of closeness that has significant effects on how society operates and how individuals perceive their role within the larger global community (Harvey 1989, 240). One consequence of time–space compression is the hastening pace of life, as rapid technological and cultural shifts contribute to a more unpredictable and unstable world (Harvey 1989, 240). Hence, in contrast to Koselleck's more abstract theoretical approach, Harvey provides a concrete, material basis for understanding the changing dynamics of experience in crisis cultures. He anchors the accelerated social processes in physical realities—how we move, communicate, and transact in the world. This real-world application, as we shall see, is especially pertinent in my analysis of crisis cultures.

In the context of modernity's focus on the present as the primary temporal axis, Michel Foucault, particularly in works like *The Archaeology of Knowledge* (1972), aims to dismantle what could be termed modernity's undue emphasis on the present as the main temporal axis, a present burdened with the responsibility of anticipating the future and revering the past. This aspiration to transcend the modern time consciousness also underpins Foucault's focus on historical critique, where he aimed to dissolve false continuities and pay heed to ruptures, thresholds, and changes in direction in history rather than assuming continuity (Foucault 1977, 4–5). Intriguingly, Foucault perceives crises not as problems but as opportunities for transformation (Roitman 2014, 35). However, within crisis cultures, the rapid pace of change and the constant state of crisis become the new norm; that is, this relentless state of crisis becomes so embedded in our collective consciousness that it effectively redefines our sense of normalcy. This normalization of crisis makes it hard to identify what Stuart Hall defines as "conjunctures"—not just periods in time but critical moments formed by a complex array of contradictions and conditions (1990, 130). It is as if the continuous noise of crisis drowns out the ability to recognize transformative moments, let alone catalyze them. Similarly, the task of conceptualizing transformative events, as Alain Badiou (2005) characterizes them—specifically, as radical ruptures facilitating new possibilities—encounters difficulties within a crisis-pervasive culture. These events are not inherently impossible; however, their potential to gain significance or to influence our dominant paradigm of transformation is diminished due to their consistent overshadowing by ongoing crisis. Such a context generates cognitive dissonance, where the theoretical recognition of potential change is overwhelmed by the predominant, crisis-driven experiential reality. Even events that one might think could prompt transformative change, like the 2008 GFC or the COVID-19 pandemic, often lead to a longing for a return to "normalcy" rather than a radical restructuring of systems and orders. Consequently, the transformation that Foucault sees as possible and even necessary becomes much harder to conceive. Hence, what Foucault identifies as transformative moments remain hidden, drowned out by the incessant noise of the ongoing crisis, preventing them from standing out as critical turning points. What emerges, then, is an atmosphere of unbroken continuity, a perpetuity of the present that is all-encompassing, and yet fundamentally unsettling.

Teasing apart the complexities of temporality in crisis cultures is a nuanced task. The aim here is not to reconcile the divergent perspectives of Koselleck, Harvey, and Foucault into a simplified, unified theory, but rather to underscore how these diverse theorizations can coexist and collectively enhance our understanding of temporality in a crisis-ridden modernity. These are not necessarily contradictions but rather the inherent complexities within our temporal experience in the context of crisis cultures. The philosophies of Friedrich Nietzsche, for example, similarly grappled with the temporal complexities of modernity. As the nineteenth century drew to a close, he tapped into a prevailing sense of unease by articulating a pervasive feeling of falsehood that infused the age, a sense of being unmoored from historical continuity and authenticity (Mishra 2017, 239). His writings not only mirrored this collective angst but advocated a desire for radical transformation, calling for a New Man and New Order (Nietzsche 2006). Central to this was his concept of the "will to power," an idea that sought to reveal latent spaces for subjectivity to reconstitute its own desires, ideological constructs, and social mythologies (Nietzsche 1968). Nietzsche provided intellectual tools for challenging established norms, defying authority, innovating new ways of living, and engaging in transformative politics (Mishra 2017, 269). What connects Nietzsche's thinking to my discussion of crisis cultures is his approach to dealing with the immutable past. Instead of resigning to historical determinism, Nietzsche advocated for a future-oriented perspective that emphasizes transformative actions to prevent the repetition of past errors (de la Durantaye 2009, 323). In such a context, crisis cultures can be interpreted as emblematic of dynamic processes of action (doing) and continuous evolution (becoming). This reflects Nietzsche's emphasis on radical change and an unwavering focus on future aspirations. Consequently, one might consider whether crisis cultures could be re-envisioned as a type of cartography, not charting physical spaces but mapping future possibilities and potentialities. In this conceptualization, the "doing" of the future becomes an entity to be mapped, comprehended, and potentially, actively engaged with and harnessed.

Nietzsche's call to shift our focus from a past-centric view to transformative future actions resonates with wider discussions about catastrophe, a concept often mistakenly equated with crisis. In contemporary scholarly discourse, the understanding of catastrophe has evolved from religious interpretations of divine punishment to secular analyses within political, economic, and technological contexts. Catastrophes are now seen as both inherent risks of modernity and catalysts for major socioeconomic changes, embodying the "creative destructiveness" of the modern era (Dole et al. 2019, 4). For Nietzsche, the catastrophes of his time were not merely endpoints but opportunities for reconstituting social mythologies and ideological constructs (1968). Similarly, Voltaire and Baudrillard contend that catastrophes should not be perceived merely as devastating, isolated incidents. Instead, in their respective philosophies, catastrophes play a significant and enduring role, shaping broader narratives and philosophical discourses. In Meiner's interpretation of *Candide* (1759), Voltaire depicts a world dominated by an unending cascade of catastrophes, which become the norm rather than the exception. According to Meiner's reading:

> The real catastrophe is not so much the earthquake in Lisbon, the Seven Years' War, rape, disease, and injustice, nor the fact that all of these catastrophes co-exist. The catastrophic aspect of these events is not so much the fact that they shatter and destroy life or that our ideas about the way of the world are destroyed, but that these cruel and destructive events do not seem to change anything in the rationalists' conception of the world. (2012, 100)

He terms this the "catastrophe effect," where the overwhelming nature of continual disasters is more impactful than their individual occurrences (2012, 100). In a similar vein, Baudrillard introduces "*la grève des événements*" (the strike of events), a concept underscoring the ceaseless nature of catastrophes (1992, 39). By effectively going "on strike," events cease to make historical sense or lose their transformative power. Eliassen cautions that perceiving catastrophe in such a manner risks its conceptual implosion, diverting our focus from distinct events to an ever-present condition that could undermine not just historical interpretation but also usher us into a state of crippling paralysis (2012, 52, 56). This presents us with the challenge of a historical impasse—a state where the "space of experience" and the "horizon of expectation" paradoxically converge and immobilize. This will be a key focus in further discussions.

Reimagining crisis cultures as cartographies of future potentialities necessitates a close look at Walter Benjamin's *Theses on the Philosophy of History* (1968), which opens with the arresting image of an angel, the Angel of History, whose gaze is fixed upon the past while the future winds propel him forward. This angelic vision serves as a poetic metaphor for the ironies inherent in our understanding of progress and catastrophe (1968, 257–261). Much like this Angel of History, who is forced to watch the accumulation of human disaster while being propelled toward an uncertain future, our collective consciousness is trapped in a similar duality: a struggle between the transformative potentialities of the present and the weight of past catastrophes. Benjamin's *Theses* presents an urgent call to reevaluate how we understand time, history, and catastrophe in this dualistic context. He specifically focuses on the idea that each moment in time contains the potential for revolutionary change, what he calls "now-time" (*Jetztzeit*), disrupting traditional linear views of historical progress (Benjamin 1968, 260). In the *Arcades Project*, Benjamin defines catastrophe as a failure to capitalize on critical opportunities, viewing it as the preservation of the status quo (1999, 473–474). He further argues that this status quo is itself a continual catastrophe. Following Benjamin's logic, catastrophe is not just a looming event but a persistent condition, woven into the fabric of historical evolution and our prevailing models of progress. Therefore, to halt this unending catastrophe, we must challenge not only the immediate events but also the foundational temporal structures that underpin them. This perpetual state of catastrophe underscores the urgency and transformative possibilities present in every crisis. Such an understanding is acutely pertinent to contemporary contexts like climate change, where failure to act may result in ongoing ecological catastrophe.

Extending Benjamin's insights into "now-time" and the awakening of historical memory, we confront a critical aspect: individuals are not devoid of experiences or expectations, yet these become obfuscated in the face of the ever-present "now." The widening Koselleckian gap between "space of experience" and "horizon of expectation" underscores how ongoing crisis forces a reconsideration of how we perceive and interact with time, disrupting traditional narratives of progress and continuity. Benjamin's *Theses* (1968), however, provide not only a theoretical lens but also a practical approach for navigating the historical and temporal challenges inherent in crisis cultures. Central to this approach is the advocacy of an ethical responsibility toward both past and future. In the context of crisis cultures, the imperative becomes to reconstruct a sense of meaningful temporality, in line with Benjamin's focus on historical accountability. This involves actively engaging with significant moments from the past and applying their lessons to the present, thereby countering the pervasive sensation of an unending present. Such engagement not only allows for a reevaluation of one's place in the world but also opens avenues for potential change and new forms of communal becomings, moving beyond the constraints of continuous crisis. These endeavors are not solely individualistic but encompass collective actions aimed at cultivating an enhanced historical awareness. By embracing Benjamin's principles of solidarity and collective memory, new paths may emerge for navigating and potentially mitigating the temporal disorientation prevalent in contemporary crisis cultures. The insights derived from these reflections on temporality lead to a deeper inquiry that lies at the nexus of understanding crisis cultures: the fragmentation of human experience itself.

THE FRAGMENTATION OF EXPERIENCE

The horizon, as a metaphor for experience, beckons with the promise of endless possibility, while simultaneously marking the limits of our current understanding (Pickering 2004, 272). The term "experience," while frequently used in a general sense, encapsulates a range of subtle meanings across various disciplines, including psychology and philosophy. Its relevance is particularly heightened in the crisis cultures under discussion, where the discrepancy between actual lived experiences and projected futures complicates the interpretation of crises. In this setting, experience serves both as an analytical framework and a reality through which we navigate temporality. This section embarks on a philosophical and psychoanalytical examination of the notion of experience within crisis cultures, integrating insights from theorists such as Koselleck, Benjamin, and Agamben, and incorporating psychoanalytical viewpoints from Arno Gruen. To anchor this exploration, I refer to Count Reinhard's observation during a dialogue with Goethe, which poignantly captures the essence of experience in relation to time:

> Experience arrives too late for individuals, while for governments and peoples, it is never at hand. Past experience consolidates into a single point, whereas future experience disperses across various temporal spans—minutes, hours, days, years, centuries. As a result, similarities appear dissimilar; the past is perceived as a unified entity, while the future is seen in fragments.
>
> (quoted in Koselleck 1985, 34)

Reinhard's insight extends beyond the unique nature of past events; it also underlines our fragmented perception of the future. This dialectical relationship is not merely theoretical; it manifests materially in various social contexts. For example, in the management of natural disasters, governments often retrospectively perceive past disasters as singular, cohesive events, while future catastrophes are anticipated as a series of fragmented possibilities. The dynamic relationship between past and future reveals that experience transcends mere recollection or foresight; it becomes a critical epistemological tool, guiding our approach to the cultural and existential challenges presented by ongoing crises.

Koselleck, as discussed above, examines how our experiences from the past inform our expectations for the future and how these expectations, in turn, reframe our understanding of the past. Rather than treating these as static categories, he underlines their fluid and mutable nature, shaped by the fluctuations of social, political, and cultural change. Agamben, however, redirects this oscillation between past and future to the nature and quality of experience itself. His *Infancy and History: The Destruction of Experience* (2007), examines the diminishing quality of authentic experience in our globalized, information-saturated world. He attributes this decline to the oversimplification of life's complexities into easily digestible facts and data, which undermines our ability to create a cohesive narrative of our experiences. This trend not only affects individual perception but also weakens communal connections and political engagement (de la Durantaye 2009, 83). Agamben thus critiques how modernity has redefined history itself, inferring that history has shifted from being a lived experience to a sterile archive of "known" events, devoid of experiential depth (2007, 17). He advocates for a return to a more unadulterated form of experience, less influenced by language and conceptual frameworks—a return to an "infant" state in human experience—in order to reclaim the depth that has been lost in the modern era (2007, 55–60).

For Agamben, the crisis of modernity transcends the philosophical; it is a "crisis that threatens the very social and political fabric of our communities" (2007, 15). As Leland de la Durantaye clarifies, Agamben's reference to the "destruction of experience" pertains to the German concept of *Erfahrung*. The German terms *Erlebnis* and *Erfahrung*, both translating to "experience" in English, carry different philosophical meanings (Casey 2023, 284). *Erfahrung*, the older term, has its roots in the concept of travel or journeying, suggesting a well-traveled path (Casey 2023, 284). It symbolizes transformative experiences that shape the individual over time. This term embodies cumulative knowledge, not only at an individual level but also as collective wisdom, passed down through tradition and serving as a cultural roadmap for daily life. Kant's use of *Erfahrung* in *Critique of Pure Reason* (1998) associates it with sense-based perceptions that are quantifiable and repeatable, aligning with a theoretical, representational approach to the world (Casey 2023, 284). On the other hand, *Erlebnis*, associated with the word *Leben* (life), denotes an immediate, personal experience (Casey 2023, 284). It implies living through something novel and fresh, distinct from the conventional wisdom passed down culturally. For this reason, *Erlebnis* is often translated into English as lived experience. Philosophically, *Erlebnis* captures the novel and disruptive experiences of modernity, such as urbanization and technological progress, which diverge from established cultural patterns and necessitate new interpretations (Casey 2023, 284). This philosophical distinction between *Erlebnis* and *Erfahrung* sets the stage for Agamben's critique of modernity. For Agamben, the modern condition leads to us becoming "expropriated" of our experience (*Erfahrung*), weakening the authority founded on it (2007, 16–17). Although our times abound with events, they are enacted "outside" of individuals, often observed with detachment or even relief (Agamben 2007, 17). This poses an existential dilemma: How can we navigate through a multitude of events without genuinely experiencing them? The dilemma points to a profound disconnect between our daily encounters and our ability to absorb and reflect upon them, leading to a superficial engagement that compromises our self-understanding. This is not just a philosophical issue for Agamben; it is a critical concern affecting our cultural values and civic engagement. For him, then, the crisis of the modern age lies in its erosion of authentic experience, necessitating a thoughtful and assertive reaction to rescue and reinstate its value.

Although Agamben suggests a diminished capacity for genuine experience in modern times, this does not imply that events within crisis cultures lack discursive contestation. In fact, the very nature of crisis cultures lies in their contested representation and interpretation, a phenomenon that can be insightfully examined through Nico Carpentier's theoretical framework of the "discursive-material knot" (2017). This concept underscores the intimate relationship between discourse and material conditions, highlighting how dominant narratives and ideologies, particularly those aligned with neo-capitalist or extractivist paradigms, are not only shaped by but also shape material realities. These paradigms may actively seek to obfuscate our perceptions of events and experiences, contributing to the confusion and disorientation Agamben describes, and simultaneously reinforce material conditions that perpetuate their dominance. In this context, the discursive contestation within crisis cultures becomes not just a battleground for different interpretations and understandings of events, but also a site where material and discursive elements are inextricably linked. While Agamben points to a loss of depth in our experiences, it is precisely within the intertwining of discourse and materiality that this depth can be contested and, potentially, reclaimed. The challenge, then, lies in navigating these complex crisis narratives and understanding how they are shaped by, and in turn shape, the cultural, social, and political terrains. Therefore, while we may grapple with the "expropriation" of experience in the way Agamben describes, it does not preclude the active engagement and contestation of meanings and material realities within crisis cultures.

Arno Gruen, in his psychoanalytic work *The Betrayal of the Self* (2007), provides a perspective that complements the discursive-material knot, exploring how social structures not only influence but are intertwined with our capacity to develop authentic experiences. He redefines autonomy not as a proclamation of self-importance or independence but as a state of being attuned to one's emotions and needs (2007, 1). Dismissing the idea that autonomy implies the perpetual reiteration of one's strength and superiority, Gruen identifies genuine autonomy as the ability to connect with affective registers, capturing feelings of joy, sorrow, and pain—a genuine sensation of being alive (2007, 2). However, he notes that in modern society, the focus on success and achievement often obscures the quest for personal autonomy, an observation that aligns with Han's critique of the burnout society (2007, 9, 63). In Gruen's view, real autonomy can reveal the power structures to which individuals conform, often as a means to avoid feelings of helplessness (2007, 10). Autonomy, therefore, emerges as a situated praxis, gained from navigating these societal constraints, rather than a mere abstract concept to be pursued. He cautions that a fear of true autonomy and its inherent vitality can become a central, yet unrecognized, aspect of our lives, leading to such a fragmentation of potential autonomy that it remains largely unnoticed (Gruen 2007, 18).

Gruen's analysis of personal autonomy problematizes the psychological and social constraints inhibiting the development of authentic experiences, subtly advocating for the creation of environments where such authenticity can be restored and nurtured. It is within the realm of these proposed environments that Agamben's concept of a "phantasmatic space," as introduced in *Stanzas* (1993), becomes particularly relevant. Agamben envisions this phantasmatic space as a domain where transformative ideas and thoughts can not only emerge but also evolve (1993, 59). In this phantasmatic space, the discursive (ideas, thoughts) and the material (the environments that enable their emergence) coalesce, fostering the rediscovery and cultivation of authentic experiences. Agamben thus shares Nietzsche's view that the current crisis in modernity presents opportunities for both exploration and potential transformation. Yet, this transformative potential is limited if rooted only in epistemological abstraction. Gruen (2007, 30) cautions against an overemphasis on abstract thinking, echoing Soren Kierkegaard's warning about reducing real challenges to mere intellectual exercises (1962, 38). Such overreliance on abstraction can be understood as a misalignment within the discursive-material knot, where the discursive (abstract thought) becomes disconnected from the material (emotional realities and needs), leading to a fragmented understanding of our lived experiences and a diminished capacity for authentic emotional engagement. Consequently, the more we immerse ourselves in abstractions, the more detached we become from the tangible aspects of our emotional lives and their potential destructive outcomes. Gruen even warns of the potential for abstraction to be weaponized, noting that those in control of abstract concepts in politics and power often equate survival with the highest good, regardless of the impact (Gruen 2007, 50). How, then, can we reconnect with our genuine emotional selves and acknowledge the real consequences of our actions in a world increasingly dominated by abstract thought and the relentless pursuit of survival? To address this question, it is essential to consider the broader historical context in which the concept of crisis has evolved. It is this genealogical lens that I now turn to, with the aim of tracing the evolution of crisis from a nuanced academic term to a prominent feature of contemporary discourse.

CRISIS, A TRAVELING CONCEPT

The concept of crisis, as it spans disciplines like medicine, sociology, anthropology, psychology, and political science, necessitates a thorough genealogical analysis. Reinhart Koselleck's "Crisis" (2006) is essential in elucidating the historical evolution of the term. Originating in ancient Greece, the term crisis was initially associated with medicine, law, and theology, symbolizing key decisions or turning points (Koselleck 2006, 358–360). As the concept evolved and spread into Latin, French, and Western languages like English and German, it began to take on social and political meanings while preserving its original medical connotations (Koselleck 2006, 360–362). By the seventeenth century, the term's discursive ambit had widened to encompass the "body politic," and extended into interdisciplinary areas such as economics and historiography, further underlining its adaptability (Koselleck 2006, 362–67). Moreover, crisis gained significant religious implications, aligning with broader historical and philosophical ideas such as the "Last Judgment" (Koselleck 2006, 370). Its evolving lexicon came to symbolize both cyclical repetitive situations and singular, decisive moments, forming a dual nature that solidified its status as a key concept in historical analysis (Koselleck 2006, 371). The ongoing evolution of the term, as detailed in this section, underscores its complex relationship with both language and politics. By tracing this evolution, I aim to highlight the intricacies and challenges that arise in its present-day usage. Understanding this evolution is key to interpreting and addressing the crisis cultures that we are immersed in.

In *Critique and Crisis* (1988), Koselleck outlines how the Enlightenment introduced a novel form of critical thinking, precipitating a significant political crisis. He connects this crisis to a utopian vision of history, where modern individuals were depicted as "destined to be at home everywhere and nowhere" (1988, 6). This teleological view redefined the present as a perpetual site of crisis and transformation, establishing a stark dichotomy between the past and future (Koselleck 1988, 9–10). This interpretation of crisis resonates with Rousseau's contemplations on the nexus between catastrophe and civilization's progress. Rousseau, in his reflections, conceives catastrophe not as a looming event but an ongoing ontological condition. This view informs his polemic against the perils of unchecked optimism about progress and the risks of new forms of subjugation (Mishra 2017, 89). In his *Emile*, first published in 1762, Rousseau critiques society's moral and spiritual contradictions, driven by envy and material pursuits (1979). His bold claim: "*Nous approchons de l'etat de crises et du siècle des revolutions*" (We are approaching a state of crises and a century of revolutions)—articulates his belief in a chronic crisis condition (Koselleck 2006, 372–373). For Rousseau, the moral decay he observed in modern society was integral to his definition of what constituted a moral crisis. Unlike Pascal, who attributed human discontent to a theological estrangement, Rousseau pinpointed a crisis stemming from self-alienation (Storey & Silber Storey 2021, 102–103). He nostalgically recalled an age of "noble savagery," contrasting it with the axiological moral decline of his time (Koselleck 1988, 170). His ideal solution envisioned a utopian return to a natural state where society and state are unified and virtue and industriousness reign (Koselleck 1988, 170). His philosophy thus advocated for a simpler ethos as the antidote to humanity's existential crises, valuing community over individuality and finding redemption in nature.

Diderot, too, perceived a crisis in modernity, echoing the sentiment of his contemporaries with his declaration: "*Nous touchons à une crise qui aboutira à l'esclavage ou à la liberté*" (We are reaching a crisis that will culminate in either slavery or liberty) (Koselleck 2006, 373). Diderot's statement extends beyond mere political commentary, pointing to the crisis as both a signifier and a catalyst for decisive actions (Koselleck 2006, 374). This perspective influenced the contemporary conceptualization of crisis, underscoring its dual character as semantically ambiguous yet efficacious in catalyzing change. In Germany, during the Enlightenment, thinkers like Herder further developed the term into a key historiographical tool, moving beyond its earlier metaphorical associations with death and rebirth (Koselleck 2006, 378). The medical metaphor, which had previously been the dominant interpretation, was replaced by a more comprehensive view of crisis as indicative of ongoing, significant changes, cementing its place as a defining aspect of modernity (Koselleck 2006, 378, 381). Although the meaning of crisis expanded and at times became less distinct, the effort to utilize it in a precise manner persisted. The concept remained a staple in historical analysis, consistently seen as a variable yet crucial element in interpreting history.

During the American War of Independence, the concept of crisis underwent a pivotal transformation. It evolved from being a predictor of revolution to symbolizing a global moment of reckoning (Koselleck 2006, 374). Drawing inspiration from Rousseau, Thomas Paine viewed the war as a critical juncture leading toward justice and equality (Koselleck 2006, 374, 377). In this context, crisis transcended its role as a mere catalyst to become an independent historical concept, signaling a philosophical shift that required insight and tactical strategy (Koselleck 2006, 377). As the newly independent nation sought to define itself, Alexis de Tocqueville arrived to explore American society in the wake of the revolution. Contrasting with Rousseau's utopic vision of the past, Tocqueville focused on the inherent contradictions of emerging democracies. He identified a paradoxical quest for "immanent contentment," where individual pursuits of happiness often exacerbated social crises (Storey & Silber Storey 2021, 160–166). Tocqueville cautioned against a subtle form of tyranny arising from conflating personal success with the overall health of a society (Mishra 2017, 269–270). This theme is explored in contemporary discussions by Michael J. Sandel in his book *The Tyranny of Merit* (2020). Sandel critiques how meritocracy, a system that should reward talent and effort, actually deepens social divides and perpetuates inequality. He argues that this focus on personal achievement undermines communal values and solidarity, echoing concerns Alexis de Tocqueville raised about individualistic societies. Hence, while Rousseau's crisis nostalgically reaches back, Tocqueville's emphasizes the unceasing pursuit of immanent contentment, reflecting the paradoxes of modern societies and the fluid and ever-evolving narratives of crisis within them, bridging the intellectual thoughts of the era from Rousseau to Diderot and beyond.

From the mid-nineteenth century onward, the term crisis began to encompass economic disruptions, reflecting the emerging global phenomena linked to capitalism (Koselleck 2006, 389, 392). In this new economic frame, crisis was perceived not as a permanent state but as a transitional phase, adaptable to both liberal and socialist historical narratives. For liberals, each economic crisis represented a step in an evolutionary process toward societal improvement. In contrast, socialist thinkers, notably Marx and Engels, interpreted crises as both triggers and harbingers of forthcoming revolutionary changes (Koselleck 2006, 393–394). This bifurcated interpretation is rooted in Marx's materialist critique of capitalism's intrinsic contradictions, notably in his seminal work *Capital* (1992). This perspective led to the development of various neo-Marxist economic theories and analyses, extending the understanding of crises beyond economic dimensions to reveal structural limitations within the capitalist framework, challenging the idea of a stable, liberal economic system. The influence of these insights has been significant in shaping contemporary economic theories and historical philosophies, especially those with a neo-Marxist orientation (Koselleck 2006, 396–397). With the contributions of Marx and Engels, the concept of crisis evolved into a powerful tool for radical social critique, closely linked to their utopian vision for social transformation. This expansion of the term's scope reflects a crucial connection between intellectual discourse and economic realities, marking a significant broadening of the term's application. It mirrors the complex changes in modern society and highlights the inherent instability of the capitalist system.

During the nineteenth and twentieth centuries, the concept of crisis continued to evolve, expanding its applicability across various academic fields while simultaneously becoming less precisely defined. Koselleck notes that contemporary media has transformed crisis into a prevalent, albeit overused, term, often associated with conflict, revolution, and feelings of alienation (2006, 398–399). He acknowledges the term's utility but cautions against its vagueness and theoretical imprecision (Koselleck 2006, 399–400). Building on this foundational understanding, recent scholars have developed nuanced theoretical approaches to better grasp the complexity of crisis in the contemporary era. The anthropologist Henrik Vigh (2008) proposes that crisis should be understood as an ongoing lived reality rather than merely a metaphor or isolated event. His concept of "crisis as context" is especially relevant to marginalized communities. For these groups, Vigh argues, crisis is not a temporary or exceptional state but a constant, pervasive condition that shapes their day-to-day existence. In such environments, instability becomes the norm, and continuous adaptation is necessary for survival. This view challenges traditional notions of crisis as a distinct and bounded period, suggesting instead that for some, crisis is a chronic backdrop to their lives (2008, 7–8). Janet Roitman, in *Anti-Crisis* (2014), on the other hand, introduces greater intricacy to the term, exploring its complex evolution from a specific critical moment to an ongoing state of being (2014, 7–8). She critiques the generalized usage of crisis as a catch-all term, emphasizing that a proper understanding of crisis requires relational judgment—crisis compared to what?—and a careful consideration of the context in which it occurs (Roitman 2014, 4).

Roitman's and Vigh's studies collectively challenge the simplistic view of crisis as a turning point, instead foregrounding its persistent nature. Vigh, in particular, prompts us to redefine the notion of "normal" within the context of crisis, asserting that "crisis, when it is chronic, may become normal in the sense that it is what there is most, but it does not become normal in the sense that this is how things should be" (2008, 11). His problematization of "normal" within the context of chronic crisis subverts conventional binaries between normality and crisis, drawing attention to how crisis shapes the very fabric of daily life (2008, 9–10). For instance, the growing precarity of labor markets, where short-term contracts and unstable employment have become "the new normal," can alter our sense of what constitutes normality. This phenomenon is more than just an alteration of what is considered "normal"; it serves as a "transcendental placeholder," a term Roitman uses to indicate a conceptual space where the label of crisis captures an array of complex, contingent circumstances and tensions (2014, 9). By functioning as a transcendental placeholder, it opens up new possibilities for rethinking the frameworks and norms that govern our conceptions of employment, stability, and the nature of crisis itself. Thus, Roitman and Vigh move away from binary categorizations of "crisis" versus "non-crisis." Instead, they portray crisis as a fluid, evolving phenomenon that impacts individual experiences and broader social structures (Vigh 2008, 11; Roitman 2014, 10).

Roitman's analysis challenges the characterization of crisis as a historical "super concept," provoking an essential question: how does such a generalized abstraction impact our comprehension of crisis? This designation, she warns, may become so generalized that specific meanings are elided, essentially creating a blind spot that obfuscates the true complexities of crisis situations (2014, 11). Roitman's contention is not merely theoretical but a call to action, likening crisis to an observation that remains unobserved, and thus transforming it into a multidimensional symbol that resists oversimplification. She thus encourages us to view crisis as an enabling force in the production of knowledge (2014, 14). This is vividly illustrated by the example of precarity in labor markets. When a crisis such as job insecurity becomes endemic, it demands new ways of thinking, compelling researchers, policymakers, and even individuals to generate fresh knowledge and perspectives on employment and social stability. In the next section, I sketch out how the production of knowledge takes on narrative form, both shaping and reflecting the cultural life of a society in crisis.

CRISIS IN THE STORYLINE

The evolution of crisis into crisis cultures represents more than just a change in terminology; it is a significant alteration in our perception and interaction with the contemporary world. Crisis narratives are partly responsible for this evolution, as they often obscure rather than clarify the underlying meanings of crisis situations. The theoretical framework articulated thus far in this chapter can be seen as a "necessary detour" (Hall 1992, 286) on the road to a deeper understanding—a notion famously articulated by Stuart Hall, who noted that "theory is always a detour" on the road to "somewhere more important" (1991, 42). This section extends this theoretical foundation, emphasizing the vital role of narrative in unraveling these entanglements, especially in a postmodern world where both new and traditional narratives converge, challenging foundational concepts of truth, reality, and meaning. In Roitman's analysis, the term crisis transcends mere categorization; it becomes a narrative device, a mechanism through which the distinctiveness of individual events is abstracted into a broader, seemingly self-explanatory historical narrative (2014, 3). When crisis is leveraged to form the basis of contemporary historical narratives, it emerges as pivotal in shaping how we perceive history. Crisis, in this context, becomes a means to underscore "moments of truth," giving them importance as reflective points in history (Roitman 2014, 3). Roitman thus reveals the polymorphic nature of crisis not solely as a concept but as an interpretative tool, acting as both a pathway to historical authenticity and a conceptual lens to contemplate "history" itself (2014, 3–4).

In *Cruel Optimism* (2011), Lauren Berlant examines our present condition as an unending crisis, a continuous state where narratives of crisis become a recurring motif, heightening our sensation of instability (2011, 7). Her elaborate mapping of what she calls "crisis ordinary" does not necessarily promise authentic encounters but does initiate an intriguing conversation on crisis narratives, focusing on the affective resonances and embodied rhythms that lie beneath. In wrestling with narratives of crisis in this book, I am similarly not simply reading stories of crises but rather flipping the sense-making priority. That is, I contend that the cultural life of crisis cultures is essentially oriented toward making sense of crisis *in the storyline*, where narratives do not merely reflect reality but actively construct it, demanding a new level of critical engagement with the stories we live by. In a world where crisis becomes a recurring motif, a crisis ordinary, how do we differentiate between authentic experiences and mere conceptual abstractions? What fresh insights might we unlock by critically examining the nature of crisis and its influence on the stories we tell about ourselves?

At the intersection of Western modernity and crisis cultures, a key narrative emerges: the erosion of traditional values as a hallmark of modern life. Hannah Arendt remarks on the phenomenon of "a global present without a common past," underlining the breakdown of shared stories and values and the resulting dominance of individualism over community cohesion (1968, 84). Similarly, Agamben's critique in *The Man Without Content* (1999a) focuses on the isolation of art and the artist in the modern world. He challenges the contemporary separation of aesthetic value from its ethical and historical contexts, rendering the artist as a "man without content," estranged from both community and the deeper purposes of art, an estrangement that has implications for the continuity of cultural traditions. This isolation manifests as the disintegration of shared cultural values and a loss of historical continuity, leaving individuals in a liminal state between a fragmented past and an uncertain future (1999, 108). Thus, the search for reference points, such as art that explores identity, literature that bridges cultural gaps, community engagement that fosters connection, or political activism that strives for shared goals, emerges as an essential existential quest, a response to the crisis cultures that define our modern condition.

The erosion of tradition not only makes present the inherent vulnerability of modernity but it paves the way for an intellectual transition toward postmodernism. This transition, involving novel epistemological challenges, has been examined by thinkers such as Lyotard in *The Postmodern Condition* (1984) and further scrutinized by Jameson (1984) and Harvey (1989) among others. At its core, this shift signals a crisis that transcends the mere supplanting of grand narratives with localized truths, leading instead to a profound uncertainty about the function of narratives and their purpose in our lives (Jameson 1984, xi). This uncertainty is a reflection of our dwindling faith in historical or political teleologies and compels us to confront less visible narratives that shape our collective consciousness. Harvey, in particular, interprets postmodernism as an inherent crisis within modernism, viewing postmodernity as a complex reaction to modernity, not as a clear break from it (1989, 111–112). He cautions that the increased fragmentation and diversity of voices could lead to political incoherence, potentially marginalizing different perspectives (1989, 116–117). He further warns that postmodernism might inadvertently ignore the critical realities of political economy or even veer toward complicity with certain political aesthetics (1989, 117). Baudrillard adds to this discourse by portraying the postmodern era as a paradoxical time marked by both catastrophic end and the end of catastrophe (1989, 34). He argues that we have reached a point where new catastrophes no longer bring about meaningful change because the ultimate catastrophe has already occurred. For instance, in the context of climate change, individual extreme weather events, while disastrous, may not lead to significant shifts in consciousness or action because, Baudrillard might say, the essential environmental tipping point has already been crossed. The real tragedy for Baudrillard lies in achieving our desires without any coherent vision for the future (Dietrich 2012, 205). Thus, in a theoretical terrain where the distinctions between modernism and postmodernism are murky at best, the question is: Are crisis cultures a direct response to the postmodern condition or are they indicative of a more complex undercurrent?

Crisis cultures, I contend, are not merely postmodernism repackaged but a more intricate manifestation of it. Echoing Harvey's critique, crisis cultures can be seen as a natural consequence of the diverse and often conflicting narratives that characterize the postmodern condition. Lawrence Grossberg

(2010) provides a pertinent example with his analysis of the Global Financial Crisis. From a postmodern perspective, different constituencies may interpret the Global Financial Crisis in different ways: economists might view it as a failure of financial regulation; politicians may regard it as a symbol of corporate greed; and those who lost their homes could interpret it as a personal tragedy. Each interpretation forms part of a mosaic of meanings, turning the crisis into a surge of multiple narratives, each striving to answer the question of what went wrong (Roitman 2014, 11). For instance, some narratives might pinpoint the housing bubble collapse as the cause, whereas other narratives might recognize that the roots of the crisis were evident even earlier. Nonetheless, multiple narratives circulate and overlap within mediated discourse, each attempting to make sense of the crisis and its contributing factors. This prompts Grossberg to observe: "not that these accounts of the crisis are not true, but that they are all true and yet, even collectively, *not true enough* to describe, let alone explain, what has happened" (my emphasis) (2010, 300). He emphasizes the need to consider and reflect upon these multiple narratives without consolidating them into a singular, definitive story. In this sense, crisis cultures partly embody this postmodern proclivity to question the function of narratives that is an inherent feature of our historical moment. As such, the phenomenon of crisis cultures is not a mere reflection of our postmodern landscape but a complex evolution within it.

Crisis cultures, while rooted in the postmodern condition, also signify a distinctive departure from traditional postmodern interpretations. This divergence is captured in the paradox articulated by Mark Hayward: "Everything is different, yet nothing is changing" (2010, 284). In postmodernism, creative destruction might have been seen as a metaphor for continual transformation and critique of established norms, a process that questions and often upends traditional structures, offering new ways of understanding. However, in crisis cultures, the clear milestones or transformative moments that might have brought clarity or guidance in a postmodern context are conspicuously absent. The constant shifts and innovations, while promising progress, often blur into an indistinguishable continuum, leaving individuals without the meaningful signposts that once marked the path of modernity (and postmodernity). Despite the array of crisis narratives that seek to explain crisis events, the pervasive sense of crisis remains constant and unyielding, underlining a situation where crisis is omnipresent, yet the overarching state of change remains static. In other words, whereas postmodern contexts enable multiple interpretations and continuous inquiry through crisis narratives, within crisis cultures, crisis narratives become diluted, losing their capacity to synthesize for us the meaning of crisis events. Crisis narratives become, instead, an ever-present background noise, a constant hum that pervades our daily lives. For example, postmodern interpretations of climate change encompass a range of narratives, from environmental catastrophe to calls for technological innovation, offering diverse insights. In crisis cultures, however, climate change becomes a continuous undercurrent of ecological anxiety. Varied interpretations recede, overshadowed by a generalized sense of impending ecological threat, constantly present but lacking specific events or turning points. This evolution exemplifies a shift from a landscape rich with competing narratives to one where crisis itself is a pervasive backdrop in our collective experience.

The evolution from postmodernism to crisis cultures signifies not just a shift in interpreting crisis narratives, but a profound transformation in the perception and practice of individualism. Han's critique of hyper-individualism draws attention to its harmful effects, such as widespread fatigue and burnout caused by the relentless pressure on individuals to continuously perform and reinvent themselves (2015). This intense focus on self-optimization echoes through Pankaj Mishra's analysis of the paradox of individual freedom within a neoliberal context. Mishra explores how this context offers both opportunities and a relentless demand for self-reinvention, creating a dynamic where individual freedom is both a promise and a burden (2017, 26). Further, Mishra argues that the consequences of embracing individualism go beyond what early thinkers like Tocqueville anticipated, leading to a profound change in people's expectations and worldviews. Individuals are now grappling with uncertainty and the destabilization of their "horizons of expectations," leading to a frantic search for new belief systems and modes of self-expression (Mishra 2017, 27). The modern individual now operates in a world where identity is fluid and constantly evolving, influenced by global crises, digital connectivity, and a reshaping of social and cultural norms. The "Western model," which once epitomized a linear progression of progress, now faces significant skepticism. Mishra suggests that future generations might question how such a once universally accepted framework came to influence global consciousness (2017, 40).

The crisis cultures we are immersed in elicit a broad spectrum of interpretations and reactions too diverse to fully recount here. However, two contrasting responses stand out. The first response can be characterized as an optimistic interpretation endorsing a utopian vision of modernity. This perspective, cogently articulated by Steven Pinker (2018), celebrates the Enlightenment's achievements, advocating for the continuation of principles that have driven substantial positive global changes. Pinker contends that any wholesale dismissal of modernity and the Enlightenment not only overlooks their tangible, life-altering contributions to human well-being but inadvertently fuels a growing cynicism toward Enlightenment tenets such as science, reason, and progress (2018, 17–18). While Pinker's perspective provides a counterpoint to critiques of current neoliberal regimes, such as Thomas Piketty's *Capital in the Twenty-First Century* (2017), it underscores both the achievements of modernity and the erosion of trust in its institutions since the 1960s. His robust defense of modernity, focusing on increased total wealth and social advancement opportunities, cautions against viewing every challenge as a crisis and warns against undue pessimism (2017, 356–360). Yet, this optimism might fall short in addressing the affective emotional atmospheres of inequality and the underlying tensions that shape crisis cultures. This contradiction highlights a significant flaw in overly optimistic views: they frequently overlook how systemic inequalities can endure or even intensify, despite apparent overall advancements. Next to Mishra and Han's analyses, Pinker's vision leaves unanswered some pressing questions. Why, despite clear evidence of progress, do individuals and communities often fail to recognize or appreciate these advances? And why, despite these significant strides, does instability's specter continue to cast a shadow on the modern world?

Although fundamentally aligned with Enlightenment values, the second response contrasts sharply with Pinker's optimism and can be considered a dystopian vision of the era in which we find ourselves. This view, expounded upon by Anthony M. Wachs and Jan D. Schaff in *Age of Anxiety* (2020), warns of the social consequences of shifting from community-centered life to radical individualism, a move they argue has led to widespread anxiety and fragmentation (2020, vii–viii). Similarly concerned with the growing fissures in contemporary society, they argue that the rise of cultural relativism and an overemphasis on multicultural "otherness," underpin contemporary crises like Brexit or Trumpism (2020, 7). Jordan Peterson provides another dimension to this discourse. Unlike Wachs and Schaff, who critique the ascendancy of individualism, Peterson (2019) shifts the spotlight to the opposite end of the spectrum, decrying the fixation on group identities that, in his view, leaves the individual self adrift in a sea of competing narratives. Peterson underscores the significance of myths and traditions as navigational frameworks for human conduct, a perspective that resonates with earlier philosophers like Mazzini, Sorel, and José Ortega y Gasset (Mishra 2017, 269). For Peterson (2019), postmodernism essentially contends that the world is open to an infinite array of interpretations, thus destabilizing any claims to a single, authoritative perspective. While he concedes that numerous interpretations of the world do exist, he argues that not all of them hold validity. The measure of an interpretation's validity, he argues, is determined by its capacity for enduring sustainability over extended periods and across diverse social contexts. Moreover, he contends that postmodernism's deep-rooted skepticism ought to render it fundamentally at odds with Marxism, a philosophy built on overarching grand narratives. Despite this theoretical incompatibility, Peterson notes a paradoxical alliance between the two—most notable in academic environments. As a result, he critiques postmodernism for lacking a coherent ethical framework, leading to an intellectually inconsistent yet influential ideology. Hence, while Wachs and Schaff see the pendulum swinging too far toward individualism and cultural relativism, thereby causing social fracturing, Peterson aims his critique at the other end of the spectrum. He contends that an excessive focus on group identities and what he describes as "cultural neo-Marxism" leads to a departure from universal principles that have historically guided Western society. Peterson specifically targets identity politics and "wokeness"—initially a term denoting awareness of social injustices, which right-wing media has since recast as a derogatory label for progressive policies (Atkins 2023, 321). These trends, according to Peterson, signal a significant moral and ideological shift away from foundational Western values. His call for a reevaluation of society's ethical and philosophical underpinnings aligns with a broader intellectual tradition spanning from Rousseau to contemporary thinkers like Agamben and Arendt, urging a reassessment of the principles that unify and sustain societal cohesion.

In *Crisis of Modernity* (2014) Augusto Del Noce adds another dimension to the issues raised by Wachs, Schaff, and Peterson by examining how the erosion of cultural heritage has resulted in a lack of stable moral frameworks in contemporary society. While Peterson emphasizes individual transcendence through myths and traditions, Del Noce shifts the focus toward communal rediscovery and renewal. He argues that modern society has moved away from the ethical principles that have historically guided human civilization. He advocates for a return to traditional values, suggesting that the rise of multiculturalism and moral relativism has weakened these foundational traditions, pushing society toward nihilism (2014, 94). Del Noce goes beyond merely invoking traditions as guiding principles; he emphasizes the need to understand the specific historical and social contexts from which these traditions originate. He advocates for a more grounded approach to tradition, avoiding idealized visions of the past and instead examining how these can be adapted meaningfully to address contemporary challenges. His critique presents modernity as an irreversible shift that has divorced reality from any transcendent order, leaving us susceptible to new forms of totalitarianism (2014, 94–99). His arguments resonate strongly with the anxieties expressed by Wachs and Schaff, underlining the urgent need for a return to coherent traditions and a stable moral compass in an age marked by fragmentation and uncertainty.

While Pinker, Wachs, Schaff, Peterson, and Del Noce provide incisive, albeit contrasting, frameworks to understand the crisis cultures we are immersed in, their interpretations may inadvertently reduce the complexities of both modern and postmodern conditions to reductive binaries—either utopian visions or dystopian warnings. This somewhat polarized discourse tends to marginalize the more variegated realities of our historical moment. For instance, Wachs and Schaff pin the crisis of modernity on what they view as postmodernity's hyper-individualism. Peterson, meanwhile, diagnoses the ontological disarray spurred by postmodernity as the primary ailment. Del Noce, on the other hand, points to a moral failure. However, these focused interpretations could potentially obscure deeper, more elaborate origins of the predicament they are describing. They also occlude the fact that classical critiques of modernity by thinkers such as Nietzsche, Koselleck, Habermas, Adorno, and Benjamin have already portrayed modernity as inherently crisis-ridden, suggesting that the crisis is not a deviation but a fundamental aspect of Western modernity. These thinkers unsettle the idea that resolving contemporary issues relies solely on a return to traditional values or an uncritical embrace of modernity. Instead, they provide a more layered assessment of modernity, one that goes beyond simplistic classifications of salvation or ruin.

In contrast, Lauren Berlant's *Cruel Optimism* serves as a compelling counterpoint to both these utopian and dystopian perspectives, introducing affect as a critical dimension in the interpretation of crisis narratives. Berlant introduces the concept of "cruel optimism," which refers to the intimate relationship between optimism and attachment, and how this relationship can turn cruel when our desires obstruct our well-being (2011, 1–2). Berlant explores how optimism propels us to seek fulfillment through external connections, whether with people, objects, or ideologies. The cruelty, however, emerges when these connections create paradoxical entanglements that inhibit the realization of our desires (2011, 2). Focusing on the post-World War II era in the United States and Europe, Berlant examines the erosion of ideals such as job security and political equality and centers on the concept of the "crisis ordinary," which undermines the dream of "having a good life" (2011, 2–3). In this context, the "ordinary" becomes marked by a permanent state of crisis, where mere adaptation is seen as an achievement (Berlant 2011, 3). Affect and sensory experience are pivotal to Berlant's analysis as they not only shape how we perceive and experience crises but also influence our ability to navigate them (2011, 10). Berlant's approach might offer a novel alternative out of what she calls the "impasse," presenting a nuanced epistemology of how optimism can turn cruel and how traditional desires can become obstacles to flourishing (2011, 1). By interweaving histories, desires, and fears into her analysis, Berlant complicates the simplistic binary of utopian and dystopian narratives. Her work introduces the dimension of affectivity into our understanding of crisis, revealing how both emotions and desire shape our lived experiences of crises and fundamentally influence our capacity to navigate through them.

Rather than advocating for a mere re-inscription of traditional values or maintaining an uncritical celebration of modernity's achievements, I propose a broader, more nuanced framework to understand our crisis-ridden era. My focus leans toward a critical and imaginative engagement with crisis as a fluid, ever-evolving phenomenon. In doing so, I contend that our contemporary anxieties are not mere epiphenomena of individual or cultural failures but are dialectically entwined with broader social transformations. What we see here intersects dialogically with Gruen's probing into modernity's paradoxes: on one hand, we are drowning in stimuli, while on the other, a sense of profound emptiness pervades (2007, 95–96). If we are so "connected," why do we feel increasingly disconnected? What does this dissonance disclose about our culture and its illusions of progress? My framework extends these queries, informed by scholars like Lauren Berlant, who contemplates the crisis ordinary through affect theory. Specifically, I search for communal becomings—practical social actions that work to counter mainstream narratives of crisis. These communal becomings function as what Michel Foucault (1977) calls "counter-memory," involving the active creation and presentation of alternative histories that challenge the conventional ways we think about crises. This goes beyond mere ideological critique; it is embodied praxis—an ongoing dialectic of becoming that aligns with Stuart Hall's call to challenge the "dominant codes" of representation and meaning (1990, 128). This strategic remapping aims to cultivate a more interconnected epistemology, one adept at hearing, reading, and responding to crises in transformative ways. It turns crises into opportunities for what Giorgio Agamben would describe as "potentiality," where each crisis becomes a site for collective emancipation (1999b, 178–81). This path leads us toward a more hopeful future, or what Derrida might term as a state where experience is no longer "out of joint" (1994). In this manner, we reorient ourselves away from stifling dichotomies and toward an understanding that accounts for the multiplicity of forces shaping our experience of present and future crises.

This approach might recall Martha Nussbaum's urgent warning about the humanities facing an existential crisis. Nussbaum claims that this crisis is not just academic; it is a threat to democracy itself: "We are in the midst of a crisis of massive proportions and grave global significance . . . a worldwide crisis in education . . . The future of the world's democracies hangs in the balance" (2010, 1). Her ominous words resonate strongly in today's context, where authoritarian regimes are on the rise globally. This leads some to wonder if the decline of the humanities in education has, perhaps, set the stage for this troubling trend in governance (De Chavez & Varadharajan 2023, 54). This notion—that underfunding the humanities might indirectly boost authoritarianism—provides a sort of dark vindication for those who champion these academic disciplines. However, the very urgency in Nussbaum's argument opens the door to a particular critique. De Chavez and Varadharajan argue that the protective "guardian" role Nussbaum assigns to the humanities can inadvertently perpetuate social divisions. Specifically, it risks excluding people who do not fit into a particular mold, fostering what they term a divisive "fear of the Other," or essentially a fear of the uninformed or the "stupid"

(2023, 55). It is against this contentious backdrop that my interdisciplinary approach finds its purpose, methodologically aligned with viola candice milton's vision of academic "disobedience" (2023, 35). She urges us not only to innovate but to embody disobedience in our scholarship, continually questioning its relevance and impact with a probing "so what?" (2023, 36). This involves actionable social practices that not only acknowledge but also integrate the diverse epistemologies and lived experiences of our communities (milton 2023, 45). This strategic remapping, then, is not just an ideological exercise but a lived praxis. It stands in line with milton's insistence on the scholar's responsibility to articulate the relevance and transformative power of their work, while also harmonizing with De Chavez and Varadharajan's view that crisis is "situated and contingent" rather than universal (2023, 51). As Keyan G. Tomaselli puts it: "Postmodernism, properly done, is basically in the business of critique, but to be socially relevant it needs to recover position, rights and justice. Diagnosing what is wrong can only occur in terms of discussions about what is right" (2023, 126). My methodological framework, then, is a step toward fulfilling this need. It stands as a challenge to both conventional metrics of academic success and to more established scholarly approaches that have proven themselves to be inadequate in navigating our multiple and overlapping crises.

As we circle back to the leitmotif of my argument—the integral role of narrative within crisis cultures—we confront the indelible urgency to rethink the storyline within these narratives of crisis. Echoing Stuart Hall, the complex theoretical journey traversed in this chapter emerges not as digressions but "necessary detours" (1992, 286). In crafting a dialogic framework that can accommodate complexity and dissonance, the aim is to forge a substantive response to the crisis in the humanities, pointing toward a new epistemological and ontological grounding for the field. The focus of this intellectual endeavor hinges on a critical reorientation, a *flipping of sense-making priorities* in grappling with crisis narratives. Such a reframing invites us to question the ontological solidity of these stories that circulate within the framework of what Berlant calls the "crisis ordinary" (2011). The narrative, then, is not merely an expository mirror reflecting the chaos of our times; it is an active scaffolding, a meaning-making apparatus that constructs the lived realities of crisis cultures. If narratives are performative constructs that wield the power to shape, and even distort, collective imaginations and lived experiences, the question we ought to pose is not just what these narratives are, but what they *do*—what affective frequencies they tune us into, what discursive spaces they open or foreclose, what forms of relationality they propagate or dismantle. In a context where crises risk becoming banal through their sheer omnipresence, it is no longer just about demarcating authentic experiences from conceptual abstractions or unveiling the hidden "moments of truth" within a saturated field of crisis narratives. Instead, the objective lies in our capacity to generate a dialogic framework robust enough to host these multiple registers of truth, meaning, and affectivity. We are tasked with creating a narrative ecology that is capable of holding complexity, dissonance, and even contradiction—a narrative space where the real and the conceptual, the unique and the ordinary, can critically coexist, reciprocally inform, and even transform one another. Such a space, rich in its polyvocality, could herald not just new levels of critical engagement but new possibilities of communal becomings. It is here, in the interstices of these crisis narratives, that we may find the transformative potential to reimagine and reconfigure our crisis-laden storylines.

CONCLUSION

In this extensive inquiry—which weaves together various theoretical threads—I circle back to the chapter's central axiom: The Experience is Out of Joint. This phrase takes inspiration from Hamlet's famous declaration that "the time is out of joint," a sentiment later philosophically examined by Derrida in his *Specters of Marx* (1994). Specifically, Derrida argued that this disjointedness is not just a temporal anomaly, but rather the very thing that makes time possible. Expanding this dialogic framework, I have reconceptualized this aphorism yet again, steering it toward the realm of "experience," arguing that the disjointedness we confront is not just a temporal aberration but a state of being that affects our very experience of life. By focusing on the experience of disjointedness, I eschew the common debate of whether to embrace Western modernity, as suggested by thinkers like Pinker, or to challenge the complex and hegemonic narratives that come with postmodernity. The point is, crises do not merely unfold "in time"; they change how we experience time itself, leading to affective feelings of dislocation and existential uncertainty. In taking this step from Hamlet's lament to Derrida's analysis, and arriving at our current immersion in crisis cultures, the disjointedness of experience becomes less an intellectual inquiry and more a site upon which our lived realities are actively scripted, re-scripted, and performed. As we move to the subsequent chapter's exploration of individual navigations within these crisis cultures, the overarching question shifts from merely the "what" and "how" of these crises to the more compelling "when" and "where to now?" The experience is indeed out of joint, yet it is precisely in this disjuncture—this liminal space between the existential and the temporal—that we find an opportunity for reconfiguration, a space where the contentious articulations of crisis cultures might be questioned, understood, and perhaps even reimagined.

Chapter 2

Crisis Ambientality

The airplane touched down at Barcelona's El Prat Airport with the first rays of the morning sun casting long shadows on the runway. I had been traveling for more than twenty hours, crossing continents to set foot in this Mediterranean city. While this was my first touchpoint in an ambitious two-week itinerary that would whisk me through five different European cities, it was a unique one: I was here specifically to meet my students. They had already been experiencing life in Barcelona as part of a transformative academic venture—a commitment to a year-long, full-scale immersion in local cultures, undertaken at a local university and taught in the local language. My role was dualistic, oscillating between that of an academic guide and a custodian of their cultural well-being amid this intense year-long journey. As my students navigated their way through Barcelona's maze-like streets and engaged with its diverse local cultures, their experiences added new dimensions to my own intellectual inquiries. I found their predicaments mirroring those of my other students in Buenos Aires, who expressed their exasperation at how difficult it was to maintain local friendships; one by one, their newly made friends would abandon Buenos Aires as economic instability forced them to seek opportunities abroad, often in Barcelona. Meanwhile, in Barcelona, the scenario was strikingly similar but reversed; young Catalans were leaving for opportunities in Berlin. Both movements were underlined by the crippling legacy of the Global Financial Crisis—also known as the Great Recession—which had disproportionately affected the youth, collectively referred to as "the lost generation." These varied experiences in different cities illustrated that the impact of economic crisis extends beyond mere financial indicators; they also disrupt the social fabric, dissolving relationships as quickly as they are formed. These firsthand observations enriched my understanding of what Berlant conceptualizes as the "crisis ordinary" (2011), reframing it for me as both an ontological and temporal paradox that not only defines our current era but also challenges traditional, linear conceptions of history.

That morning of October 14, 2019, set the tone for an emotionally charged atmosphere that would pervade my entire stay in the city. The Supreme Court of Spain had just handed down its verdict: nine Catalan leaders were sentenced to between nine and thirteen years for sedition and misuse of public funds. The referendum of 2017 had left its scars on the city, leaving Barcelona a city torn in two: pro-independence supporters on one hand, unionists on the other. But the streets I walked told a different story. The pro-independence movement that day had more to fight for, more to be angry about, and they were not afraid to make their voices heard. Their list of complaints was long: Spanish police used violence against Catalan voters on the day of the referendum; the central government invoked Article 155 of the Spanish Constitution that dissolved the Parliament of Catalonia and instituted direct rule from Madrid that lasted for eight months; political leaders involved with the process were imprisoned, branded "political prisoners" by Catalan nationalists and largely ignored by Europe and the rest of the world. The Autonomous University of Barcelona, where my students were studying, had become a hotbed of pro-independence activism. Yellow ribbons smothered the campus buildings, signaling support for imprisoned political leaders. My students empathized with the suffering of their Catalan counterparts but could not reconcile the region's historic legacy of repression under Francoism and the emerging international context of populist nationalisms. This global trend, marked by the rise of movements asserting national sovereignty and distinct cultural identities, sets the stage for Catalonia's own distinct expression of nationalism, which uniquely intertwines aspirations for independence with a deep historical narrative of resistance and cultural preservation. The students looked on in awe at the passionate expression of national identity that is far removed from the less spirited or conventional articulation of their own national identity. And as I wandered through the barricaded streets in those first couple of days, the heightened police presence was a palpable reminder that the city was holding its breath, bracing for an expected social upheaval. As I walked, I reflected on how these divergent landscapes were but different facets of a single, complex phenomenon—each piece shaped by its own unique blend of histories, crises, and troubled identities. The city in crisis, I observed, powers on—verbalized through the language of the nation. And with each different nation comes different emotional capacities. For some the nation is so deeply felt it *wounds;* others have the privilege of having no emotional investment at all.

Later that evening the eerie quietness had slowly given way to small crowds of protesters who had taken over some squares and blocked some intersections. The atmosphere was tense. One young woman approached a group of young independence supporters and unfurled a Spanish flag. *Fuera, fuera, fuera, la bandera española* ("Go away, go away, go away, Spanish flag"), the crowd chanted at her until a police officer approached and led her away, advising her not to provoke the crowd for her own safety. The seeming duality between those who identified as Catalan nationalists and those who identified as Spanish, apparent on those streets, seemed to occlude the silent majority of Catalans who regard themselves as both Catalan and Spanish without identifying with any of the two homogenizing discourses that have dominated the public narrative of the Catalan independence issue, also known as "*el procés*." Over the next few weeks, protests turned violent. Demonstrators torched more than one thousand trash containers, destroyed street furniture, and threw rocks at police. Within just the first five days, 600 people were injured in the clashes (Martín 2019). Where did the anger and resentment of the young people protesting come from? Like my students, I was confounded by the passion that their desire for an independent nation-state stirred within them. But was there something else underpinning the protests? Carles Feixa, a researcher of student movements at Pompeu Fabra University of Barcelona, links the protests to a wider phenomenon:

> There are a series of circumstances that have fed the flame: precarious jobs, mini-jobs, university fees and a sense of injustice. This is the first time since the Transition [to democracy after the death of dictator Francisco Franco in 1975] that young people are seeing that they are going to live worse than their parents. An independent Catalonia is *the only concrete utopia they have* (my emphasis).
>
> (Martín 2019)

Does a crisis truly have a beginning and an end, or does it merely shift and morph into another form, leading us to seek our own utopias? This question finds resonance in the voices of young Catalans, who, caught amid competing narratives of crisis, find themselves gravitating toward what might seem like utopian aspirations. Recalling Koselleck's (1985, 271–276) temporal dimensions of the "horizon of expectation" and "space of experience," these young Catalans navigate a tumultuous intersection of lived realities and future possibilities. Their responses serve as oral testimonies to the way expectations and experiences are continually negotiated and renegotiated within crisis cultures. According to Julia Termens, a twenty-two-year-old protester:

> I am protesting because I need change. I need to look toward the future and see a way out, and an independent Catalonia could improve the situation. Of course, I am not saying that it is going to be that easy. But when I look at the horizon, I see nothing.
>
> (Martín 2019)

Pau, another young Catalan, echoed Julia's sentiments, emphasizing the dire economic conditions: "In my home, my mother and I struggle to make ends meet. . . I believe an independent Catalonia would be better economically. The protests bring together all the frustration about our living conditions" (Martín 2019). Viewed in this light, the protests in Catalonia are not simply an expression of nationalism gone mad. While it might be tempting to dismiss the quest for independence as a simple psychological defense strategy—a way to project collective anxieties onto an ontological object of hope such as an independent nation-state—the stories of Julia and Pau reveal deeper layers. They grapple not just with an external political crisis but also with an internal terrain marred by disillusionment, poverty, and instability. The crisis has created a blurred line between the privileged and the "Wretched of the Earth." Some are invisible. Some are no longer silent.

I lived in Spain during the worst years of the economic crisis, and frequent protests became part of the political landscape. The austerity measures put in place by successive Spanish governments under pressure from the European Union and other international financial institutions led to mass mobilizations of young people, most notably through the *indignados* (indignant) movement. When I traveled to Greece, the situation was even more intense. The crippled economy meant young people had really nothing to lose. For some Greeks, the utopia became a desire for a purified nation (Golden Dawn), a nation free of immigrants and the constraints of European Union membership. For others, the utopia was pure anarchy; simply the freedom to tell the troika and the financial markets to go to hell (see the 2015 Greek bailout referendum). Both Spain and Greece were often shamed in international media for their failure to live up to the ideal of liberal capitalism that demands AAA credit ratings. It was as if their closeness to the Mediterranean limited their capacity to discipline their finances.

Indeed, the Mediterranean basin can be seen as a microcosm for evolving global dynamics that have been taking shape over the past decade or two. The region has witnessed diverse forms of dissent, including the Israeli social justice protests opposing the rising cost of living (2011); the Tunisian protests that sparked the broader Arab Spring (2010–2011); protests in Cyprus demanding the reunification of the island (2013); Türkiye's Gezi Park protests (2013); protests against corruption and economic stagnation in Slovenia (2012–13); unrest in Bosnia and Herzegovina (2014); and the Syrian Civil War (2011-present). More recently, the list has grown to include protests in Italy against the populist government (2017); the Yellow Vest movement in France (2018–19); student protests in Albania opposing higher tuition fees (2018–19); widespread protests in Lebanon against economic malaise (2019); renewed protests in both Egypt and Algeria (2019); and anti-government protests in Malta and Montenegro (2019). The Global Financial Crisis, moreover, did more than amplify long-standing narratives that cast the Mediterranean as unruly; it spotlighted the region's role in a larger matrix of global crisis. This extends from the impassioned calls for racial justice via the Black Lives Matter movement in the United States, to the resilience displayed in the Hong Kong democracy protests, the unyielding solidarity in the Indian farmer protests, and even demonstrations against government restrictions instigated during the COVID-19 pandemic and against Russia's invasion of Ukraine. These global threads of dissent, each with their unique blend of grievances and aspirations, have one thing in common: they are underpinned by fragile economies that make a certain section of the population feel like they have nothing to lose. It is not that they believe in utopias, but rather they cannot bear a world without them.

While I observed from the periphery, I could not help but sense a cautious optimism pervading the climates in Spain and Greece during this period—an inkling that the protests and social unrest could perhaps be the catalysts for meaningful political transformation. The air was thick with dissatisfaction, but also punctuated by moments of hope and resistance. Yet, years have passed, and the financial system remains largely intact; the tenets of neoliberal economics still stand strong, and political parties that once promised revolutionary change, such as SYRIZA in Greece, have been ousted. How can we make sense of this incongruity? Why does this atmosphere of crisis, this vociferous call for change, often seem to yield only more of the same? Adam Przeworski's *Crises of Democracy* (2019) offers a valuable lens to think through this question, spotlighting the multifaceted stressors that challenge democratic governance. These range from the diminishing sway of traditional political parties to an all-encompassing erosion of institutional trust, which collectively hinder substantive reform. Such factors go beyond mere political dysfunction; they represent a deeper, ontological crisis where public disaffection morphs into vocal, sometimes even violent, resistance. In this volatile environment, Przeworski's commentary on the rising polarization seems especially pertinent. Citizens, increasingly fragmented by political and cultural differences, view each other less as democratic participants and more as existential threats. Polarization, in this charged context, becomes not an agent for change but a spectacle—political theater that is more performative than transformative. Consider Greece at the peak of its economic crisis. Despite sparks of hopeful resistance, such as the "*Oxi*" (No) vote in the 2015 bailout referendum, the stagnation identified by Przeworski effectively diminishes the impetus for genuine change. Even when public outcry crescendos and parties promising change ascend to power, the collective "space of experience"—scarred by economic hardships and political disappointments—does not evolve toward a brighter "horizon of expectation" (Koselleck 1985, 271–276). Instead, the crisis becomes perpetual, trapping societies in a temporal limbo where the pressing demands of the "now" overshadow meaningful engagement with the lessons of the past or prospects for the future. This phenomenon is clearly evident in both Spain and Greece, where clamors for change often devolve into ritualistic performances that serve to perpetuate the crisis rather than bring it to resolution.

The potential for violence that Przeworski outlines—where democratic tools like voting give way to "fists, stones, or bullets"—is not merely theoretical but maps onto tangible experiences of people living under conditions of economic and political precarity (2019, 13). In Barcelona, each spray-painted slogan and shattered window reverberates with Przeworski's cautionary narrative. These are not isolated acts of defiance; rather, they embody a culture steeped in anticipatory anxiety, shaping both the future we envision and the present we navigate. In this context, the winding, unpredictable streets of Barcelona's Barrio Gótico serve as more than a poetic metaphor; they become the physical terrain of crisis cultures, a labyrinth that lacks the organized geometry of L'Eixample, and one that defies any straightforward path toward social transformation. Why, then, in an era marked by heightened activism, do people find it so challenging to experience these crisis moments as transformative experiences? To try and understand this, it is essential to consider how crisis cultures intensify existing tensions, where emotional vacillations between hope and apprehension, narrativistic dichotomies of utopia and dystopia, and temporal antinomies of history and futurity, interact dynamically. These oscillations, far from being abstract constructs, manifest materially, particularly in socioeconomically fragile contexts like Spain and Greece. The undercurrents of despair and disillusionment amplified by austerity and political stasis suppress the spark of hopeful activism. These nations, therefore, exist in a sort of recursive tension: an endless loop of emotional and social imbalance with no clear way out. The lived experience here is not just affected by economic downturns; it is fundamentally disoriented by them. Far from being solely fiscal catastrophes, these crises corrode the core categories through which individuals understand and experience their lives: emotion, narrative, and temporality. They disrupt not just economic structures but the very frameworks of human experience, turning the act of living within these crisis cultures into a perpetually disorienting endeavor.

This chapter explores the intersection of individual subjectivity and the narratives borne out of crises, zeroing in on the Global Financial Crisis and the COVID-19 pandemic as critical case studies. I begin with "crisis ambientality," a concept I introduce to underscore the often-underestimated role of smartphones in shaping our experiential encounters with crises. These devices actively mediate crisis, embedding it within our emotional and cognitive capacities. Events such as the street protests in Barcelona serve to illustrate the dual role of crisis ambientality as both an observatory lens and a measure for broader uncertainties, particularly those related to democratic governance and economic stability. Transitioning from this digital paradigm, I shift the focus to the crisis narratives that emerged during the Global Financial Crisis as it unfolded in Greece. These are not just a cacophony of disorienting narratives but rather a sophisticated matrix of meanings that deeply influence our ability to make sense of—and engage with—ongoing crises. Yet, amid this terrain of narrative ambivalence, there emerge latent opportunities for what may be termed a "remapping" of the crisis topology. This remapping is aligned with the previous chapter's objective to foster a more pluralistic narrative ecology—one resilient enough to absorb dissonance, complexity, and even contradiction without fracturing. This involves a reorientation not just of the stories we tell but of their collective emotional and social resonances. Consequently, remapping enables the emergence of alternative modes of relationality—novel emotional engagements that challenge the normative limits set by pervasive crisis cultures. The chapter concludes with a discussion on the COVID-19 pandemic, spotlighting its manifestation within the framework of a digital crisis ambientality. I aim to describe both the realities of the pandemic and also the innovative emotional responses it has spawned that push against the boundaries established by dominant crisis narratives. By building on prior discussions that viewed narratives as both reflective and constitutive agents in what Berlant terms the "crisis ordinary" (2011), this chapter extends the conversation to address lived experience. It shifts from merely reading these manifold narratives to interrogating their generative potential: what forms of relationality they enable or foreclose, the emotional registers they activate, and ultimately, how they can be reconfigured to foster more equitable and meaningful communal becomings.

THE VIRTUALIZATION OF CRISIS

In *Infocracy* (2022), Byung-Chul Han explores a new power structure termed the "information regime." This regime is governed by information, algorithms, and artificial intelligence, affecting social, economic, and political processes (Han 2022, 1). Unlike previous disciplinary regimes that relied on physical control and rigorous work regulation, the information regime leverages communication and connectivity (Han 2022, 2). People in this regime are seen as free, authentic, and creative, capable of self-generating and performing their identities. The focus of control has shifted from physical dominance to psychological influence, a phenomenon Han calls "psychopolitics" (2022, 2–3). This shift is marked by the transition from rigid, isolated structures to open, pervasive communication networks (2022, 4). In pursuit of visibility and recognition, people willingly sacrifice their privacy, rendering traditional external control mechanisms unnecessary (2022, 5). Consequently, surveillance becomes an integral part of everyday life, subtly evolving from a tool of punishment to one of motivation and optimization (2022, 7). Han argues that power is now intricately woven into the fabric of freedom and community, fundamentally transforming its operation within society. As Han puts it: "Power now depends on the possession of information" (2022, 11).

Han's *Infocracy* (2022) aligns with the idea that the widespread adoption of smartphones since 2007 marks a significant shift toward an information-centric society, a shift that has redefined our interactions with the world (Arthur 2012). This transition signifies more than a technological evolution; it represents a paradigm shift in human cognition and social interaction. By 2022, with over 6.4 billion users (Statista 2023), smartphones have transcended their role as mere technological artifacts. They have emerged as indispensable tools in shaping human perception and engagement with global events, especially in contexts of crisis. To encapsulate this phenomenon, I propose the term "crisis ambientality." This concept articulates a transformative shift in our existential experience, fundamentally mediated through the pervasive influence of technology, particularly smartphones. As Han argues: "The smartphone is the new medium of domination. Under the information regime, people are no longer passive spectators who surrender to amusement. They are all active transmitters" (2022, 170). In this new terrain, the smartphone's ubiquity and the constant stream of information it delivers have reconfigured our engagement with the world. We find ourselves in a state of perpetual connection to global events, leading to a redefinition of how crises are perceived and experienced. This continual awareness and connectivity to worldwide happenings, made possible by the smartphone, signifies not just a technological advancement but a profound shift in the cognitive and emotional consciousness of society.

Crisis ambientality has roots in philosophical thought, inviting comparisons to Martin Heidegger's notion of *Dasein* or "being-in-the-world" (1962, 78) and Guy Debord's "society of the spectacle" among others. Heidegger's "*Dasein*," often translated as "being-there," is not just a mere conceptual understanding of human existence but a deeply existential one, emphasizing how individuals always find themselves already embedded within a particular world. In other words, our existence is not isolated but is always deeply connected to the world and the context in which we find ourselves (Heidegger 1962, 36–42). If we consider "crisis ambientality" in Heideggerian terms, the smartphone can be seen as a tool that not only extends but also modifies our *Dasein*. The device does not merely inform us of crises; it integrates these crises, weaving them seamlessly into the fabric of our everyday lived experiences. In a world where technology has the potential to overshadow or make us forget the genuine, direct experience of "Being," crisis ambientality underscores how our understanding and perception of crisis is being shaped by what Heidegger might term the enframing nature of modern technology. Similarly, Guy Debord's concept of the "society of the spectacle" (2014) suggests that authentic social life is being replaced by its representation. In this society, images and media dominate, overshadowing real experiences and relationships (Debord 2014, 2–11). Central to Debord's critique is the commodification of life, where experiences are transformed into consumable spectacles, distancing individuals from active participation in their realities (2014, 16). Crisis ambientality is thus a contemporary manifestation of this Debordian diagnosis. That is, the spectacle of crisis—the continuous feed of breaking news alerts, the scrollable tragedies, the dramatized narratives—often overshadows and detaches us from the actual, material conditions and sufferings that give rise to them. Instead of being connected to the genuine struggles and implications of these crises, we are presented with mediated versions, ready for consumption. For example, economic crises presented as "market corrections" in news apps might obscure the real impacts like unemployment or economic hardship. Thus, crisis ambientality reflects a contemporary iteration of Debord's "society of the spectacle." It involves a continuous cycle of consuming and reproducing crises, often ignoring their root causes or solutions. This phenomenon diverts attention from systemic issues and normalizes a constant state of crisis. It conditions us into accepting a certain level of relentless crisis as the "new normal," thus limiting our capacities for collective mobilization and resistance.

In a world where the smartphone serves as the lens through which we perceive reality, crisis ambientality becomes not just an academic construct but a lived, existential condition. These devices fundamentally reshape the contours of our individual subjectivity, alter the syntax of our social interactions, and redefine our roles as citizens and consumers. Through software architecture that ranges from news alerts to social media apps, smartphones not only grip our attention but also serve as outlets for affective and emotional responses to crises. For example, during the Australian bushfires of 2019–2020, social media platforms on smartphones became hubs for real-time updates, emotional support, and fundraising (Cox & Davidson 2020). Many people expressed genuine grief, solidarity, and even mobilized resources, proving that the smartphone's capabilities for emotional engagement are far from illusory. However, this leads to a certain paradox: while smartphones could theoretically deepen our *Erfahrung*—the transformative, lived experiences that can enrich our existential understanding of crises—they often result in what I term "*Erlebnis*-saturation." This represents a flood of shallow yet very real emotional engagements that can obfuscate our ability to process these crises meaningfully. The ephemeral nature of digital interactions—scrolling through distressing news one moment, liking a friend's picture the next—creates an environment where the affective charge of a crisis can be intensely felt but rarely synthesized into deeper understanding. It is not that our emotional or affective responses are false; it is that they are dispersed and fragmented, distributed across a myriad of issues presented to us in rapid succession, each demanding a slice of our emotional bandwidth (Han 2022, 18). This barrage clouds our ability to critically engage with any single crisis, suggesting that our state of hyper-connectivity may paradoxically be hindering rather than helping our ability to effectively address and respond to crises.

Over time, smartphones have undergone a transformation that mirrors the evolution of our collective crisis-consciousness: once celebrated as tools of liberation that enhanced individual agency, they have increasingly become mediums that cultivate a pervasive crisis ambientality. An early example of the cell phone's positive impact (pre-smartphone era) was in Spain in 2004. Following the terrorist attacks incorrectly attributed to the Basque group ETA by the government, millions used text messages to organize protests, showcasing the phone's power in enabling immediate, transformative collective action (Suárez 2016). Similarly, during the Arab Spring, cell phones were not just communication tools but also platforms for citizen journalism and activism, helping to disseminate authentic, grassroots narratives globally (Khamis & Vaughn 2014). These events highlighted the potential for cell phone technologies to facilitate *Erfahrung*, or rich, lived experiences that can drive social change. However, with the widespread adoption of smartphones in 2007, as this technology grew more sophisticated and became more embedded in daily life, its influence was not solely restricted to these grand moments of social revolution. Ironically, the same devices that once symbolized empowerment began to also symbolize a new kind of pervasive unease on a more intimate scale. For instance, the capability of smartphones to deliver real-time notifications means that parents can be immediately informed of potential threats in nearby areas, whether it is suspicious activities around schools or incidents of local violence. While this immediate flow of information might seem beneficial, the unceasing barrage of alerts can amplify perceptions of danger, leading to heightened anxiety. Consequently, parents find themselves in a perpetual state of increased alertness regarding their children's safety due to the omnipresence of the smartphone, fostering an environment where every moment feels fraught with potential peril, even when actual risks remain low. Moreover, the tailored crisis information provided to different groups by smartphones can divert attention from broader social issues, potentially deepening social divides (Han 2022, 20–21). Smartphones have thus morphed into double-edged instruments: on one hand, they offer unparalleled connectivity and serve as outlets for genuine affective responses; on the other, they enmesh us in an environment saturated with crisis narratives. The design of these devices, along with the ecosystem of social media, breaking news alerts, and live updates, keeps us in a constant state of vigilance. This paradoxical situation results in an overload of emotionally charged, granular information, yet this barrage often dissipates before it can lead to meaningful action or deeper understanding of situations.

The case of climate change vividly exemplifies the limitations of our digitally mediated crisis-consciousness. Described as a "hyperobject" by Timothy Morton (2013), climate change is so vast and temporally distributed that it exceeds the limitations of human cognition and the narrow framing capacity of our devices. This expansive nature renders it resistant to the kind of bite-sized, simplified understanding that smartphones are designed to deliver. Through a Heideggerian lens, our "*Dasein*," or "being-in-the-world," becomes refracted through the smartphone's screen. In this refracted state, crisis morphs from an external event into a component of our lived reality. Yet this form of *Dasein* is, to use Heidegger's term, "inauthentic," as it distances us from an authentic understanding and engagement with the world (1962, 186). In a similar vein, Debord's (2014) "society of the spectacle" can be invoked here to describe how climate change becomes another ephemeral scene in the theater of crisis. Its existential import is diluted as it turns into yet another spectacle, a topic to scroll past, to "like" or "share," but seldom to deeply engage with. While smartphones keep us continually updated with real-time data on climate anomalies, these updates are often decontextualized snippets that lack the nuance and gravity the issue demands. Of course, it is worth noting the efforts in technological innovation, political mobilization, and grassroots activism to address the climate emergency. Still, for many, this superficial digital interaction with such critical matters diminishes our emotional and cognitive engagement, establishing a gap between passive recognition and active involvement. Although we have unparalleled access to information about the planet's predicament, our heightened alertness often fails to convert into a commensurate understanding or action. Our devices are thus more than mere conduits of information; they shape the very texture of our collective consciousness. The design of these devices, optimized for constant connectivity, ensures that we are forever tuned into a real-time feed of crises, a factor that contributes to an existential detachment. This detachment manifests as a dissonance: we find ourselves submerged in an ocean of crises, aware but aloof, informed yet impotent. The smartphone leaves us navigating a vast expanse of issues we can neither fully comprehend nor effectively confront.

The smartphone thus functions not merely as a technological device but as a metonym for our prevailing ontological state—capturing what Han describes as a burnout society characterized by unending yet ineffective forms of rage and distraction (2015, 22–23). This condition echoes Pankaj Mishra's *Age of Anger* (2017), where the technology becomes a conduit for channeling our collective response to crisis, transmuting it into anger, even as it ostensibly promises connectivity and information. Within an ecosystem of incessant notifications, each demanding our emotional and cognitive bandwidth, the smartphone reveals a unique tension between distraction and impotence. Our emotional reservoir is continuously drained, yet rarely deeply engaged. This leads to a sort of emotional attenuation, a dilution of emotional intensity that serves as both a safeguard against emotional exhaustion and a pathway to apathy. For instance, news about the Amazon rainforest fires rapidly disseminates via smartphone alerts. While we receive a barrage of updates on the devastating blaze, how many actually channel this information into actionable support or even take a moment to understand the underlying causes behind such environmental disasters? In line with Mishra's analysis, this creates a potent form of misdirected rage; our smartphones channel our emotional energies into easily digestible but superficial concerns—such as trending hashtags and viral news—diverting us from the deeper, structural issues that demand more nuanced engagement. In this way, the smartphone functions as a "pharmakon," both a remedy and a poison (Han 2015, 23). While the device keeps us informed, it simultaneously sustains an affective cycle that perpetuates our existential inertia (Gruen 2007, 45–46). Thus, the smartphone perpetuates crisis ambientality, systematically dismantling both the temporal and existential conditions required for meaningful transformation.

In both our everyday interactions and extraordinary moments of social upheaval, smartphones fundamentally recalibrate our mode of existence, acting not merely as passive conduits of information but as active shapers of our reality. This is vividly illustrated by the street protests in Barcelona, where the tension between active engagement and digital distraction highlighted a broader crisis flagged by Agamben: the shift from authentic, transformative experiences to a form of sterile archiving (2007, 17). Amid the passionate cries for justice, I witnessed protesters momentarily disengaged from the immediacy of collective action, absorbed instead by their screens—tweeting, scrolling, capturing. Such acts, while appearing to amplify the cause via social media, risk what Agamben calls an "expropriation" of transformative experiences (2007, 39). This process can dilute the emotional intensity of the moment and contribute to the perpetuation of crisis ambientality. Affectively, we thus find ourselves entangled in a recursive loop of crisis awareness and existential inaction, equipped with digital tools that tax our intellectual and emotional bandwidth without meaningfully exercising them, and trapped in a complex labyrinth of crises that we can neither fully navigate nor escape.

Adam Przeworski's *Crises of Democracy* (2019) serves as a compelling lens through which to examine the systemic scale of crisis ambientality.

Much like how smartphones act as a conduit for magnifying personal anxieties and distractions, they can also be seen as microcosms for the larger social and political issues that Przeworski engages with. In his incisive analysis, Przeworski portrays a world teetering on the edge of democratic crises, laden with puzzling political contradictions and unsettling trends. One such contradiction is the case of a billionaire presidential candidate, who, despite proposing to slash taxes and social programs, gains traction among the working class. Meanwhile, a candidate advocating for taxing the rich paradoxically receives support from Wall Street (2019, 81). These incongruities exist against the backdrop of disintegrating traditional party systems, burgeoning xenophobia and racism, and diminishing public enthusiasm for democratic governance (2019, 83). Equally disturbing is the concurrent economic crisis that Przeworski identifies. He points to three main trends: declining growth rates in developed countries, widening income inequality, and the transformation of industry into low-paying service sectors (2019, 103). These shifts have engendered disconcerting outcomes, such as stagnant incomes among lower economic strata and a growing disillusionment with the prospect of material progress (2019, 106–107). Most strikingly, Przeworski cites research suggesting that a majority of people in the United States and Europe now believe their children will be financially worse off than they are (2019, 106). This loss of faith in intergenerational progress is not a minor concern but rather a monumental shift in societal outlook, rupturing long-held beliefs that have persisted since at least the early nineteenth century (2019, 107). In such an economic landscape marked by uncertainties, gig employment and spiraling debt, one would anticipate a heightened collective awareness and coordinated action to respond to such challenges. Yet the crisis exists in an uncanny proximity—close enough to form the background noise of our daily existence, but too distant to spur us into action. In Heideggerian terms, we might say that the preoccupation with immediate concerns and technologically mediated distractions diverts us from questioning the more foundational aspects of existence itself. As a result, our existential attention is deflected away from authentic *Dasein* ("being-there") toward an "inauthentic" mode of existence—consumed by a public world that obscures deeper existential reflection (Heidegger 1962, 186). The result is a curious type of inertia, a stagnant urgency replaced by ambiguous dread. This is not merely an epistemological crisis questioning our ways of knowing but an ontological crisis that unsettles our very ways of being. Narratives that once clarified or synthesized crises contribute to a disorienting white noise, blurring the lines between real crises and their simulations in a Baudrillardian "hyperreality" (1994, 22). Amid this backdrop of crumbling democratic institutions, economic disparities and ontological disarray, we therefore find ourselves caught in a recursive loop of crisis awareness and existential inaction, exacerbated and perpetuated by the very technologies designed to keep us connected and informed. What does it mean to "be" when crises are everywhere yet nowhere, immediate yet deferred, urgent yet inconsequentially routine?

To unravel the existential struggle of "being" in an era of omnipresent crises, we must critically examine the structural foundations underpinning our individual and collective narratives: specifically, the role of neoliberalism. David Harvey, in his *A Brief History of Neoliberalism* (2005), demonstrates that far from being a waning force, neoliberalism has demonstrated remarkable resilience. This is a testament to its adaptive capacity, and in spite of myriad critiques and declarations of its impending collapse, neoliberalism continues to be a pervasive influence that orchestrates global governance, economic systems, and the texture of social life itself. Broadening the lens from neoliberalism to capitalism, Žižek (2017) offers a thought-provoking counterpoint. He disputes the very idea that capitalism is in crisis. According to Žižek, what is frequently construed as a crisis should instead be understood as an integral operational feature of capitalism itself, a system that thrives on the dichotomies of global expansion and localized suffering (2017, 23). While Žižek interprets these recurring crises as inherent features that ultimately fortify capitalism, I argue that these crises underscore an ongoing state of instability intrinsic to capitalism—a state that does not rejuvenate the system but rather sustains it in perpetual imbalance. In such a state, the architecture of smartphones, replete with personalized news feeds and notifications, serves to atomize crises, transforming individuals into isolated curators of their own personal crisis portfolios. For instance, a smartphone user who receives real-time notifications about stock market fluctuations, local crime rates, and climate change disasters may interpret each notification as an individual challenge requiring a personal response, whether it is investment diversification, enhanced personal security measures, or sustainable lifestyle choices. This insular focus on individual action and responsibility synergizes with the overarching neoliberal agenda, thereby compounding the complexity of "being" within a crisis ambientality. It is as if the smartphone becomes a personalized dashboard of neoliberal governance. To exist in this setting is to navigate an ontologically precarious terrain, where crises are simultaneously ubiquitous and elusive, immediate yet deferred. Within this framework, neoliberal resilience is more than an ideological perspective; it becomes an ontological condition that shapes our interpretations of crises and delineates our roles within them. Consequently, our existential predicament is not merely a product of this intractable cycle of crises and resilience but also contributes to its perpetuation, thus complicating any attempts to conceptualize a form of existence beyond this paradoxical framework.

If neoliberal resilience informs our very ontology, might we then question to what extent it also dictates the narratives we construct and readily embrace? For example, a freelance graphic designer navigating the gig economy may have her narrative framed as one of "individual hustle," where late-night work and inconsistent income are not seen as systemic flaws, but rather as "necessary sacrifices" on the path to individual success. Yet, beneath these compelling tales of grit and determination lies a deeper architecture, one that drives our gaze away from broader structural challenges and focuses us on isolated individual experiences. Such narratives, as they champion personal trials and victories, serve to fragment collective crises, making them seem like a series of unrelated personal challenges (Maher 2023). This not only detaches us from the systemic roots of these challenges but implicates us in perpetuating an ideological paradigm that often hides more than it reveals.

In an age where crisis ambientality is not the exception but the rule, the individualized experience of crises, accentuated by relentless digital notifications and media channels, often feels both urgent and intensely personal. This individual focus obscures the systemic dimensions of various crises, from economic to ecological and political, thereby perpetuating their elusive and persistent nature. This is not to say that attempts at remapping the landscape of crisis cultures are futile; rather, it underscores the inherent complexity and obstinate resistance these crisis cultures often display against straightforward reconfigurations. A remapping in this sense would demand an unsettling of accepted narratives. Instead of portraying crises as singular episodes of individual hardship, we could engage in a deliberate act of reframing to expose their structural and systemic roots. Such a reframing would not necessarily mitigate the crises at hand, but it would contest the hegemony of neoliberal narratives that individualize and isolate these crises. The goal of this reframing is not transformation per se, but rather a nuanced interrogation—a shift from narrowly focusing on individual resilience to questioning the very systems that produce and perpetuate crises. This makes room for a more expansive narrative ecology, one that does not simplify crises into tales of individual overcoming, but complexifies them, laying bare the tensions, paradoxes, and interdependencies that conventional accounts often elide. By recasting these crises as collectively experienced epiphenomena that resist simple solutions, we approach a more honest portrayal of our tangled, collective involvement in these enduring challenges. This lens of nuanced interrogation enables, in the following section, an exploration of the crisis ambientality within the specific national context of Greece. This investigation serves not only as a case study but also as a critical reflection on the broader dynamics of crisis cultures, illustrating their reciprocal influence on individual experiences and societal structures.

FROM RUINS TO RUIN

The Global Financial Crisis of 2008, precipitated by the collapse of the U.S. housing market, marked a significant shift from typical economic downturns. Unlike previous cycles of boom and bust, this crisis transitioned into a pervasive condition with far-reaching social, cultural, and economic ramifications. The persistent state of crisis underscored the fallacy of treating financial downturns as temporary aberrations destined to self-correct. It spotlighted the fragility of existing systems, amplifying financial precarity and nurturing a pervasive distrust in political institutions. Prolonged austerity, skyrocketing unemployment, and eroding public faith in institutions shifted the topology of crisis from a linear trajectory with a beginning and an end to one deeply embedded in what Bourdieu would describe as the "habitus" (1984)—a system of dispositions, shaped by past experiences and expectations of the future, that guide the behavior and thinking of individuals. This shift demands a reconsideration of established ideas about the self-correcting nature of capitalist economies and the durability of sociopolitical systems, particularly when the sociocultural structure appears resistant to immediate repair or regeneration.

The crisis that engulfed Greece in the aftermath of the 2008 Global Financial Crisis became emblematic of a crisis culture in its most relentless form. Far from being a temporary setback to be resolved, the Greek crisis became a permanent fixture, indelibly altering the economic, social, and psychological fabric of the nation. Rather than a mere event to be overcome, it revealed deeper structural vulnerabilities, including unsustainable debt, governance failures, and fiscal mismanagement. From the second quarter of 2008 to early 2014, Greece's economic trajectory was marked by consistent decline. In this timeframe, the country's real GDP contracted by about 26%, and unemployment surged from 13.1% in June 2007 to 27% by December 2012 (Siani-Davies 2017, 11). This downturn draws parallels with the U.S. Great Depression in terms of economic contraction, though the latter was relatively short-lived (Siani-Davies 2017, 8). Areti Stabelou, a young Greek who graduated from university in 2012 amid the height of the crisis, captured its affective impact succinctly: "It was very difficult to talk about in those early years. The crisis was affecting everyone's mood, but we all assumed we were the only ones feeling that way" (Bateman 2019). Beyond numbers, austerity measures imposed a social cost, degrading public services, precipitating acute poverty, and heightening mental health concerns. Katerina Morfoniou, grappling with the personal tragedy of her husband's suicide, decided to focus her energies on operating the online radio station affiliated with the sole suicide prevention clinic in Greece: "I made a decision to close my eyes and ears to the shame," she declared (Bateman 2019). By hosting shows and inviting doctors and other patients from the center to share their experiences, Morfoniou created an outlet for open discourse on mental health. Her journey is not simply an individual narrative arc of overcoming adversity. The metamorphosis she underwent—from shame to advocacy—parallels the collective existential renegotiation that the Greek populace has been subjected to. This is more than a story of personal resilience; it is a story through which to explore the phenomenology of crisis, the deeply rooted alterations in the very being and self-understanding of individuals and, by extension, their community. The Greek crisis therefore not only serves as a poignant lesson on how economic downturns can metastasize into holistic crisis cultures, but it also underlines that any evolution in public discourse only served to further deepen, rather than resolve, the ambientality of crisis. Consequently, in this crisis ambientality, there is no "making sense" of the crisis; there is only a continual reconfiguration of life within it.

The financial relationship between Greece and its international creditors—namely the European Union (EU), European Central Bank, and the International Monetary Fund, collectively known as the Troika—unfolded as a deeply contested discursive terrain between 2010 and 2015. Greece's persistent advocacy for debt relief and restructuring stood in stark contrast to the Troika's unyielding commitment to austerity measures as a precondition for further financial aid (Siani-Davies 2017). This dissonance, however, was not merely a financial or technical disagreement; it was imbued with asymmetries of power and conflicting ideological frameworks. Applying Michael Herzfeld's concept of "crypto-colonialism," which refers to the subtle or unacknowledged control exerted by a more powerful entity over a less powerful one, often disguised by shared history or cultural ties (2002, 900–901), underlines this discord. In the case of Greece, crypto-colonialism refers to how the nation, traditionally esteemed as the birthplace of Western democracy, finds itself in a subordinate economic position within the European Union. This relationship could theoretically operate under the guise of partnership or mutual benefit but in reality manifests itself in unequal power dynamics. With its status as the cradle of Western civilization, Greece therefore often found itself oscillating between historical pride and contemporary moments of national introspection and shame. This incongruence between external perceptions and internal self-understanding cultivated what Herzfeld (2016) refers to as "cultural intimacy," where certain practices or beliefs might contrast with the nation's international image yet are embraced internally as markers of identity. These moments of cultural intimacy and the push-pull dynamic of crypto-colonialism in Greece's relationship with the European Union are emblematic of more significant debates surrounding fiscal responsibility and the extent to which supranational bodies can intervene in the affairs of a sovereign state. When Greece eventually conceded to its creditors' conditions, signing its third bailout agreement in August 2015, it marked a surrender not only in economic terms but also in its struggle for self-definition and autonomy within the European integration project. Yanis Varoufakis, Greece's finance minister at the time, underlines this sentiment by framing the terms imposed by the EU and the Troika as exacerbating rather than resolving the crisis: "What they propose is not a solution. It is a perpetuating of the crisis. We don't have a mandate to perpetuate the crisis" (Simantke & Schumann 2015). The public's vehement disapproval and mass protests that followed the signing of the memorandum attested to a broader skepticism toward the bailout conditions. Varoufakis's description of the failed negotiations as a "war against Greece," underlines Herzfeld's crypto-colonial dynamics (2002), illustrating how the fiscal crisis was both a symptom and an accelerant of deeper ideological fissures within the European project itself, drawing attention to the internal contradictions that compromise the purported solidarity among member states. In this multifaceted crisis, Greece emerged as a focal point, a symbolic battleground where larger ideological conflicts regarding the nature and future of European collective governance were fought, putting the ethical and pragmatic dimensions of collective European governance and economic policy under intense scrutiny.

Emerging as a political force amid Greece's deteriorating economic and social conditions, the SYRIZA (Coalition of the Radical Left) party rose to prominence as a staunch critic of the austerity measures imposed by international creditors. Winning the general elections in January 2015, SYRIZA, led by Alexis Tsipras, promised a radical departure from the belt-tightening policies that had aggravated the country's recession and contributed to social unrest. Explicitly challenging the austerity narrative, the party galvanized a public yearning for drastic change, advocating for debt renegotiation and the revocation of austerity measures. However, this political ascent led to a puzzling denouement: Why did a party rooted in anti-austerity ideology ultimately sign a third memorandum in August 2015 that committed Greece to further austerity measures? The capitulation of SYRIZA to austerity measures is not merely a strategic repositioning but a stark admission of the unavoidable economic and political frameworks constraining states and their governance. In effect, SYRIZA, for all its revolutionary zeal, found itself enmeshed in a web of structural constraints that necessitated a drastic shift in its original objectives. Employing Giorgio Agamben's notion of the "state of exception" (2005)—a political situation in which the normal legal rules and rights are temporarily suspended—one might argue that SYRIZA's decision represents less an abdication of principles than a reluctant conformity to crisis-defined governance. In this exceptional condition, the conventional rules that dictate what is politically achievable are either sidestepped or completely disregarded, ostensibly in the service of crisis management. This bending or breaking of rules serves to compound the difficulties of maneuvering through polarized economic and political landscapes, especially for insurgent parties like SYRIZA that gained traction through a rhetoric of defiance. Consequently, the experience of the SYRIZA government underscores an unsettling paradox that has implications well beyond the Greek stage: political actors who rise with a mandate to challenge prevailing systems may, ironically, end up perpetuating those very same systems. This quandary further solidifies the concept of crisis ambientality as a deeply ingrained, structural condition that eludes straightforward solutions or unilateral efforts at change.

The repercussions of the Greek economic crisis and comparable crises in other locations reverberate well beyond mere statistical indicators into the human experience. For those ensnared in this reality, the tangible hardships such as unemployment, social exclusion, and eroding trust constitute their "space of experience," while their "horizon of expectation" is constricted by the unrelenting nature of the crisis (Koselleck 1985, 271–276). In illustrating the real-world ramifications, Dimitra Kotouza's *Surplus Citizens* (2019) argues that economic crisis unequally burdens the marginalized members of society, thereby unmasking systemic inequities often glossed over or normalized. This disproportionate impact is glaringly evident in the plight of undocumented migrants who are doubly marginalized—first, due to their uncertain legal status, and second, because they lack access to social safety nets. The 2023 wildfires in Greece offer a grim parallel: the tragic deaths of eighteen refugees and migrants hiding in forests near Alexandroupolis underscore that crises—whether economic or environmental—accentuate the vulnerabilities of those already on society's fringes (Avramidis & Konstandinidis 2023). These disparities reveal complex ethical and sociological questions regarding identity, justice, and belonging. Furthermore, crises often lay bare underlying social rifts, such as gender imbalances, that were previously veiled by periods of seeming stability or economic prosperity—conditions often facilitated by Greece's European integration. In this crisis ambientality, women become doubly disadvantaged, falling victim to both traditional gender roles and systemic wage gaps, thereby becoming more susceptible to job losses and domestic abuse (Vaiou 2014; Kontos et al. 2017). Consequently, these crises should not be regarded simply as economic anomalies but as indicators of sociopolitical structures that both reveal and reinforce existing inequalities. It is a self-perpetuating cycle in which the ambientality of crisis both exposes and exacerbates systemic inequities, rendering the marginalized even more vulnerable.

Polarization thus emerges as a defining characteristic of crisis cultures, fundamentally altering the political field and facilitating the rise of populist movements that often displace traditional centrist parties. Botanova identifies this realignment as a manifestation of an "encompassing cultural and identity crisis" (2017, 10), further aggravating an already precarious national mood. In the wake of the Global Financial Crisis, the rise of SYRIZA (radical left) and Golden Dawn (extreme right) represented more than just ideological outliers in Greece; their narratives became formidable forces in shaping public perception and sentiment during this period. Acting as both barometers and architects of Greece's crisis ambientality, these parties offered competing narratives intended to either mitigate or exacerbate the nation's pervasive uncertainties. Both parties thus seized the opportunity to provide a semblance of ideological coherence to a political landscape engulfed in chaos. However, their visions diverged considerably: SYRIZA advocated for a more equitable, anti-austerity future, seeking to dismantle existing financial constraints, whereas Golden Dawn promoted a more exclusionary, ethnonationalist agenda (Ellinas 2013). Notwithstanding these glaring ideological differences, both parties emerged from the same nexus of systemic vulnerabilities—economic instability and social fragmentation—that served as the impetus for their rise. Their ability to redefine the boundaries of conventional political discourse was not an aberration but a direct reflection of these underlying systemic conditions.

SYRIZA and Golden Dawn are thus more than just ideological opposites; they are symptomatic of a deep-rooted disillusionment that pervades Greek society. Both parties served as disruptors that challenge the existing political order, albeit in diametrically opposite directions. SYRIZA, recognized for its strong anti-austerity position, initially captivated the public with its utopian promise to liberate Greece from the shackles of crippling financial constraints. Policies such as debt relief and the reversal of labor market reforms were at the forefront of their agenda. However, as Botanova would put it, their idealistic vision required significant "unlearning" (2017, 8). By "unlearning," Botanova refers to the need for a fundamental reevaluation and rejection of entrenched ideologies and practices that have led to the current crises, advocating for a radical shift in perspective and approach. The party's eventual capitulation to EU and Troika pressures not only tempered public enthusiasm but also deflected attention away from enduring systemic inefficiencies and corruption (Botanova 2017, 8). Conversely, Golden Dawn tapped into a distinct form of despair—the fear of cultural and national dissolution. Their ethnonationalist platform, featuring stringent immigration policies and a call for Greek ethnic purity, attempted to fill the ideological vacuum created by the failures of mainstream politics (Kotouza 2019, 5–6). Far from being an abstract ideology, Golden Dawn's extremist narrative found visceral expression in real-world acts of violence, such as the 2013 murder of rapper Pavlos Fyssas (Ferguson & Lavalette 2014). Despite their apparent opposition, these movements are different responses to the same predicament: the failure of existing political systems to adequately address multi-layered crises. Both

SYRIZA's challenge to EU-endorsed neoliberal policies and Golden Dawn's advocacy for an insular Greek identity underscore a deep disillusionment with traditional politics, signaling an urgent call for systemic transformation that has implications beyond Greece.

Yet, in the sociopolitical theater of crisis, what Guy Debord (2014) would term the "spectacle" takes center stage. The compelling narratives offered by movements like SYRIZA and Golden Dawn become the compelling emplotments of this spectacle, filling newspapers and igniting public sentiment. Drawing upon Debord's ideas, one could argue that the spectacle mediates our relationship with our social realities, potentially transforming crises into narratives that are either more palatable or more mobilizing. Both movements leverage this power of narrative to frame crisis ambientality in ways that resonate deeply with different segments of the Greek populace. They function not just as reflections of collective anxieties but also as scripts for potential futures, offering visions that can either assuage or aggravate the prevailing crisis conditions. In this capacity, they serve dual roles: as symptoms of the crisis culture and as agents shaping it. But while these narratives may dominate the public imagination, they are constantly tempered by a yearning for normality. Despite the allure of radical change, a counternarrative of reverting to the familiar—be it through aligning with European norms or through continuity of local traditions—remains potent. Regardless of whether the political narratives propagated are utopian or dystopian, they are locked in a perpetual struggle with a more latent but equally compelling story of a return to the status quo. Hence, in the Greek context, while political parties such as SYRIZA and Golden Dawn emerged to offer diverging paths out of the crisis—each tapping into unique facets of the collective Greek mood—they inevitably confronted the omnipresent narrative of normality, which served both as a foil and a boundary to their own stories. Consequently, the question became not which narrative would prevail but how these contrasting stories interact under societal strain, further influencing and reshaping the overarching spectacle. This is where the concept of "unlearning" gains its greatest relevance, for it beckons a critical reassessment of long-held assumptions and paradigms (Botanova 2017, 8). The challenge is not only to navigate between these polar narratives but also to confront the limitations of the spectacle itself, understanding that while it may capture public imagination, it is not an end in itself. Thus, the spectacle of crisis ambientality—whether in Greece or globally—demands not merely spectators but critical actors capable of both storytelling and story questioning.

One might ask, why is there such a potent yearning for a return to "normality," especially when the very notion of normality might be the bedrock upon which crisis cultures are built? Ontologically, the concept of normality serves as an anchor, a baseline reality to which individuals and societies aspire to return. It provides a comforting frame of reference, a set of familiar conditions and expectations that offer a semblance of control in a world turned awry. Phenomenologically, normality becomes the lived experience of stability, the sensorial assurance of continuity in the midst of chaos. However, this quest for normality is not as straightforward as it appears. As Vigh astutely observes, "Crisis, when it is chronic, may become normal in the sense that it is what there is most, but it does not become normal in the sense that this is how things should be" (2008, 11). This casts the Greek situation, and indeed the concept of crisis ambientality, in a new light. The normality we seek may be fraught with the very systemic conditions that precipitate crisis in the first place. In the Greek context, for example, aligning with European norms might exacerbate rather than resolve underlying socioeconomic tensions. The normality that is sought might itself be a mosaic of neoliberal policies, social inequalities, and cultural erasures that feed into the perpetual state of crisis. In this vein, the pursuit of normal is far from neutral; it is imbued with the power dynamics and imbalances that can foster crisis conditions (Botanova 2017, 10). This paradox underscores the limitations of the "spectacle" as described by Debord (2014). While narratives of crisis may captivate the public's imagination, rallying them toward radical change or reactionary provocations, they often obscure the more insidious workings of the very "normality" they either seek to restore or upend. In this light, "unlearning" becomes an existential imperative (Botanova 2017, 8). It calls for a deeper contemplation of what we accept as normal, challenging us to unravel the complex array of forces that shape both the crises we experience and the crisis cultures in which we are embedded.

The concept of the "new normal" within Greek crisis ambientality offers an additional dimension, especially concerning its performative aspects in governance. Crisis, within this framework, is understood not merely as an ontological backdrop but also as a strategic instrument leveraged by political authorities to shape the collective imagination and social realities (Boletsi et al. 2020, 4). Thus, the very cultural manifestations of crisis, so crucial for the production of collective narratives, are subject to manipulation by the governing structures that they, in turn, influence. Agamben's warning that "crisis has become an instrument of rule" (Agamben 2013) finds renewed urgency here, suggesting that crisis narratives in Greece are not merely a spectator's drama; it is a participatory theater where the performative enactments of crisis have potential power, though at times such power is difficult to perceive. The challenge is transitioning from a merely interpretative lens to a genuinely engaged and dynamic interaction with these potentialities. The key lies in the utilization of this performative power. It can either restrict us to the confines of pre-existing narratives, thereby solidifying the new normal as a limiting framework for imagination, or it can give rise to new expressions that actively challenge these boundaries. Boletsi's notion of an "arrested temporality" thus functions as both a warning and an open question (2018, 6). It warns against the perils of letting the new normal solidify into a status quo that perpetuates systemic failures. Simultaneously, it questions whether this arrested temporality can be ruptured by new cultural expressions and social movements that redefine what we consider as "normal," thereby serving as catalysts for systemic change. This dual nature of arrested temporality calls for vigilance in examining the rhetorical strategies employed across the Greek political spectrum, recognizing that crisis narratives can either uphold or challenge existing power dynamics. As such, any understanding of the "new normal" within the context of chronic crisis should be neither static nor complacent but a dynamic field ripe for critical intervention and reimagination.

In a political landscape where crisis has been normalized, Benedict Anderson's (1991) concept of "imagined communities" takes on renewed significance. Anderson's term designates a form of collective identity that is not grounded in daily, face-to-face interactions but is rather constructed in the imagination by those who identify as part of the community. Taking this a step further, Dimitrios Theodossopoulos (2013) posits that imagined communities can also form around collective grievances, beyond their traditional roots in nationalism. His research into peripheral Greek communities finds that local actors perceive themselves as part of an "imagined community," one that is held together not just by national or cultural ties, but also by shared grievances against global politics and neoliberal capitalism (2013, 200–201). Within the crisis-ridden topology, these imagined communities evolve to serve dual roles. They become both a foundational structure for creating collective identity and a vital apparatus for interpreting and responding to an unending state of crisis. Drawing from Herzfeld, Theodosopoulos examines the role of blame attribution as a culturally coded discursive tool (2013, 202). This tool is particularly useful for deciphering the citizen-state relationship, an exercise that becomes increasingly complicated in a globally interconnected world where lines of blame and accountability are often blurred (Theodossopoulos 2013, 204; Herzfeld 1992). Within these evolving imagined communities, internal tensions emerge. There are "indignants" who are also "indignant with the indignants," underlining that frustrations can be directed both outward, at global systems, and inward, at one's own community members (Theodossopoulos 2013, 201). These contradictions and complexities signal that imagined communities themselves are not static but are shaped and reshaped by the "new normal" of ongoing crisis.

In reimagining a social terrain devoid of the perpetuity of crisis and its ensuing imagined communities, one cannot help but wonder: Can new identities also be forged within these very cultures of crisis? And if so, what might these identities look like? If imagined communities, as posited by Anderson, are constructed through shared narratives and understandings, then what narratives are possible within a culture deeply embedded in crisis, and yet not wholly defined by it? Navigating these questions necessitates confronting a troubling meta-crisis: the collapsing semantic utility and ontological value of the term "crisis" itself. Karen Emmerich scrutinizes this semiotic dilution, suggesting that the traditional conceptualization of crisis—as a fleeting yet pivotal moment offering a unique opportunity for transformation—has become woefully inadequate in capturing the current atmosphere of sustained, omnipresent crisis (2020, 28). She further contends that to navigate this "epistemological impasse" requires a shift from theoretical introspection toward concrete interventions capable of dynamically reshaping both political discourse and social justice (2020, 39). This introduces an inherent incongruity: If crises have become ambient features of our sociopolitical landscape, their omnipresence undermines their traditional characterization as events or phases to be overcome or transcended. The task before us, therefore, is not to overcome a temporal or epistemological impasse, but rather to seek transient and fleeting instances of communal becomings within these all-encompassing crisis cultures. These ephemeral instances of communal becoming possess intrinsic merit, as they serve as potential sites for the incubation of alternative forms of relationality and identity. They offer not wholesale solutions to the unyielding presence of crisis but moments of respite and possibility, brief interruptions in an otherwise monolithic narrative of perpetual crisis. These transient spaces might cultivate new idioms of community, solidarity, and resistance, which, although temporary, could serve as the building blocks for more sustained forms of collective resilience and, perhaps, regeneration.

Athens offers a compelling terrain to explore the potency of these transient spaces. The city attracts a diverse demographic—from artists to activists—and epitomizes a concentrated embodiment of Greece's crisis ambientality (Misouridis 2017, 77–78). In Athens, the complex nature of the crisis is evident as a dual phenomenon: it not only undermines existing social norms but also inspires novel social and cultural expressions (Boletsi 2018, 9–10). When traditional institutions crumble and prevailing narratives prove insufficient, an ontological void appears that beckons, if not necessitates, a collective reimagination of lived reality. Cédric Klapisch's TV series *Salade Grecque* (Greek Salad) (2023)—a spin-off of sorts to his trilogy of films *L'Auberge Espagnole* and its sequels—taps into this void, spotlighting Athens as a canvas where European youth navigate and reimagine their shared crisis experiences. Through its depiction of Athens—a city uniquely characterized by its crisis ambientality—*Greek Salad* captures the city's dual role as both an emerging international hub for art and culture and a focal point for local youth-driven artistic ventures. This portrayal is consistent with a larger trend toward community-based artistic practices and grassroots movements in Athens, underscoring the city's significance in the European collective imagination (Tzirtzilakis 2017, 142). Artistic practices in this context are not just aesthetic endeavors but instrumental catalysts that create the space for this reimagination, offering fertile grounds where new social configurations may emerge (Misouridis 2017, 82). Athens, within this schema, has thus entered a stage of cultural "myth-making," a transformation further ignited by its ongoing crisis conditions (Misouridis 2017, 82).

Yet, the relationship between crisis and imagination necessitates a discerning approach. Stafylakis's skeptically asks: "Does the 'exceptional state' of Greek society produce the need for collectivity?" (2017, 237). On this point he observes: "There is a local—yet rather global—pseudo-anthropological mantra" contending that impoverishment and precarity invariably foster collectivity (2017, 238). For him, this amounts to mythological discourse—a "myth of national survival"—alerting us to the possibility that the rise of artistic collectivism in Greece may not be an unmediated expression of communal solidarity (2017, 239). Instead, he intimates that it might emerge as a narrative strategy, perhaps crafted to counteract global neoliberal influences (2017, 239). With these considerations in mind, we face a critical obligation to avoid oversimplifying or mythologizing the complex social dynamics at play, even while recognizing the potent human desire for collective action that a state of crisis often invokes. What Athens presents, then, is an intricate social topology—a vibrant, ever-evolving landscape where not only can the contours of crisis be critically re-mapped, but also where the seeds of "communal becomings" might just take root (Misouridis 2017, 81). That is not to suggest that the surge in creativity in the Greek context, particularly among the youth, is a cure-all, but rather it reflects society's resilient instinct to turn to communal forms of expression when traditional structures fail (Tzirtzilakis 2017, 112, 142; Misouridis 2017, 82). Art, in a sense, preserves imaginaries of the future when they no longer exist in the present world, becoming a repository of what has been lost. In this light, Athens serves less as a backdrop for a cultural renaissance than as a living, evolving cartography of crisis, constantly reinterpreted and revised by its residents. The aim here is not to propose a resolution to the crisis or to transcend it, but to pinpoint those temporal and spatial intersections within it where communal becomings may occur, however ephemeral. This shifts the understanding of both the city and the nation from fixed entities to mutable, dynamic, "in-progress" terrains, offering intermittent but meaningful ruptures in an otherwise monolithic narrative of perpetual crisis.

Dimitris Papanikolaou's concept of "Archive Trouble" offers a compelling framework for understanding the city "in-progress" within such a crisis ambientality. Archive Trouble, as described by Papanikolaou (2017), is a dynamic, interconnected series of acts that form a public manifesto, democratizing history by promoting active public participation and making the archival process a collective venture. Building upon Foster's idea of the "Archive Impulse," Papanikolaou examines how Greek artists and the public at large grapple with their historical legacy amid ongoing crises (2017, 40). The traditional notion of the archive as an organized, stable repository of the past loses its footing in this crisis-laden context. Here, Archive Trouble flips the sense-making priority, transforming archival efforts into acts of resistance and resignification. One of the most provocative examples of this reimagining of traditional archives is seen in Yorgos Lanthimos's film *Dogtooth* (2009), a standout piece of the Greek Weird Wave. In the film, the narrative revolves around a secluded family where the patriarch, seeking to protect his children from the outside world, creates an alternate reality for them. Within their fenced compound, the children are led to believe that they are in danger from the outside world and are fed a reconfigured version of language and knowledge. Any outside influence is considered perilous, and they remain oblivious to the true nature of their existence. The film thus troubles normative social "archives" by challenging commonly held understandings about family, authority and socialization, with the family's manufactured vocabulary, behavioral norms and disturbingly idiosyncratic worldview operating as an archive that is perpetually interrogated and reinvented within the film's narrative (Papanikolaou 2017, 45). The film thus exemplifies what Papanikolaou identifies as the "cruelly optimistic archival impulse" in Greek art. Drawing on Lauren Berlant's concept of "Cruel Optimism," this impulse represents an unrelenting drive to explore and reshape stories, even those anchored in painful histories, fueled by a sense of hope and a desire to confront and reconfigure entrenched narratives (Berlant 2011; Papanikolaou 2017, 40–42). This reimagining fosters a nuanced dialogue between past and present, grounding an understanding of civic participation within the complexities of a crisis ambientality. In *Dogtooth*, the patriarch's fabrication of reality is not merely an individual act but an emblematic manifestation of how crisis ambientality can deeply penetrate even the most intimate spheres of life, such as the family. Though offering no easy answers, this relentless engagement with crisis ambientality, as seen in films like *Dogtooth*, amplifies rather than resolves the dysfunctions it portrays, compelling the audience into a state of discomfort and questioning that echoes the unresolved nature of Archive Trouble (Papanikolaou 2017, 50). In this way, Archive Trouble underscores the contradictory ways individuals and communities navigate crisis cultures. It beckons us to continuously question and reframe our narratives, pushing back against the complacency of accepting a static version of history. And even amid the existential weight of ongoing crises, Archive Trouble persists as a powerful tool for resistance and reimagination, defiantly challenging the inertia of what Agamben terms the sterile archive (2007, 17).

As the Greek capital's ancient ruins stand juxtaposed against graffiti-splattered walls, art emerges not as a conclusive resolution but more as an iterative inquiry that resonates through diverse expressions which grapple with the complexities of identity and community. Cinema, particularly within the innovative Greek Weird Wave movement, represents a significant medium in this dialogic exploration. The poetic voice, too, offers a unique lens into the symbiotic relationship between personal autonomy and national identity. The "Generation of the 2000s" poets, such as Adrianne Kalfopoulou and Yiannis Doukas, compose works that, while not overtly rooted in crisis, echo with the somber reverberations of its presence (Lambropoulos 2016). In Kalfopoulou's poem "Ungodly" (2015, 65), her verse navigates the complex terrain of belonging and exile, capturing a poignant struggle faced by many Greeks during the economic crisis—the tension between the desire to escape a deteriorating situation and the profound connection to one's homeland:

> You want to flee, but flee where? The urban concrete elsewhere does not seethe, does not breathe the scent of carob trees.

Kalfopoulou's metaphorical dialogue evokes a visceral connection to place, with the poem's opening lines problematizing the concept of geographical escape against a backdrop of existential rootedness.

> "Flee" you hear it everywhere, the taxi driver, the farmer at the
> *Laiki*
> tell you "Go!" and are puzzled that you are still here,

The performativity of the verb "flee" reveals the widespread feeling of despair and the compulsion to escape. The voices of everyday people like the taxi driver and the farmer amplify a collective sentiment, adding a layer of societal critique to the individual's dilemma.

> you who actually could—with your American passport,
> your several tongues—you could translate home into longing, so
>   why not go?

This line interrogates the intersections of privilege and displacement, suggesting that mobility does not equate to freedom from cultural ties. Kalfopoulou's mention of her American passport thus symbolizes potential mobility and opportunity, seen as an escape from the national crisis. The verse then evolves into a deeper philosophical inquiry:

> Greece with its tales of flight
> and light, returns, rebirths, keeps teaching the stubborn human
> > lesson

These lines synthesize the lure of flight with a gravitational pull toward the homeland, imbued with its legacies of myth and rebirth. The dialectic presented challenges the binary of difference/stasis, propelling a dynamic interaction with the concept of home and identity. Kalfopoulou's work thus serves as a reflection on how crises mediate the understanding of belonging and identity, resonating through the lenses of personal and national experiences. According to Badiou:

> In poetry it is clear that the real potential of the poem lies in its piecing together a certain saying that is manifestly the saying of that which cannot be said . . . The saying of the unsaid makes no sense, and yet that is what the poem strives for. (2019, 44)

The attempt to say the unsaid is vividly illustrated in the closing lines of poems by Yiannis Doukas and Nikos Erinakis. Doukas in "Epitaph" (2015, 139) writes:

> We lay wreathes and weep
> but we are what we burn, we are what we bury deep.

And in the final two lines from "The New Symmetry" (2015, 203), Nikos Erinakis writes:

> We have always had the sun with us
> And from what I see the sun is still here

In Doukas's verse, there is a palpable sense of despair and resignation, a reflection on loss and the inevitability of fate, as expressed through the metaphors of burning and burying. Conversely, Erinakis's lines project a contrasting emotional repertoire, one that harbors resilience and an unwavering hope symbolized by the enduring presence of the sun. The use of the plural first-person pronoun "we" in both poems creates an intimate bond between the poet and the reader, making the poetic experience simultaneously deeply personal and universal (Orr 2002, 46). This linguistic choice engenders "affective atmospheres" (Anderson 2009) where the emotional undertones of the poems resonate with the readers' own experiences and perceptions of crisis. As Orr contends, poetry's power lies in its ability to bring us to the brink of our emotional thresholds, to resonate with our deepest feelings

(2002, 55). By identifying with the collective "we" and the individual "I" in these poems, we momentarily dissolve the barriers of separateness, sharing in the poets' emotional spaces. Consequently, Greek poetry transcends mere artistic expression; it becomes an instrumental medium for any attempt at making sense of the affective experiences associated with crisis situations. It offers a space where the present can be reinterpreted and felt with a renewed sense of clarity and possibility.

Within the enfolding ambience of crisis, a symbiotic relationship emerges between artists and their audiences, reflecting how the Greek crisis transcends mere economic downturn to resonate deeply within the foundational rhythms of national consciousness. This resurgence of artistic expression aligns with the poetic imagery of Nobel laureate George Seferis, who depicted Greek poetry as a "shy nightingale," a steadfast companion to the nation in its moments of turmoil. Seferis's allegorical representation of a pepper metamorphosing into a dragonfly symbolizes the subtle yet profound metamorphoses that art can intimate—providing, if not resolution, a momentary respite (Barley 2015). As tourists once again fill the Acropolis and the city squares, a veneer of "business as usual" pervades the Greek cityscapes. Yet, the reemergence of center-right parties and the dissolution of extremist groups like Golden Dawn mask deeper tensions beneath a façade of normalcy. The emotional tension between hope and apprehension is palpable in the lives of ordinary Greeks, who traverse a terrain where future prospects remain uncertain, and the national narrative oscillates between revival and despair. In the poetry of Adrianne Kalfopoulou and Yiannis Doukas, we see this tension articulated—a grappling with identity and belonging amid economic and social upheaval. Kalfopoulou's verses in "Ungodly" encapsulate the absence of transformative events, as individuals feel anchored to their crisis-laden reality, illustrating how such stasis intensifies the emotional turmoil between the desire to escape and the pull of ancestral ties. Similarly, Doukas's reflections on loss and renewal in "Epitaph" illustrate a communal meditation on fate and continuity, suggesting that even within ongoing crisis, there remains a stubborn, underlying hope—a sentiment that shines through Erinakis's optimistic lines about the enduring presence of the sun. Narrative tensions between utopian aspirations and dystopian realities further complicate the Greek experience of crisis. The rise and fall of SYRIZA, captured through public and political discourses, reflect a broader narrative struggle within Greece—a yearning for a radical break from austerity contrasted sharply with the entrenchment in crisis-induced political and economic constraints. These narratives are not just political but permeate everyday Greek life, influencing how individuals perceive their agency and future possibilities within a framework that feels both imposed and inescapable. Consequently, in this enduring crisis ambientality, there is no ultimate "making sense" of the crises at hand.

Instead, what emerges is a constant reconfiguration of life within these perpetual crisis cultures, where the intensification of underlying tensions—emotional, narrative and temporal—continues to redefine our understanding of historical continuity, illustrating how crises are not mere interruptions but formative elements in the narrative of human experience. The "Archive Trouble" (Papanikolaou 2017) concept flips the sense-making priority, transforming archival efforts into acts of resistance and resignification, complicating narratives and offering alternative pathways in a reality that is both anchored in the past and tentative about the future. Amid this crisis ambientality, moments of communal becoming do arise—not as preludes to a grand transformation but as fragmented instances that challenge, catalog and nurture, lived experience.

DIGITAL CRISIS AMBIENTALITY

Amid a backdrop of recurrent global crises, the 2019 onset of the COVID-19 pandemic that seemingly emerged from Wuhan, China, represents not just a biological anomaly but a cultural inflection point. Cities, from the emblematic skylines of New York to the architectural silhouettes of Milan, did not merely experience a stillness; they became sites of collective reflection as societies were suddenly confronted with their inherent, biopolitical, vulnerabilities. In grappling with this unprecedented circumstance, governments, recognizing both the existential stakes and the challenges to communal cohesion, deployed measures that were a blend of control, caution and containment. Borders transitioned beyond their traditional function as geopolitical lines, becoming emblematic of security and containment policies. Parallel to this, the domestic sphere, traditionally regarded as a space of familial comfort, was recast as a primary line of defense against the external viral onslaught. The healthcare sector, while visibly strained, served as a mirror to larger societal challenges. Beyond the immediate medical concerns, these institutions waded through the murky waters of ethical decisions, particularly as they pertained to the allocation of primary care, the judicious distribution of resources and the equity of access in crisis situations.

In the early phases of the pandemic, the collective sentiment in response to the COVID-19 crisis pointed unmistakably toward *Erfahrung*—a deep, reflective and transformative experience. Situated within Koselleck's conceptual framework, individuals found themselves immersed in a "space of experience" but constantly weighing it against a formidable "horizon of expectation" (Koselleck 1985, 271–276). While the immediate implications of the pandemic were medical and epidemiological in nature, its deeper resonance lay in its ability to prompt a broad-based existential reevaluation. Daily life, replete with its newfound challenges—enforced isolation, disruption of established routines, and an ever-present threat of contagion—pushed individuals toward introspection. For Arundhati Roy, the pandemic could open up portals or gateways to new worlds to "break with the past and imagine their world anew" (2020). Within the constrained physical space of lockdown, emotional and cultural potentialities seemed to expand. As Žižek put it, physical distancing paradoxically underscored the true essence of our close relationships, noting: "It is only now, when I must avoid many of those close to me, that I truly perceive their presence, their importance to me" (2020, 3). The indiscriminate nature of the virus also ushered in a sentiment of shared vulnerability. To say "we are now all in the same boat" (Žižek 2020, 31) was not a mere observation of collective risk, but an existential assertion that the specter of the virus rendered all individuals equally vulnerable. Emphasizing this egalitarian threat, Iran's deputy health minister, Iraj Harirchi, declared: "This virus is democratic, and it doesn't distinguish between poor and rich or between the statesman and an ordinary citizen" (quoted in Žižek 2020, 42).

While the pandemic's existential undertones highlighted shared vulnerabilities, it simultaneously revealed entrenched social disparities. Despite the virus's universal biological threat, not everyone faced equal risk. Individuals in middle-class professions had the advantage of transitioning to remote work, thus protecting themselves within their personal enclaves. Conversely, "essential workers" in roles ranging from healthcare to retail, remained exposed on the frontlines, underscoring occupational disparities. This inequality extended to the broader spectrum of global responses. Different countries adopted varied strategies: Italy implemented early, strict lockdowns, while Sweden pursued a strategy banking on herd immunity. The United States exhibited a disjointed approach, with states operating under diverse regulations. Such inconsistency not only complicated a unified global response but also highlighted socioeconomic divides and differing policy approaches. In this scenario, two distinct temporalities surfaced. One, propelled by institutional assurances, clung to temporary timelines—short-term online school transitions with educators and parents alike believing in a swift return to physical classrooms, ephemeral travel bans with airlines offering optimistic rebooking options for postponed vacations, and hopeful lockdown durations with businesses often extending their "temporary" closure dates month by month. This narrative, laden with hope, implied a brief interruption before a return to normalcy. On the other hand, the concept of a "new normal" suggested a lasting departure from the past. Examples of this include the swift adoption of telemedicine, long-term remote work commitments, and urban reconfigurations for pedestrian prioritization, indicative of a shift toward sustainable urban futures. The pandemic, exposing the fragility of our constructed realities, raised doubts about the long-standing paradigms of progress that had been shaped by decades of optimism and technological growth.

This was magnified by the emergence of the phenomenon known as the Great Resignation—mass departure of employees from their jobs, particularly in the United States, during and following the COVID-19 pandemic—which, while ostensibly about occupational discontent, hinted at a broader societal introspection. The fundamental concepts of work, community and "the good life" appeared to be at an inflection point. In the face of these dual temporalities, the global narrative teetered between the allure of familiar comforts and the unsettling yet invigorating prospect of forging a new recalibrated world order.

Even as the immediacies of the pandemic occupied global consciousness, there was a parallel discourse unfolding that sought to understand its long-term implications. This was not merely a matter of crisis management, but a deeper inquiry that questioned foundational structures, with the debates around China's governance serving as a case in point (Žižek 2020, 39). The COVID-19 pandemic thus materialized as a watershed moment, captivating global attention, but not in the introspective depth many had hoped for. As Naomi Klein points out in her book *Doppelganger: A Trip into the Mirror World* (2023), this global crisis arrived alongside a distinctive confluence of digital technologies. These technologies, particularly smartphones and social media, transformed the pandemic's pervasive ambience into a constant stream of data points and alerts. Digital interfaces not only kept us updated with the progression of the virus but also channeled our anxieties, hopes and fears, proliferating conspiracy theories and a bewildering array of explanations that could not be neatly categorized within the traditional left/right political spectrum. The digital platforms, initially seen as heralds of connectivity and enlightenment, paradoxically became spaces of confusion and obfuscation. The *Erlebnis*-saturated digital ecosystem—quick, ephemeral, sensation-seeking—prioritized the sensational over the substantive. The relentless pace of digital interactions—posting, sharing, commenting—and the blending of distinct voices diminished the potential for authentic contemplation and reflection. Consequently, the opportunity for a profound, global *Erfahrung* through the pandemic was eclipsed by the overwhelming cacophony of digital *Erlebnis*-saturation.

Klein's analysis underscores an important reality: digital crisis ambientality is not a mere backdrop but an active participant in our cultural experience. Digital crisis ambientality, as defined here, refers to the digital navigation of ongoing crises, perpetuated by constant, surveillance-driven anxieties. Such a terrain is primed for the proliferation of conspiracy theories, which feed on emotion and bypass critical interrogation. Conspiracies, often dismissed as fringe ideas, become in this context valuable cultural markers. Narratives about "Algorithm Overlords" or "Data Harvesters" transcend mere fantasy; they echo genuine anxieties about privacy, autonomy, and individual agency.

Klein argues that these conspiracy-oriented narratives emerge from an underlying surveillance crisis (2023)—a reality characterized by invasive monitoring technologies that track our movements and interactions. This crisis, marked by unchecked digital surveillance, data collection, and privacy erosion, she argues, has been largely overlooked by progressive groups and the broader left. This neglect has inadvertently created a space where conspiracy theorists propagate their ideologies, using legitimate surveillance concerns as a foundation for far-reaching, often baseless dystopian narratives. The current *Erlebnis*-saturated era, which emphasizes immediacy, further magnifies these conspiracy theories. Platforms like Facebook, YouTube, and Reddit have been awash with COVID-19 misinformation, from bioengineered virus origins to unverified vaccine side effects. Such a digital architecture, by amplifying the sensational and speculative, distorts our "space of experience" and "horizon of expectation," fostering not only a perpetual sense of urgency but also a distorted perception of reality that feeds into the very conspiracy theories it disseminates, thus perpetuating a constant state of crisis. For example, pervasive conspiracy theories proliferating in the digital ecosystem include that the pandemic was an orchestrated event by covert global elites aiming for worldwide domination, while others undermined the efficacy of masks and vaccines, insinuating broader schemes to encroach upon individual liberties. Such theories, fueled by digital dissemination, not only play into entrenched social fears but are, in themselves, manifestations of this digital crisis ambientality. At their core, they reveal a society that feels under siege, constantly embattled, and forever in crisis conditions. Underlying these theories is an angst about manipulation, a diminished sense of personal agency, and a profound mistrust in proposed solutions, painting them as just more facets of an unending crisis. Every new theory, every piece of "evidence" pointing to deception, further entrenches the sentiment that we are entrapped in a ceaseless cycle of crisis with no discernible way out.

Within such a digital crisis ambientality, it is important to clarify that not every critique stems from conspiracy-oriented thinking. Prominent intellectuals like Giorgio Agamben have articulated well-founded critiques regarding pandemic measures, grounded in philosophical and moral reasoning. Agamben's argument centers on the concept of a "state of exception," where he observes a global tendency for the suspension of constitutional rights, leading to what he terms "sanitation terror" (Agamben 2021, 8). This phenomenon, he argues, morphs into a "religion of health," transforming a once-valued right in bourgeois democracy into a near-absolute obligation. This transformation is epitomized by the term "biosecurity," highlighting the merging of health-focused doctrines with expanded state authority (Agamben 2021, 9). Agamben extends his analysis to include the pandemic response as indicative of a larger shift in governance. He posits that in an era of dwindling institutional trust, governments increasingly rely on states of emergency to capitalize on the public's craving for stability (Agamben 2021, 10). He depicts a society deliberately maintained in a "state of precarity and fear," setting the groundwork for "mass panic" that incidents like the pandemic readily trigger (Agamben 2021, 13). In seeking security, the public inadvertently relinquishes freedoms, paradoxically empowered by the very institutions pledged to protect them. Central to Agamben's critique is a fundamental query: "What is a society that values nothing more than survival?" (Agamben 2021, 18). He perceives the arising "new normal" as life reduced to mere biological existence, devoid of its rich cultural and emotional resonance (Agamben 2021, 18). Rather than realizing true liberty, society remains trapped in a cycle of "perpetual fear and insecurity" (Agamben 2021, 18). This trajectory not only endangers individual liberties but also jeopardizes the essence of "public space," the arena for discourse, debate, and democratic engagement (Agamben 2021, 19).

In the face of such a somber dystopian narrative, one might wonder, as Agamben does, why there has not been a more significant opposition to this apparent state of exception. After all, in situations of significant social crisis, resistance often arises as a countermeasure. However, Agamben proposes that the pandemic "was somehow already present, even if only unconsciously and that people's life conditions were such that a sudden sign could make them appear as they really were—which is to say, as no less intolerable than a plague" (Agamben 2021, 23). Agamben's interrogation into the muted societal response—or lack thereof—to the pandemic's measures is, therefore, emblematic of a larger epistemic phenomenon that underlies crisis cultures. The collective response was not simply borne out of complacency or resignation, but perhaps derived from a deeper phenomenological crisis. The pandemic, within this schema, did not materialize as an aberration, but rather as an extension or intensification of extant crises. Such congruence with an established crisis ambientality influenced both how society perceived the pandemic and how we collectively internalized its implications. The reaction, it appears, was less about steering through an uncharted ontological territory and more about grappling with a persistent, albeit amplified, existential condition. Deducing from Agamben's perspective, the understated resistance to the pandemic's severe protocols may stem from this ingrained crisis mindset. It was not necessarily that people agreed or were apathetic, but perhaps they were already so submerged in pre-existing crises that the pandemic's emergence felt like an expected, albeit overwhelming, addition to an ongoing crisis culture. Thus, rather than manifesting a novel rupture, the pandemic magnified what had already been festering beneath the surface.

Agamben suggests that our shift toward predominantly digital interactions, often lacking physicality, is not merely a result of the pandemic but part of an ongoing transformation (2021, 9). Increasingly, digital-mediated interactions are eclipsing traditional engagements, pushing the digitally non-versed to the periphery (Agamben 2021, 10). Yet, as Žižek asks: "Where does data end and ideology begin?" (2020, 55). This question blurs the distinction between objective reality and constructed narratives, thus underlining that not even profound events like pandemics can invariably offer transformative experiences (*Erfahrung*). Amid this digital crisis ambientality, however, moments of communal becomings become poignant interludes in our daily scripts. The pandemic, while heralding an accelerated march toward digitization, concurrently underscored our indelible longing for community, for human touch. These interstices of human solidarity were reminders of our unyielding desire to connect, to empathize and to be together, albeit sometimes from a distance. The widespread practice of clapping for frontline workers during lockdowns, for instance, was not just a gesture of gratitude; it was a communal ritual. Neighborhoods reverberated with the symphony of applause, pans and whistles, transforming balconies and windows into shared spaces of mutual appreciation and hope. In Italy, impromptu balcony concerts saw individuals share their musical talents. And in countless cities, candlelit vigils were held for those who succumbed to the virus, illuminating the dark times with collective mourning and remembrance. Grassroots initiatives, like mutual aid collectives, blossomed globally, with neighbors aiding neighbors, from provisioning for the elderly to extending emotional support amid isolation. However, there is no denying the underlying fact that there was no mass mobilization to improve the conditions of essential workers, reflecting, perhaps, an era of individualization that overdetermines responses to such crises. Yet, these acts and gestures stand as testimony to Agamben's assertion that human interaction, when constrained or redefined, will seek alternative, often more profound modes of expression and serve as a counterpoint to the dominant digital narrative. They suggest that, even when faced with unprecedented challenges and an overpowering push toward digitization, there remains an undying collective yearning for the tangible, for the humane.

In contextualizing the COVID-19 pandemic within Koselleck's temporal theory, it becomes evident that the event was not merely a series of disruptive incidents, but rather a manifestation of an ongoing constitutive crisis. The pandemic served not as a breakpoint, but as a magnifier of the pre-existing crisis culture, compelling a reconsideration of the narrative of the pandemic as a standalone event and recognizing it as a continuation of a perpetual state of crisis. This shift in perception moves the understanding from viewing crises as isolated episodes to seeing them as enduring conditions that shape and are shaped by societal structures and individual experiences. Thus, the pandemic emerges not just as a public health emergency but as a novel revelation, exposing the chronic crises embedded within modern existence and highlighting existing fault lines from healthcare inequities to digital divides.

This realization underscores that crises should be viewed not merely as acute incidents but as a chronic state that exacerbates latent societal fractures. The "new normal" of the pandemic and its accompanying rapid digital transformation illustrates a clash between a utopian vision of technological prowess and the dystopian reality of digital surveillance and misinformation. The phantasmatic relationship between digital interaction and physical solidarity during the pandemic exemplifies this dialectical process, revealing the dual forces of alienation and community. These moments of crisis are not mere interruptions but are constitutive of our ongoing historical narrative, continuously influencing and being influenced by underlying crisis conditions.

CONCLUSION

In Pablo Larraín's film *El Conde* (2023), the reimagining of Augusto Pinochet as a vampire serves not merely as narrative novelty but as a poignant allegory for the enduring nature of crisis cultures. The vampire is often regarded as a metaphysical and timeless figure that perpetually rejuvenates itself by drawing life from others. Is it not suggestive of how crises, much like vampires, linger within societies, deriving their sustenance from historical traumas and perpetuating crisis ambientality? The choice of the vampire metaphor hints at a deeper philosophical proposition: that the nature of crisis is not episodic but ambient. Just as a vampire continually adapts and metamorphoses, remaining eternal, so too does a crisis shape-shift within the sociopolitical terrain. It does not wither but transforms, absorbing new realities and manifesting in different guises.

In *El Conde*, Margaret Thatcher is depicted not merely as a historical character but as an emblem of the prevailing neoliberal order. Her representation as the influential force behind figures like Pinochet indicates an intimate intertwining of neoliberalism and authoritarianism. These ideologies display a disturbingly synchronized capacity to adapt and reassert themselves, akin to the perpetual cycle of a vampire. Through Thatcher, the film examines the ubiquity of these conjoined ideologies—forces that extend beyond shaping economies to subtly influencing societies, both overtly and covertly. Larraín's narrative hints that such ambient crises do not arise in isolation. They are the product of both individual actors and larger systemic forces. As *El Conde* concludes, transitioning from monochrome to color, paralleling Pinochet's change into a young boy, Thatcher's reflective monologue during a school drop-off underscores the cyclic dialectic of power and vulnerability inherent in these crises: "He says that the most dangerous leftists of all are right here . . . Perhaps I shall find it interesting, being rich in a country of the poor," she muses. *El Conde* demands an understanding that extends beyond the visible manifestations of crises to their underlying origins. The film portrays Thatcher not just as a symbol of neoliberalism but implicates her in the creation and perpetuation of the vampiric Pinochet. Such an approach suggests that crises are byproducts of deliberate decisions, policy frameworks and ideological alignments. In the ambient shadows of such enduring crises, societies are called to introspect on their histories, reassess their foundational tenets, confront their realities and also cautiously chart their futures.

Just as the vampire in *El Conde* is not a mere isolated creature but a manifestation of broader societal dysfunctions and imbalances, the Greek economic downfall and the COVID-19 pandemic are not isolated episodes. They are symptomatic of deeper, entrenched structures and systemic failures in global societies. The vampire's continuous cycle of rejuvenation by drawing life from others can be equated with how the Greek economy, drained by austerity measures and financial constraints, sought to rejuvenate itself, only to find that the sources of its sustenance—international bailouts and financial aids—were themselves fraught with conditions that perpetuated its weakened state. Similarly, the COVID-19 pandemic, while a health crisis on the surface, unearthed deep-seated disparities and inefficiencies. The virus did not merely infect bodies but spread through cracks in social structures, drawing attention to deficiencies in healthcare, governance and global cooperation.

If the vampire in *El Conde* serves as a compelling metaphor for the persistent and adaptive nature of crisis, then our contemporary reality is no less illustrative of this concept. Just as the vampire persistently morphs to its surroundings, crises in our modern era are deeply influenced by and continually evolve within the sociopolitical and technological terrains they inhabit. As Bauman suggests, the digital age propels individuals into a relentless pursuit of visibility and validation (2002, 34), revolutionizing how individuals perceive their sense of self and place within society. Indeed, technology does more than merely record or amplify crises; it interlaces with them, transforming both their nature and our perception. Platforms and digital ecosystems become arenas for displaying resilience, adaptability and reinvention. However, while technology facilitates adaptability, it also paradoxically exacerbates the pressure to continually evolve. Every scroll, swipe or click confronts one with another individual's triumph over adversity, setting a benchmark and feeding into the insatiable desire to "capture the eye" (Bauman, 2002, 34). This "always-on" digital culture creates an almost Sisyphean task of self-improvement, where the hill to climb seems never-ending (Bauman, 2002, 40). Digital spaces, while ostensibly a place of connection and opportunity, often magnified the dissonance between their lived realities and the narratives that propagated the "good life." Stories of resilience and innovation often served not as inspiration, but as a "cruel optimism" (Berlant 2011) a stark reminder of a world moving at a pace they could scarcely match. The onset of the COVID-19 pandemic, too, prompted many to seek solace and understanding in the virtual world, only to find it rife with paradoxes. On one hand, it offered the allure of global community and shared struggle; on the other, it echoed with narratives that seemed distant from the immediate and pressing challenges at hand. This disjunction—between the digital promise and the material, often painful reality—accentuates the widening gap between our "space of experience" and the "horizon of expectation" (Koselleck 1985, 171–176). This dual-edged nature of technology, as both savior and oppressor, forms a core component of crisis ambientality. However, the key lies in discerning genuine pathways to adaptability from the incessant noise of validation, and in recognizing that while we are influenced by the stories we encounter, we remain the sole authors of our manuscripts (Bauman 2002, 40).

Similar to the vampire's need for constant adaptation, individuals in modern societies are compelled to continuously evolve, engaging in a perpetual cycle of visibility and self-affirmation (Bauman 2002, 34). Digital platforms do not merely act as passive observers; they transform into spaces where these personal transformations are displayed and celebrated. In this digital theater, skills are not merely about one's *savoir-faire* (knowing how to do), but increasingly about one's *savoir-être* (knowing how to be)—a continuous adaptation to an ever-evolving script set against the backdrop of crisis (Boltanski & Chiapello 2000, 151). But herein lies the paradox: as digital platforms champion adaptability, they concurrently set relentless benchmarks of success, akin to the vampire's insatiable thirst.

In the next chapter, I shift the metaphorical lens from the ever-adapting vampire to the concept of confabulations. Just as individuals craft narratives to navigate the ambient nature of personal crises, nations too weave tales—stories of survival, resilience and reinvention. These national confabulations, often constructed at the intersections of history and politics, become essential tools as countries grapple with their identities amid the disorientation caused by crisis cultures. If our lives, as Ulrich Beck (1992, 137) suggests, become "the biographical solution of systemic contradictions," then are nations not scripting tales of relentless adaptation and endurance? Through these stories, nations not only seek to make sense of their place in a crisis ambientality but also shape their trajectories, illustrating the adage that sometimes, to survive, we must first learn to tell our stories.

Chapter 3

Confabulations

Amid the ambience of crisis cultures, my positionality, both as an individual and an academic, underscores a tension situated between the contrasting worlds of the "elite" and the "working class." My father, a factory worker, and my mother, a homemaker, embodied the diligent working-class spirit, building a stable, albeit modest, life for our family. In this environment, narratives were constructed from actual struggles rather than theoretical abstraction, such as the challenges my migrant parents faced navigating the educational system of their adopted country. When I stepped into academia—becoming notably the first in my family to traverse the terrains of higher education—I found myself somewhat unexpectedly anointed with the label "elite." This label, with all its variegated implications and inherent expectations, resonates dissonantly against my working-class origins and the potent narratives of perseverance and struggle that shaped my upbringing. I thus exist in a strange duality: seen as part of a demographic often criticized for being detached from the "real" or "common" people on one hand, while also being deeply connected to lived experiences that defy being defined by my current socioeconomic position on the other. Within the constraints of such dualities, "elites" are frequently depicted as disconnected from material everyday realities, while "real" people are presented as those firmly rooted in the practicalities of daily struggles, unencumbered by the often-abstract dialogues of intellectual discourse. However, such portrayals often overlook the rich, heterogeneous textures of lived experiences.

Does my present engagement in what could be considered elite pursuits—like authoring this book—inherently limit my capacity to understand and empathize with the realities of families like mine? The very act of reflection, of questioning one's place amid such pervasive and polarizing narratives of crisis, only serves to underline how tenuous such divisions really are. Many young individuals, for instance, emerging from working-class neighborhoods, embody a progressive ethos typically ascribed to the "elite." They champion causes such as climate change activism and Black Lives Matter (BLM), demonstrating a convergence between grassroots struggles and progressive narratives that confidently transcend socioeconomic boundaries. Meanwhile, it is not a rarity to witness individuals who are well-educated and economically privileged subscribing to retrograde, reactionary narratives that stand starkly incongruent with their socioeconomic status, thereby propagating discourses that reinforce exclusionary and regressive social structures. This phenomenon, what Leicht and Fennell term a "cultural backlash," often celebrates the "common man" (gender intended) in opposition to the high-minded claims of experts and elites who profess to know what is best for everyone (2023, 41). Can it ever be plausible, then, to entirely disengage from one's foundational narratives, especially when one is perceived as being starkly divorced from those origins?

In a pivotal moment of the 2016 U.S. Presidential Election, Hillary Clinton—a seasoned politician with a career deeply steeped in navigating through the corridors of power—coined a phrase that inadvertently, yet indelibly, became emblematic of crisis cultures: the "basket of deplorables." In this moment of political spectacle, Clinton sought to critique what she viewed as the more hateful and divisive segments of her opponent, Donald Trump's support base—those who were openly racist, sexist, homophobic, xenophobic, Islamophobic—by labeling them "deplorables." This characterization ignited widespread analysis and debate, informing various media and academic discussions and even being analyzed in Clinton's autobiography (2017). Within the dominant, yet sometimes overgeneralized, account of the incident, Clinton's "deplorables" descriptor created a stark divide, crafting an us-versus-them dichotomy between the supposedly enlightened, progressive "elite" and the purportedly regressive, unenlightened masses. Indeed, Clinton's remark, likely intended to spotlight divisive and sometimes hateful rhetoric from some of Trump's supporters, unintentionally generalized a larger demographic, attributing to them a single identity that lacked nuance and individuality. Her "basket of deplorables" comment, filled with dismissiveness and assumptive undertones, is therefore often highlighted as revealing a subtle, possibly unintentional, disdain within certain elite circles toward those with differing perspectives. In such accounts, Clinton's declaration goes beyond a simple dismissal of a substantial portion of the U.S. electorate; it is viewed as a manifestation of the dynamics of social, cultural, and symbolic capital that underscore such pronouncements (Bourdieu 1986). Within such an interpretation, the "deplorables" label symbolically devalues the social and cultural capital of those to whom it is assigned, placing them outside the realm of legitimate discourse and, therefore, power. The label thus implies an intrinsic lack of worth and erases the struggles and genuine frustrations that pervade many individuals' engagement with contemporary politics. As such, it ignores the possibility that beneath divisive rhetoric and ideologies, there is a collection of individual stories united by threads of socioeconomic disenfranchisement and political disillusionment, as well as a legitimate desire for recognition and change.

Upon closer examination, however, Clinton's use of the phrase "basket of deplorables" might not be seen solely as an expression of disdain. Instead, it could be interpreted as a vivid expression of the frustration felt within certain segments of the "elite." This perspective prompts, or even necessitates, a reflection: whether Clinton's remark should be strictly, and perhaps simplistically, seen as an act of social and moral distancing and consequent dehumanization of the "Other." Alternatively, might it instead be construed as a sharply-targeted critique of the specific rhetoric with which some of Trump's supporters had chosen to align themselves? In other words, rather than merely being a disparaging epithet, it might be a bold, if not incisive, commentary on the rhetoric and ideology that was gaining traction. This perspective invites an analytical shift, interpreting Clinton's comment not just as an "us" versus "them" dichotomy, but potentially as highlighting a significant, affective threat in a context already fraught with discord. That is, the remark may also, upon deeper, more empathetic consideration, be viewed as an exasperated call for collective consciousness: a plea for society to recognize and assiduously address the dangerous allure of divisive ideologies in an already fractiously delineated climate. While this argument does not explicitly endorse or defend Hillary Clinton—who, it is recognized, embodied the archetypal establishment candidate with no clear signs of having planned to overturn the foundational dynamics fomenting crisis cultures—it seeks to engage with how singular moments can reflect broader, more profound, social anxieties.

Clinton's loss in the election serves as a compelling case study for a common phenomenon in modern politics: the dominance of immediate, intense emotional experiences (*Erlebnis*) over deeper, reflective understanding (*Erfahrung*) of crisis events. Following her defeat, there was a significant public outcry filled with raw emotion, underscoring how, within crisis cultures, individuals often focus more on their initial, personal responses rather than on understanding the complex systemic factors behind such political outcomes. In the aftermath of the election, the roles of Hillary Clinton and Donald Trump took on symbolic significance that extended far beyond their individual political personas. They became emblematic of two deeply entrenched cultural narratives that reflected the nation's wider existential crisis. Clinton, with her extensive political background, represented the narrative of the political establishment, symbolizing continuity, expertise, and, for some voters, the undesirable continuation of the current political system. Her candidacy was thus perceived as an endorsement of the status quo, which critics equated with the system's stagnation and shortcomings. Conversely, Donald Trump presented himself as the complete opposite of this establishment narrative. His campaign and eventual victory embodied a counternarrative advocating for a radical break from traditional political praxis. Trump's image as a political outsider appealed to voters disillusioned with conventional politics, resonating with their existential frustrations and desires for a different political direction. In such a crisis culture, figures like Clinton and Trump became focal points, not for their individual merits or flaws, but for the larger, often conflicting, narratives they came to represent in the public imagination.

In the context of the rise of populism, particularly during the U.S. election, the spread of crisis cultures is becoming an increasingly common and widespread phenomenon. Political sentiments, traditionally contained within national boundaries, are now resonating globally, transforming and re-establishing themselves in different contexts. The Brexit referendum is a poignant example, having channeled similar emotional undercurrents to those seen in the United States, culminating in a vote that was as indicative of anti-establishment sentiment as it was a manifestation of the U.K.'s entrenched political divisions (Hobolt 2016; Clarke et al. 2017). The 2018 presidential election in Brazil further illustrates this pattern, with Jair Bolsonaro positioning himself as the antithesis to a perceived apathetic elite, artfully capitalizing on legitimate social grievances to fuel his populist narrative (Hunter & Power 2019). In a more recent echo, Argentina's 2023 election saw presidential victor Javier Milei embracing aspects of Trump's rhetoric. Milei, an outspoken proponent of libertarian economics, co-opted the Trumpian discourse, incorporating unexpected elements like advocating for gun ownership—an issue that resonates oddly in a nation without the U.S.'s gun culture (Nicas 2023). This trend is not exclusive to Argentina; it finds parallels in European nations like Italy, Hungary, and Poland, where leaders like Giorgia Meloni from the Brothers of Italy (FdI) similarly embrace populist rhetoric, such as hardline immigration policies (Roberts 2023). They assiduously attempt to forge a unified national identity by casting immigrants, and occasionally the European Union itself, as threats to national stability (Szabó 2020; Lipiński & Szabo 2023). The persistence and adaptability of these crisis narratives underline their deep-seated influence on local and national politics, irrespective of the diverse contexts they infiltrate.

Within this schema of political polarization, I find myself grappling with the dualities inherent within my own identity, a constant to-and-fro between a firm grounding in working-class roots and a perceived elite status within academia. My positionality, shaped by ties to both working-class roots and an academic arena often viewed as elite, recognizes that members of my own family and circle might be encompassed by labels such as "the deplorables." This personal connection underlines the imperative to construct a discourse that, while sharply critical, upholds an empathetic lens. The task then is twofold: sustaining a staunch critique against the proliferation of harmful, extremist ideologies, while concurrently embarking on an empathetic exploration of the variegated narratives residing within these categorically demarcated demographics. Attuned to the lived experiences and disenfranchisements permeating these communities, a strategic remapping might emerge, wherein critique and empathy intertwine into a singular, purposeful strategy. Navigating this dialogue with precision ensures that the scrutiny of harmful ideologies neither overshadows the multiple experiences and systemic influences within these demographics nor dismisses the disruptive impacts of polarizing labels like "deplorables." The approach, therefore, amplifies nuanced voices while staunchly opposing adversarial elements, forging a discourse wherein critique and empathy coexist without diminishing one another.

The fundamental architecture of a nation not only requires the initial formulation of a shared identity but also its ongoing recalibration and refinement, wherein it attempts to merge varied, and sometimes conflicting, narratives into a cohesive national story. This process involves a delicate balance—or indeed a confrontation—between inclusion and exclusion, acknowledgment and denial, a process whereby certain narratives gain privilege, while others are marginalized or outright dismissed. In examining a spectrum of global events, including Clinton's "basket of deplorables" commentary, the Brexit campaign, and Brazil's polarized election, a recurring pattern emerges: a pronounced dependency on simplistic, dichotomous narratives that contribute to a pervasive crisis ambientality. A superficial assessment of these incidents might suggest a straightforward dynamic where pervasive crisis cultures trigger a reflexive, and arguably existential, retreat into sharply demarcated identities. However, this chapter disputes the simplicity of such a perspective, proposing instead that these reactions, rather than being merely instinctual retreats, are psychological strategies for coping with crisis cultures. In this chapter, I therefore introduce the concept of "confabulations"—meticulously fabricated narratives that, albeit potentially grounded in fragments of truth, are chiefly characterized by exaggerations, omissions, or nuanced distortions rather than outright falsifications—that serve as cognitive mechanisms to make sense of the inherent disorientation caused by living in crisis cultures (Hirstein 2005). This analysis recognizes the compounded complexity brought about by the digital era, where national identity undergoes continuous construction and articulation in online environments, necessitating an even more considered understanding of narrative formation and perception (Han 2022). This engagement with confabulations in national contexts offers new insights into how nations, through their formative and transformative stages, utilize selective narratives that might diverge from factual accuracy yet fulfill critical and multifaceted purposes. Highlighting the depth behind these constructed narratives, the chapter posits confabulations not as reactionary or superficial, but as sophisticated tools employed—usually subconsciously—for national survival and coherence. They potentially reveal the structural, emotional, and psychological modalities that nations might employ to navigate the treacherous balance between cohesion and fragmentation, unity and discord, particularly when their core identity is under siege. These narratives, while offering refuge or an illusion of stability, also carry the danger of deepening political polarization, underlining the paradoxical nature of confabulations as both unifying and divisive forces. This positioning of nation and confabulation proffers a fresh analytical perspective to examine the manifold, complex methods through which nations engage in such narrative construction during the formation of identities, especially within crisis cultures, demonstrating how these crafted stories—though sometimes detached from objective truth—remain integral, operating at the very heart of nation-building efforts. The chapter, therefore, underscores the critical role of these narratives that are at once fictional and functional, fallible and fundamental, in the ongoing project of nation-building. It invites readers to reassess the dynamics of national narratives, especially within cultures of crisis, considering them not as mere fabrications but as crucial instruments in maintaining national unity and social cohesion.

Moving forward, this chapter is structured into three primary sections. In the first section, I trace the historical evolution of the nation from the pivotal Peace of Westphalia to its present-day conceptions, providing an essential contextual foundation by illustrating the dynamic and transformative nature of national identities across historical eras. The section does not merely chart a course through history but also endeavors to reflect these historical insights into contemporary contexts, emphasizing the critical importance of recognizing the nation's inherent historical instability to fully grasp its present-day manifestations. The following section brings into focus my contention that nationhood today is frequently enveloped and, to an extent, confined within confabulatory narratives. Such an argument underscores the strategic crafting of narratives that mediate, manipulate, and, at times, malign the collective national consciousness, particularly during times of crisis, thereby offering a theoretical lens to explore the intimate intertwining of national narratives and crisis management. This theoretical discussion then leads to a material exploration in the final section, which considers the January 6, 2021, U.S. Capitol Hill insurrection as a case study, attempting to decode the mechanics of national confabulations and their affective impacts on real-world events. Through this, the chapter underlines the dialectic between nation-building and crisis, rendering insights into how national narratives, especially those crafted within crisis cultures, can inadvertently shape, dictate, and perpetuate the project of nation-building.

NARRATIVES OF NATIONHOOD

Recognizing that the "nation" operates not merely as a territorial or political entity but, critically, as a dialectical construct where manifold narratives are continuously shaped, contested, and reimagined, tracing its historical evolution through the lens of how crises have shaped nation-building efforts becomes fundamental, especially through the lens of ongoing crisis. This extensive historical exploration is thus necessary, offering a foundation to appreciate how nations have historically navigated and merged varied, sometimes conflicting, narratives into a cohesive national story. Such an exploration into history is indispensable for fully understanding how contemporary digital environments and crisis cultures both influence and are shaped by national narratives. While this inquiry gleans insights from an expansive historical trajectory, its primary focus on European nation-building is a reflection of Europe's prolonged history of nation-states, not an oversight of other global nation-building efforts. The exploration is not merely historical but inherently philosophical, examining the very ability of these entities to conjure a semblance of unity and stability amid social, economic, and political challenges. In an era where crisis is chronic, how can we evaluate the historical proficiency of nations in formulating and maintaining collective narratives? And further, does the nation, as a construct, retain its capacity to foster unity and stability amid the enveloping crisis ambientality that characterizes contemporary crisis cultures?

The concept of the nation-state, a pivotal structure in modern politics, can be traced back to a critical moment in European history: the Peace of Westphalia in 1648. This treaty, a response to the catastrophic Thirty Years' War, was a turning point in defining state sovereignty and territorial boundaries (Croxton 1999). It established the framework for a system of independent, sovereign states across Europe. It is within this historical context that the idea of the "nation" began to form, characterized by shared cultural, ethnic, and linguistic traits that fostered a collective identity. Simultaneously, the "state" developed as a political entity with recognized sovereignty and specific geographical borders. Zygmunt Bauman points to a subtle yet important interdependence between nations and states, where nations endorsed the state's quest for governance and, conversely, states validated the nation's aspiration for unity (2002, 5). Europe's territorial landscape during this era was thus one of constant negotiation, marked by power struggles, shifting alliances, and fluid borders. The period following the Peace of Westphalia until the dissolution of the Holy Roman Empire in 1806 witnessed considerable transformation and upheaval across Europe, illustrated by events such as the War of the Spanish Succession (1701–1714) and the War of the Austrian Succession (1740–1748) (Whaley 2012; Wilson 2016). These events, unfolding amid a confluence of political, religious, and social crises, prompted a strengthening of the concepts of statehood and sovereignty, laying the foundation for the modern nation-state (Lynn 2013; Browning 1995).

Parallel to these political and social evolutions was the intellectual upheaval caused by the Enlightenment during the eighteenth century. This philosophical revolution, marked by its emergent principles such as empiricism and humanism, confronted and questioned entrenched hierarchies, heralding an era that accentuated individual liberties, secular ideologies, and rational thought. The Enlightenment planted the early seeds of dissent against conventional monarchical and religious authority, gradually undermining their unassailable status through the propagation of ideas that advocated for greater individualism and reason-based governance (Outram 2013). The dissolution of the Holy Roman Empire in 1806 further accelerated this ideological shift, simultaneously creating a conceptual void and a fertile ground for emerging nationalistic movements, which went on to define the political ideologies of the nineteenth century. The pivotal nexus within this evolutionary trajectory was, undoubtedly, the French Revolution (1789–1799), a period not just of monumental political restructuring but also of the nation-state's revelation as a potential anchor in times of extensive civil and political crisis (Hunt 2004). During the Revolution, symbolic acts such as the hoisting of the tricolor flag and the proclamation of *laïcité* (secularism) were strategies designed to engender a unified national consciousness. These actions sought to replace the regal symbols of the *ancien régime*, thereby integrating the concept of state sovereignty with citizen identity under a common banner and purpose (Bauman 2002, 6). This era thus marked a decided shift where symbols and rituals were strategically employed to cultivate a collective imagination, fostering a shared identity that transcended regional and class differences.

Equally pivotal in the evolution of nationhood and indicative of a global crisis in traditional power dynamics was the American Revolution (1775–1783). This revolution, emerging from the colonies' struggle against British imperial rule, played a crucial role in redefining modern concepts of national sovereignty and democratic governance. It was instrumental in challenging traditional notions of monarchy and colonialism, representing a crisis point for the established order. The Declaration of Independence in 1776 not only signaled the birth of a new nation but also embodied Enlightenment ideals, emphasizing individual rights and self-governance. This event marked a significant departure from Eurocentric ideas of statehood, setting a precedent for the emergence of nations grounded in the principles of democracy and republicanism amid a crisis of legitimacy for the old regimes (Wood 2011). Furthermore, the Haitian Revolution (1791–1804) stands as a seminal event in the history of nationhood, representing the world's first successful slave revolt leading to an independent nation. This revolution marked a major crisis in the French colonial regime in Saint-Domingue and fundamentally challenged prevailing global narratives of racial hierarchy and colonial exploitation. The establishment of Haiti as a sovereign state in 1804 was not just a groundbreaking moment but also a crisis point for colonial powers, symbolizing the triumph of oppressed peoples and influencing anti-colonial struggles worldwide (Dubois 2004).The subsequent collapse of the Spanish Empire in the Americas, a significant crisis in colonial hegemony, further reshaped the global landscape of national sovereignty. The early nineteenth century witnessed a series of independence movements across Latin America, sparked by both the weakening of Spanish imperial power and the spread of revolutionary ideas, signaling a systemic crisis in the old colonial order. Nations such as Mexico, Colombia, Argentina, and Chile emerged from the remnants of the Spanish colonies, each forging unique national identities and governance structures (Lynch 1986). As newly independent states navigated the complex process of nation-building, they also grappled with the crisis of creating a new identity and defining their place in the international order, a challenge characterized by both opportunities and obstacles.

Within the context of the late nineteenth century—a critical era marked by the deepening imprints of industrialization, imperialism, and the rise of nationalism—the political and cultural foundations of Europe, especially in France, underwent significant transformations. These transformations were embedded within a series of political and economic crises, demonstrating that the foundations of the nation-state were not static but flexible entities, influenced and shaped by diverse forces and exchanges. Nationhood, with its inherent aura of stability, thus emerged as a central focal point in both scholarly and political arenas, often acknowledged as a potential anchoring entity in the face of prevailing crisis (Anderson 1991; Hobsbawm 1990). Yet, nationhood, which for a brief moment had seemed impervious to scrutiny, began to show signs of strain under the weight of evolving crises, exemplified by pivotal events like the Franco-Prussian War of 1870–1871 that paved the way for the French Third Republic, alongside the ensuing discrepancies between established narratives and actual historical events (Howard 2013). The "Dreyfus Affair," which unfolded from 1894 to 1906, dramatically illustrates the internal conflicts that challenged France during a critical period of national identity crisis. Alfred Dreyfus, a Jewish French army officer, was wrongfully accused and convicted of treason, sparking widespread controversy and debate across the nation. This incident not only highlighted the deep-seated anti-Semitism within French society but also exposed significant divides over militarism and the conflicting perceptions of truth and justice. As a result, the Dreyfus Affair became emblematic of a profound struggle within France's national narrative, revealing a stark contrast between the proclaimed ideals of unity and the harsh realities of societal divisions (Read 2012).

Before the upheaval of the Dreyfus Affair, French historian Ernest Renan delivered a pivotal lecture in 1882 entitled "What is a Nation?" (2018). This lecture did more than merely provide a lens through which national phenomena could be examined; it also sparked a critical discourse that questioned the stability and continuity of the very concept of a nation. He described it as "a soul, a spiritual principle," signaling that it is more than just shared history; it is also a spiritual bond (2018, 261). Renan clarified this concept further, stating: "To have common glories in the past, a common will in the present; to have performed great deeds together, to wish to perform still more, these are the essential preconditions for being a people" (Renan 2018, 261). Significantly, for Renan, the nation is perpetually reconstructed through a delicate balance of collective memory and selective historical forgetfulness—a crucial element that finds resonance within France's internal and external conflicts and their aftermaths, wherein selective narratives and collective forgetfulness were frequently utilized to weave a semblance of national unity and cohesiveness (2018, 251). A tangible instantiation of this can be observed in France's entanglement with Algeria, where despite a protracted and violent conflict, the narratives surrounding the Algerian War (1954–1962) have often been minimized or altered in the French collective memory, subtly perpetuating a selective forgetting to maintain a cohesive national narrative (McCormack 2010). Renan thus underscored that while a nation's narrative necessitates a shared memory, it often strategically excludes inconvenient truths, thereby underscoring the performative and fabricated nature of national identities. His assertion: "The act of forgetting, I would even say, historical error, is an essential factor in the creation of a nation" (2018, 251) underlined that the formulation and perpetuation of national identity is not merely a passive reflection of shared experiences and collective memory but is, instead, an active construct, often manipulated, revised, and even obscured to navigate through the dissonances of a nation's past and present.

Bauman's perception of the nation-state as an "unfinished project" finds substantial historical anchorage here, particularly within the broad developments in European history, where fluctuations between nationalism and statecraft have been markedly pronounced, all set against a backdrop of overlapping crises (2002, 9). The deliberate elevation of state power, overcoming diverse cultural, religious, and linguistic pluralities, was essentially a strategy aimed at nurturing a standardized national identity that, theoretically, could suppress dissent and promote political stability (Bauman 2002, 9). This was not merely a governance mechanism but also a form of defense against the constant crises that threatened the meticulously crafted structure of the nation-state (Bauman 2002, 10). In a vivid historical context such as Germany's unification in 1871 under the Prussian crown, the nuanced relationship between state and nation is especially pronounced. Otto von Bismarck, with his audacious foreign policy and adroit manipulation of nationalist sentiments, engineered a series of crises, namely through wars against Denmark, Austria, and France, to consolidate the fragmented German states into a single nation under Prussian leadership (Steinberg 2011). These orchestrated crises were instrumental in stimulating a collective German identity, effectively subsuming regional particularities and rivalries beneath a dominant, overarching umbrella of pan-German nationalism (Bauman 2002, 9). Nonetheless, despite the establishment of the German Empire, the inherent heterogeneity and particularism among the distinct German states continued to pose a constant challenge to the homogenized national identity, a phenomenon not unique to Germany but also evident in other European nations at the time, such as Italy, Spain, and the United Kingdom, where diverse regional identities similarly challenged the formation of a unified national identity. The "unfinished" nature of nation-building was also markedly evident in the ensuing political crises of subsequent decades, especially during the Weimar Republic (1919–1933) following the Revolutions of 1918–1919. This era not only underscored the tensions and disparities within the ostensibly unified German nation but also exemplified the struggles to establish a coherent national identity amid political, economic, and social crises (Peukert 1991; Weitz 2007). These historical exemplars underscore that, notwithstanding the perpetuation of a unified national narrative, the underlying crises of identity, legitimacy, and allegiance—often sparked by geopolitical upheavals, internal discord, economic downturns, and regional resistances—constantly lingered, perpetually shaping—and being shaped by—the state's endeavor to construct a coherent and unchallengeable national identity (Bauman 2002, 10). These crises not only challenged the legitimacy and continuity of the pre-established national identities but, in various instances, precipitated further state interventions and recalibrations of national belonging (Bauman 2002, 10).

Renan envisioned the nation as an "everyday plebiscite," suggesting that a nation's existence is continuously affirmed and redefined by its people's daily decisions to participate in civic life, uphold common values, and consciously remember (or forget) key aspects of their shared history (2018, 261–262). This idea highlights the active role citizens play in shaping their nation, implying that national identity is not static but rather an ongoing, collective project forged through both consensus and shared memory. Building on this, Anthony D. Smith (1991) points out that even within what may appear as a united front, nations are often internally divided, with different groups interpreting the national narrative through their distinct lenses of experience.

These divisions, a natural outcome of diverse regional identities and social classes, contribute to the ongoing discourse that shapes a nation's self-perception. It is vital, therefore, to understand that the narratives forming the backbone of national identities are not just top-down constructions imposed by the state or elites. They are also the result of bottom-up influences, such as grassroots movements and regional identities, as well as the result of responses to crises that feed into the larger story. Hence, there is an ongoing dialectic between nation-building and the crises that both challenge and shape them, such as rebellions, wars, and ideological transformations. While the mantra "my country, right or wrong" may seem pervasive, its acceptance is neither universal nor consistent (Bauman 2002, 9), indicating a constant tension between citizen and state, and underlining the perpetually unstable and negotiated nature of national identity.

While national identity has been shown to be a product of continuous negotiation and redefinition, Ernest Gellner introduces a pivotal shift in this understanding, arguing that nations are less "discovered" through cultural ties than they are "invented" with specific objectives in mind, driven by modernity and industrialization (1964, 168). In this vein, he posits that the forces of modernity and industrialization compel nations, especially during their formative phases, to deliberately craft cultural and linguistic commonalities. These are not reflections of pre-existing heritages, but strategic tools to forge a unified identity conducive to new socioeconomic realities. These meticulously constructed foundations serve not merely to establish a solid and coherent nation-state but also to navigate the complex demands of modernity and industrialization. Within this framework, a unified culture becomes indispensable, specifically engineered to facilitate communication and cooperation in an environment defined by economic integration and rapid industrial advancement. Unlike Renan, who posited collective memory and "soul" as the cornerstone of nationhood, Gellner thus advances the discourse by presenting the nation not as an inherent cultural entity but as a deliberately engineered one, underscoring the essential role of a shared culture, cultivated within the dynamics of modernity and industrialization (Renan 2018, 261–262; Gellner 1964, 168). Gellner's discussion thus centers around the notion that shared culture is not merely a spontaneous alignment but a systematic orchestration meant to meet and facilitate the economic demands of a modern nation. The deliberate crafting of a national identity during the 1871 unification of the German Empire—achieved through the standardization of language and culture across various states—clearly illustrates Gellner's theoretical framework (1983, 99–100). In this context, a nation surfaces not as a spontaneous expression of inherent cultural kinship but as a pragmatic, strategically structured entity, cultivated in response to, and facilitated by, the socioeconomic necessities of modernity. In a parallel vein, the Italian

Risorgimento was not merely a romantic, cultural resurgence; rather, it was a strategic orchestration driven by the need for economic consolidation and political unification amid the burgeoning pressures of modernity and industrial advancement (Duggan 2008). This period of national unification did not lean on the spontaneous surge of cultural commonalities. Instead, it required a deliberate shaping of a new national narrative, integrating diverse dialects, cultures, and histories, often in the face of pronounced regional distinctions (Duggan 2008). The Risorgimento thus embodies Gellner's assertion that the creation of a nation is less about the discovery of an inherent identity and more about the intentional and strategic construction of a new one, a process invariably tied to the imperatives of modernization and industrialization.

Eric Hobsbawm (1990, 1992) takes a different approach to understanding the fabrication of nations, diverging from Gellner's emphasis on socioeconomic forces, and instead focusing on the deliberate crafting of what he terms "invented traditions" by the ruling elites. Unlike Gellner, who emphasizes the strategic engineering behind nation-building, Hobsbawm contends with the machinations of power, particularly examining how elite classes manipulate "invented traditions" to formulate, perpetuate, and control the collective national narrative. Hobsbawm identifies nation-building as a reflection of the strategic pursuits of ruling elites who, with astute manipulation, construct cultural and national narratives that not only consolidate their hold on power but also reinforce their authority. Nationalism, in Hobsbawm's exposition, is not a benign byproduct of shared cultural and historical identity, but a tool—sharpened and wielded with precision by elites to channel the masses toward specific political endpoints. These "invented traditions," as described by Hobsbawm, are not relics of bygone eras but modern creations. They are deliberately crafted norms and practices, ostensibly timeless, yet often modern inventions designed to convey a concocted continuity with a selectively glorified past (Hobsbawm 1990). A striking example is post-revolutionary Mexico, where the government initiated a comprehensive cultural synthesis known as "*Indigenismo*." This movement sought to integrate diverse Indigenous cultures into a unified national identity. Muralism, led by artists like Diego Rivera, played a key role in this, depicting a harmonized narrative of Mexico's history, where pre-Columbian cultures and the mestizo population were intertwined in a shared heritage (Coffey 2012). This deliberate cultural policy, while celebrating the country's Indigenous past, also served to strengthen the post-revolutionary government's legitimacy and power, masking the ongoing social inequalities and political contradictions in the country (Knight 1990; Dawson 1998; Coffey 2012). This deliberate shaping of "invented traditions" emerges as a vital instrument, serving not just as a cultural compass but also as a mechanism for crisis management within the nation-state. It goes beyond merely reacting to the imperatives of industrialization, as posited by Gellner, and extends to the strategic shaping of a collective consciousness. This process aims to unify, direct, and sometimes manipulate perceptions and actions in a manner that preserves the stability and continuity of the nation-state amid the manifold challenges it faces.

Similar to Mexico, Spain offers a further compelling illustration of Hobsbawm's thesis on the invented nature of nationalism and nation formation (Hobsbawm 1990). During the nineteenth century and well into the twentieth century, nationalism in Spain was utilized both as a tool for unity and as a means of crisis generation. Efforts to forge a unified Spanish identity were in conflict with the country's inherent regionalism and significant cultural and linguistic diversity (Conversi 1997; Guibernau 2004). This was particularly manifest during Francoist Spain (1939–1975), when an imposed national narrative sought to diminish regional identities and languages in favor of a uniform Spanish identity under a single authoritarian state. Franco's regime appropriated and amplified notable events and Catholic symbols, such as National Day parades and religious ceremonies, to establish a distinct, cohesive narrative of nationalism (García Sebastiani 2020). However, the flexibility of this national identity became most evident in its problematic imposition, leading to multiple social crises. A striking example was the Francoist suppression of the Catalan language and culture, representing more than cultural erasure. It was a strategic political move by the regime to undermine regional identity, evidenced by policies such as the prohibition of Catalan in public spaces and the systematic renaming of streets with Spanish names (Guibernau 2004; Rupiérez Núnez & Dinas 2023, 4). This aggressive approach ignited deep social and political crises, fueling resistance movements within Catalonia (Llobera 2005). Despite these repressive efforts, the resilient regional identities, deeply anchored in distinct historical, linguistic, and cultural contexts, continued to challenge the imposed unified Spanish narrative. The enforcement of a singular national identity, alongside the suppression of strong regional identities, not only generated crises during the Francoist period but also left lasting impacts into the contemporary era, vividly illustrated by events like the 2017 Catalan independence referendum. This push for independence, rooted in a historical identity and long-standing grievances against the centralized Spanish state, underscores the ongoing interaction between nationalism and crisis, continuously shaping Spain's contemporary political and cultural landscape. But beyond the crises and the struggles for cultural survival, one might ask: to what extent does the concept of the nation itself, as propagated by regimes like Franco's, rely on the "imagined" coherence of community? Indeed, in the face of rival "imagined communities" within the single state, how do these imagined constructs hold sway over real, material cultural expressions and allegiances?

In *Imagined Communities* (1991) Benedict Anderson delicately narrates nationhood through the lens of shared and constructed imagination, wherein the concept of a nation transcends geopolitical or ethnocentric dimensions to embody a universally pervasive, yet distinct, entity—an "imagined community." Anderson posits: "The nation is imagined because the members of even the smallest nation will never know most of their fellow members, meet them, or even hear of them, yet in the minds of each lives the image of their communion" (1991, 6). However, the term "imagined" does not imply a lack of reality or substance, nor does it negate the legitimacy or the tangible impacts of national identity. Rather, it demonstrates the potency of shared narratives, collective imaginations, and a perpetual quest for communality, thereby underpinning a complex thread between interconnected identities, loyalties, and social frameworks. Indeed, members of the nation, while possibly not interacting or directly communicating with one another, draw upon the collective strength, narrative, and emotive belonging to this imagined entity, finding a unifying thread in a shared purpose and destiny. Anderson predicates the existence of nations on a "deep, horizontal comradeship" (1991, 7), envisaging a unified fraternal bond while simultaneously revealing the internal disparities and divergent imaginations within their diverse citizenry. A subtle yet pivotal undercurrent to this fraternity is an acknowledgment of its inherent contradictions and tensions, including the challenges of inclusivity, such as the difficulty of integrating traditionally marginalized groups like women into these imagined constructs of national unity. Crises, therefore, act as mirrors that reflect the divergences within the narrative and as laboratories testing the nation's communal resilience and adaptability. This is compellingly demonstrated in Japan's interaction with its "imagined community" during the transformative era surrounding the Second World War. The Meiji Restoration (1868–1889) was a crucial period during which Japan forged a national story that endorsed modernity while preserving profound respect for its imperial and cultural heritage, crafting an imagined collective identity that spurred its rise as a global power, despite internal diversities and distinct regional identities (Morris-Suzuki 1997). Post-World War II, Japan confronted a seismic shift, necessitating a reevaluation and recalibration of its national identity. This period marked a harmonization of its newfound pacifist ideals with an enduring collective ethos characterized by resilience, innovation, and an unwavering focus on economic revival (Orr 2001; Hashimoto 2015). The nation did not merely transition from its past nor passively accept foreign influences; instead, it underwent a sophisticated, collective reimagination that merged historical reverence with forward-looking optimism, consolidating its people around a rejuvenated national identity and shared aspirations. This reimagined identity fostered unity and propelled Japan from economic ruin to economic dynamism, demonstrating the potency of an "imagined community" in galvanizing a nation, especially in times of existential crisis. Hence, although Anderson's insights on imagined communities directly reflect the idea of nations as fabricated entities, as argued by Gellner and Hobsbawm, he does so with a nuanced understanding of the psychological and emotional cohesiveness that defines and binds a nation.

In the aftermath of the Second World War, decolonization marked a significant geopolitical and cultural juncture, signaling the end of colonial empires and the rise of sovereignty among formerly subjugated nations. This period, characterized by a transition from colonial rule to self-governance, saw the proliferation of diverse narratives—stories of nation-building and cultural redemption (Loomba 1998). Postcolonial theory emerged alongside these transformations, becoming a critical lens to examine the vestiges of colonial domination embedded in the cultural, social, and political fabrics of newly emancipated nations. Key figures such as Frantz Fanon (1961) and Gayatri Chakravorty Spivak (1988) made significant contributions to the corpus of postcolonial thought, deconstructing the latent colonial traces and exploring how they perpetually infuse and complicate the pathways toward establishing cohesive national identities in the aftermath of colonial rule. Fanon, for instance, eloquently demarcates the psychological impacts of colonialism and asserts the necessity for a violent catharsis to truly liberate colonized nations, not only politically but also psychologically and culturally (Fanon 1961). Meanwhile, Spivak (1988) underscores the subaltern's inability to find a voice within the hegemonic power structures left in the wake of colonial departure, thereby highlighting the implicit challenges faced by postcolonial societies in articulating and actualizing their newfound identities. Critics of Spivak counter this view by arguing that the subaltern has always spoken; their voices, however, may have been overlooked or unheard by metropolitan critics. In any case, Homi K. Bhabha (1990) integrates Anderson's "imagined communities" with postcolonial insights, positing the nation as an ongoing narrative spectacle. This theory accentuates the critical role of narrative in both forming and continually redefining a nation's collective identity, proposing an active, participatory function of narratives in the process of nation-building. Bhabha thus suggests that nations "lose their origins in the myths of time and only fully realize their horizons in the mind's eye" (1990, 1). He envisions the nation as a symbolic entity, motivated by cultural mandates and marked by a fleeting unity that is constantly challenged by its inherent contradictions, echoing through national discourse and the daily lives of its people (1990, 1). Therefore, Bhabha argues that this ever-changing nature of the nation plays a pivotal role in forming the stories that attempt to articulate the idea of "nationness" (Bhabha 1990, 2–3). This endeavor is more complex than mere wordplay or rhetorical strategies; it fundamentally transforms how we understand the concept of a nation.

In the historical context of India's anti-colonial resistance, Bhabha's "nation as narration" aptly mirrors the country's efforts to forge a unified national identity amid its deep-rooted social and cultural divisions. This was particularly evident during the careful orchestration of India's collective narrative in its fight against colonial rule. Leaders such as Mahatma Gandhi did not merely strategize but aptly constructed and disseminated a potent narrative that sought to mobilize a disparate and multifaceted populace around a unified vision of an independent Indian nation (Roy 2007). The narrative was infused with symbols (like the spinning wheel), rituals (such as non-violent protests and boycotts), and discourses (foregrounding self-rule and collective action) that were meant to forge a sense of shared destiny and collective identity among the incredibly diverse population (Brown 2009, 2010). Post-independence, the narrative malleability of India as a nation was again brought into stark relief as it sought to negotiate its existence during the traumatic partition and subsequent creation of Pakistan in 1947. In attempting to embody a secular and inclusive nation, India faced the formidable task of fabricating a national narrative that would accommodate and represent its multiple languages, religions, and ethnicities. The postcolonial Indian narrative had to perform a delicate balancing act: acknowledging and respecting the vast diversity within its borders while simultaneously crafting a unifying and encompassing narrative of a single nation. In *Beyond Belief* (2007), Roy challenges the conventional wisdom that nation-states emerge primarily through a shared cultural ethos. Instead, she positions the state itself as a central figure in crafting a distinct national identity. This approach reframes the concept of the nation-state, painting it not as a reflection of a pre-existing cultural community, but as an active architect of national identity, carving out its place as the definitive emblem of the nation. Roy analyzes the role of the Films Division of India in creating a sense of national identity, showing how state-produced films made the concept of the state tangible and integral to everyday life for its citizens (2007, 58). Celebrations such as Republic Day became annual festivities that were also instrumental in promoting this principle, showcasing the country's varied cultural diversity while asserting the state's role as the harmonizing force amid this diversity (2007, 81). Roy's argument effectively extends the conversation on nation-building beyond ideological imperatives, spotlighting the state's pragmatic strategies to weave a cohesive national narrative from the diverse threads of a pluralistic society. Bhabha's narrative theory thus becomes particularly relevant as the leaders and constitution-makers sought to narrate a nation that respected its diverse cultural and religious practices yet was cohesive in its commitment to a democratic and secular national entity. This "performance" of nationhood underscores the continual reimagining and deliberate crafting intrinsic to national identity formation.

In the period following the end of the Cold War, the perceived ascension of late-stage globalization was often portrayed as an inexorable process, one that seemingly signaled a diminution of the nation-state's capacity, relevance, and potency in a progressively borderless world. This era, defined by the collapse of the bipolar power structure emblematic of the Cold War, witnessed Francis Fukuyama (1992) audaciously proclaiming what he perceived as "the end of history." He suggested that liberal democracy and global capitalism had ascended as dominant and unchallenged paradigms, intimating a global order that would sideline the traditional mechanisms and sovereignties of the nation-state. This supposed "end" alluded to a future where national boundaries, previously inviolable markers of power, identity, and governance, were becoming increasingly permeable, even antiquated, in the face of unrelenting global flows of capital. Indeed, this geopolitical and cultural shift seemed to suggest a historic rupture, where the enduring bond between nation-building and its attendant crises appeared weakened, if not entirely broken, within the dissolving contours of traditionally solid national borders and identities. Consequently, Anthony Giddens, reiterating Daniel Bell's argument, underscored a dilemma in the nation-state's capacity and relevance. He critiqued it as too unwieldy to manage the nuances of individual experiences and yet too constrained to grapple with global phenomena (1994, 65). This observation underlined the nation-state's unsuitability for addressing both personal human affairs and extensive international challenges. Within these limitations, national identities precariously walk a fine line: balancing the continuity of shared histories, cultures, and languages on one hand, against the ephemeral liquidity of global flows, crises, and transformations on the other. Echoing Zygmunt Bauman's (2000) concept of "liquid modernity," nations existed in a realm of simultaneous consolidation and disintegration, with national narratives ceaselessly reconfigured at the intersection of local and global forces. Hence, at the close of the twentieth century, Manuel Castells' (2010) idea of the "network society" emphasized the critical function of informational networks, which had evolved from supplementary elements to essential tools for social, economic, and political engagement, profoundly changing the landscape of community bonds and collective identities in this globalized era. Notably, professional elites across nations might discover more commonalities with their counterparts abroad than with citizens within their own territorial bounds. A case in point is South Korea's cultural ascendancy, epitomized by the "Korean Wave" or *Hallyu* (Kim 2013). This cultural phenomenon, marked by the international spread of K-pop, Korean dramas, and films, transcends mere entertainment; it represents a breaching of the confines of its national borders, not just commercially but also in terms of soft power, nurturing hybrid cultural identities and communal experiences across the globe (Nye & Kim 2013; Kim 2021). Thus, professional elites in the cultural industry or technological sectors in Korea might find their experiences resonating more with those of their peers in, say, Silicon Valley or Bollywood, rather than with those of a local farmer or factory worker. These dynamics underscore the sometimes contradictory nature of identity in the global era, where shared professional or cultural interests might supersede traditional national allegiances or identities.

The historical trajectory of the nation-state, cursorily sketched above, underscores a crucial paradox: despite predictions of its demise in the face of rampant globalization, the nation-state's relevance, particularly in geopolitical events post-September 11, has not only persisted but, in many instances, even strengthened. Amid the push and pull of globalization, the nation-state has notably maintained its emotive capacity, continuing to invoke a sense of belonging and identity among its citizens. This emotive capacity reveals itself most prominently during high-stake events, which, while leaving an indelible mark globally, invigorate and reify the emotional significance of the nation-state. For instance, the dismantling of apartheid in South Africa represented more than just a political and social revolution; it became a powerful symbol of endurance and collective emotional investment in the nation's fundamental ideals, both nationally and globally (Guelke 2005). Nelson Mandela's 1994 inauguration, transforming decades of systemic segregation and oppression, not only ushered South Africa into a new era but also embodied a universal potential for healing, reconciliation, and unity (Chandhoke 2022). It showcased a potential passage for nations to transition from despair to collective hope through appeals to egalitarianism. Conversely, the September 11 attacks in the United States, though geographically localized, sent emotional repercussions around the world, simultaneously amplifying the "imaginary scripts" that steer national narratives and collective emotions (by, for example, escalating U.S. patriotism and a "with us or against us" narrative) (Illouz 2008, 14). Similarly, the universal crisis embodied in the COVID-19 pandemic, which perforated national boundaries and imposed global challenges, paradoxically instigated a retreat into and reinforcement of national identities and sovereignties (seen, for instance, in the initial vaccine hoarding by wealthy nations and an emphasis on safeguarding their own citizens first), as countries scrambled to seal their borders (Kupferschmidt 2020). Moreover, although national responses are by no means monolithic, significant military actions and terrorist attacks, such as Russia's invasion of Ukraine in February 2022 and the attacks on Israel by Hamas in October 2023, demonstrate how pivotal events reemphasize national solidarity and identity, evidenced, respectively, through apparent widespread domestic support for the war in Russia (Hill 2023) and the formation of a unity government in Israel in the aftermath of the attacks (Sharon et al. 2023). These events, though deeply entwined with power politics and territorial disputes, also anchor themselves to the emotional fabrics of nations, eliciting fervent nationalistic sentiments and coalescing domestic collectives in response to these external crises, even amid the diversity of perspectives that naturally exist within any nation.

Recognizing the emotional strength and resilience inherent within nations necessitates an earnest exploration of the enduring "love" or affinity that individuals harbor for their homeland. This love, as emphasized by Martha Nussbaum (2013) and reaffirmed by bell hooks' assertion that "love is an act of will . . . both an intention and an action" (hooks 2000, 4–5), transcends mere passive sentiment; instead, it becomes a dynamic and often intensifying framing during times of crisis and uncertainty. Nations, even if they sometimes contribute to crises, remain pillars of stability and are seen as sources of recovery and, importantly, hope during periods of collective distress. Within this dynamic, nations not only provide an outlet for collective grief but also promote visions of a future that promises recovery and stability. For example, concepts like the "American Dream" play crucial roles, symbolizing the ongoing pursuit of socioeconomic betterment and casting the nation-state as a symbolic "object of hope" (Ahmed 2014, 155). However, this emotional framing is challenged by contemporary economic realities, as highlighted by Leicht and Fennell (2023). They point out an increasing scarcity of secure, well-paying jobs, noting a decline in earnings and benefits for those in such positions compared to past generations (2023, 35). Alarmingly, prestigious careers, such as doctors, lawyers, scientists, managers, and university professors, now face a troubling precarity, signaling what Leicht and Fennell ominously describe as a "dark age" for American professions (2023, 13). Employing Lauren Berlant's concept of "Cruel Optimism" (2011), this scenario becomes emblematic of an attachment individuals maintain to unachievable goals that are integral to their sense of flourishing, even when these goals are unattainable or harmful. It embodies the nation's promise of a better life, a promise that fuels hope and aspiration, yet often results in disappointment and precarity, creating a perpetual cycle where the yearning for a more prosperous future is both a driving force and a source of continual deferral and disillusionment (Berlant 2011, 2–3). Consequently, the nation emerges as a dual phenomenon: a purveyor of a potentially hopeful future and a safeguard against perceived threats to economic and cultural stability within complex socioeconomic challenges, embodying the cruel optimism that Berlant portrays—a longing clung to despite its potential for heartbreak and unattainability.

Berlant's assertion that "nations provoke fantasy" (1991, 1) effectively captures the deep psychological and emotional integration of the nation in the minds of its citizens, a development spanning from the Peace of Westphalia to our present-day crisis cultures. Thinkers like Jacqueline Rose (1996) and Luisa Elena Delgado (2014) accentuate this embeddedness, highlighting the astute, yet often illusory, narratives of loss, resistance, and longing that nations propagate. These national fantasies can starkly contrast with lived realities. In Brazil, for example, a common narrative that often champions a peaceful, multicultural, and multiracial society can contrast sharply with the concrete experiences of racial and social disparities prevalent within the nation (Lesser 1999; Eakin 2017; Davis 2018). This contrast underscores a possible disjunction between the fanciful image of the nation and the lived realities of its citizens, leading Marshall Eakin to claim that Brazilian national identity is a "story of how one myth of national identity became history" (2017, 1). Further complexity arises when considering Indigenous nations, often as nations surrounded by hegemonic national territories and claims. These nations often find themselves caught in a dichotomy within national narratives: their cultures are either romanticized, resulting in a simplified, exoticized depiction of their identities, or they encounter marginalization and negation of their historical presence and contributions (Smith 2021). This paradox plays into the national fantasy, contributing to a narrative that alternates between the fetishization of Indigenous cultures for exotic appeal and the whitewashing or outright erasure of these same cultures from mainstream national history, thereby fostering either a misleading tokenism or a void where genuine recognition should reside.

Crises, whether they be economic, political, or social, often prompt a reevaluation of these romanticized national narratives, spurring essential conversations among citizens about their authenticity, attainability, and resilience. A notable example of this dynamic occurred during the October 2023 Australian referendum on a Voice to Parliament for Aboriginal and Torres Strait Islander peoples, which resulted in a resounding defeat. The referendum debates often framed the proposition as an elitist divergence from "real" concerns, such as the cost of living. This discourse underscored the pronounced disparity between lofty national aspirations and the daily struggles that people navigate, accentuating the disconnect between imaginative constructs and lived realities. Furthermore, the referendum sparked deeper discussions about Indigeneity, the enduring legacy of colonialism, and the principles of liberalism. Critics of the Voice to Parliament argued that it would unfairly favor one group over others, showing a hesitancy to confront historical wrongs and a preference for maintaining the status quo, which continues to marginalize Indigenous perspectives (Norman 2023). Notably, significant opposition also came from within the Indigenous community, particularly from those on the left advocating for a treaty rather than the Voice, reflecting a range of perspectives within the Indigenous community itself. The defeat of the referendum reveals a complex relationship between national identity and the collective fantasy that sustains it. In this case, the proposal to establish a distinct Voice appeared to disrupt the national fantasy of equality, unearthing an underlying narrative that equates uniformity with fairness. The resistance to altering the national story, even in the face of the material needs and rights of Aboriginal and Torres Strait Islander peoples, vividly demonstrates the enduring power of national fantasies in upholding specific ideologies and power structures. This scenario underscores the mutable and often contested nature of national narratives. In this context, it becomes evident that national fantasies, while aiming to unify, can inadvertently deepen divisions, particularly when they prioritize a singular national narrative over the diverse realities of its citizens. The friction arises from a clash between the inclusive ideals that nations profess and the exclusionary realities they enact. This underscores the continual tension within national identities, which, far from being monolithic, are subject to ongoing reevaluation and contestation. Consequently, the pursuit of a cohesive national identity must reckon with these inherent contradictions, balancing the desire for collective unity with the imperative to acknowledge and address diverse individual experiences and histories.

Important questions regarding the essence of national identities thus arise. Are nations inherently fluid, forever oscillating between the poles of aspiration and reality, collective memory and selective forgetting? And how can nations maintain a semblance of unity without glossing over the genuine adversities their citizens face? These queries become even more pertinent as we consider the idea of national confabulations—the stories nations tell themselves, which may range from embellished truths to outright fabrications. The Australian referendum is a case in point, illustrating how national stories, even those founded on misrepresentations or half-truths, can significantly sway public opinion and policy trajectories. Investigating these unintentional, yet potentially misleading, stories offer important perspectives on how we understand nations, particularly when they face numerous crises that emerge, overlap, foment, and build mass, ultimately forming crisis cultures.

THE MECHANICS OF CONFABULATION

In his book *Confabulations* John Berger contends: "The horizons of past and future are being blurred. We are being conditioned to live an endless and uncertain present, reduced to being citizens in a state of forgetfulness" (2016, 77). This assertion, while situated in the context of the twenty-first century, resonates strikingly with the foundational ideas proposed by Ernest Renan more than a century earlier, when he famously declared that nationhood is a culmination not only of shared glories and collective memory but also of significant historical events that groups of people deliberately choose to forget (2018, 251). Berger's observation hints at a contemporary reformulation of Renan's thesis. While Renan emphasized the active, conscious process of forgetting in nation-building—the willingness to overlook certain historical realities to foster national unity—Berger indicates that in our current digital era, this phenomenon has potentially morphed into something passive and involuntary. He speaks to a condition that is not about selective memory used as a unifying tool, but rather about an imposed forgetfulness, a blurring of historical eras that disorients and detaches individuals from their collective pasts and futures. This is not the deliberate forgetfulness of Renan's nation-building but a systemic byproduct of contemporary life, where relentless change and information overload might lead to a people disconnected from its history, living in a perpetual present.

Berger's perspective thus raises the idea that nations today might be experiencing a collective form of confabulation, a recognized phenomenon in psychology and neuroscience that seems particularly exacerbated in the digital era. Rather than meticulously curating their histories and identities through conscious selection and omission, nations might be unwittingly confabulating—forming and believing in fabricated or distorted narratives not through deliberate intent but as an unconscious response to the overwhelming uncertainties and rapid changes characteristic of the contemporary world (Hirstein 2005, 2). This interpretation of national identity calls for a profound reassessment of what it means to belong to a nation in our contemporary era. It compels us to question: How does this confabulatory condition, as implied by Berger, alter the essence of communal bonds and the integrity of the shared narratives that nations have traditionally relied upon? What happens when the collective memory, rather than being selectively forgotten or remembered, is inadvertently confabulated? Moreover, this interpretative possibility challenges us to contemplate the repercussions of such a shift on citizens' interactions with these national stories, particularly when these narratives clash with tangible lived experiences or empirical historical facts. In essence, Berger instigates an important philosophical and cultural introspection into the stories we subscribe to, the histories we hold on to, and the threads that weave our collective identity. While prevailing scholarship acknowledges that national identities are often anchored in constructed myths rather than empirical history, my argument is intimating at something deeper: the possibility that collective entities—nations, to be precise—might engage in a form of collective confabulation, a process where these entities continuously and unconsciously reconstruct their narratives, thus reflexively shaping memories to align with current ideologies or exigencies. The essence of this comparison is not just the accuracy of these national narratives, but rather their spontaneous transformation—perhaps a byproduct of the digital age's influence on collective memory—similar to how individuals might inadvertently reshape their own memories. In this light, we might consider whether nations too can undergo an analogous, yet more expansive, form of narrative evolution: a kind of collective confabulation where stories are unconsciously modified and perpetuated, without a collective recognition of the alteration.

In *Brain Fiction: Self-Deception and the Riddle of Confabulation*, Hirstein clarifies that confabulation, from the Latin *confabulari* (a term combining *con*, meaning together, and *fabulari*, meaning to talk or chat), is distinct from lying (2005, 6–7). This differentiation hinges on the absence of crucial components found in lying, namely the intent to deceive and the consciousness of falsehood. Confabulation arises not from deliberate falsehood but from what Hirstein describes as a dual-layered cognitive error (2005, 2). It begins with the generation of an incorrect response, borne not out of a desire to deceive but rather from cognitive confusion or disarray. This error is then compounded when the individual, hampered by cognitive limitations, lacks the capacity to critically evaluate or recognize the inaccuracy of their statement (Hirstein 2005, 2). This is not a simple case of fabrication; it points to a cognitive deficit in self-assessment and the authentication of reality. Originally perceived as a unique form of memory disruption, confabulation manifests when individuals, particularly those grappling with cognitive impairments, are posed questions about their past. The responses they generate, though factually incorrect, are believed with conviction to be true: "Confabulation occurs when patients produce stories that fill in gaps in their memories" (Hirstein 2005, 2). This mechanism, I contend, mirrors the way nations create their own stories, essentially fabricating narratives to bridge discontinuities in collective memory.

The inclination to confabulate goes beyond simply not knowing; it also manifests as an absence of doubt where doubt is warranted—whether about the trustworthiness of one's own memories, the integrity of one's abilities, or the accuracy of one's sensory experiences (Hirstein 2005, 4). Social expectations frequently prize confidence and clear-cut communication, creating a disincentive for showing uncertainty or confessing a lack of knowledge, even when situations would naturally call for careful consideration. Hirstein exemplifies this pressure to appear confident with the scenario of a military general, whose position requires bold choices, irrespective of underlying uncertainties (2005, 4). This cultural inclination indicates that, in some scenarios, an assertive answer, albeit possibly incorrect, is valued more than hesitancy or indecisiveness (Hirstein 2005, 5). Expanding on this, Hirstein draws upon the philosophical insights of Daniel Dennett (1991), who posits that our sense of self is essentially the protagonist of a continuously unfolding narrative, a story we author and communicate to define our identity (2005, 5). This narrative impulse, intrinsic to human nature, could be a foundational factor in the phenomenon of confabulations. We are more than mere narrators of events or facts; fundamentally, we are creators of stories and architects of our identities. We feel driven to bridge the gaps in our memory and comprehension with narratives. While these narratives may not always mirror reality accurately, they fulfill a crucial role in preserving the consistency and ongoing narrative of our self-identity (Hirstein 2005, 5). Thus, confabulation can be seen not merely as a cognitive anomaly but also as a testament to humanity's unyielding drive to narrate, interpret, and make sense of our existence, even when our mental faculties may lead us astray.

Within human cognition, confabulation stands as a striking phenomenon, one not driven by the intent to deceive but seemingly propelled by deeper, more instinctual motivations (Hirstein 2005, 15). Individuals who confabulate often generate narratives that, though contradictory, are asserted with unwavering conviction, with the confabulators showing little to no inclination to reconcile these inconsistencies (Hirstein 2005, 9). Remarkably, they are not lying in the traditional sense; their narratives, however flawed, are beliefs held with steadfast sincerity (Hirstein 2005, 18). Hirstein (2005, 16) identifies three primary reasons behind confabulation. First, there is an underlying desire to mask one's cognitive deficits. For instance, a person who, due to memory impairments, cannot remember a significant public event might unconsciously fabricate a detailed account of their "experience" during the event to conceal their inability to remember. This is not a conscious lie but a psychological defense mechanism, filling the void left by memory loss. Second, confabulation may serve as a shield against catastrophic reactions or the daunting acknowledgment of a stark reality. For example, an individual who has lost a loved one might confabulate conversations with the deceased. In this case, the confabulated interactions may act as a buffer, protecting the individual from the full brunt of their grief or the overwhelming reality of their loss. The third motivator is a fundamental human discomfort with admitting ignorance. Faced with questions to which they have no answers, individuals might confabulate rather than simply conceding "I don't know." This could be as mundane as a person confidently giving directions when asked, despite being unsure, because the social pressure to provide an immediate and confident response overshadows the acceptance of their lack of knowledge. These underlying motivations highlight a human tendency to favor narrative coherence over factual ambiguity, even when these narratives are unconsciously crafted in direct opposition to reality (Hirstein 2005, 16).

Hirstein asks: Are confabulations the result of delusions? (2005, 19). Confabulation and delusion, while superficially similar, are distinct phenomena, particularly in their manifestation and persistence. Delusions are characterized by enduring, unshakable beliefs that remain steadfast even in the face of starkly contradictory evidence. They are defined as "ill-grounded beliefs"—false or misguided convictions—often outlasting the circumstances that gave rise to them and resistant to counterarguments, no matter how persuasive

(Hirstein 2005, 19). For example, a person with delusions might persistently believe they are under surveillance, despite clear evidence to the contrary. In contrast, confabulations are essentially "ill-grounded claims"—false or unfounded assertions rather than beliefs—fabulations that do not necessarily have the persistent adherence that delusions command (Hirstein 2005, 19). They are typically transient, often fading shortly after they are expressed, and they lack the durable conviction characteristic of delusions (Hirstein 2005, 19). For instance, a confabulating individual might recount a detailed trip to Paris they never took, but this fabricated memory may quickly dissipate, replaced by other, equally unfounded recollections. While both confabulators and those experiencing delusions can show resistance to evidence that contradicts their claims or beliefs, confabulators generally do not exhibit the same level of tenacity as individuals with delusions. This is not to say that confabulators readily abandon their false narratives when presented with contradictory facts, but their adherence to these fabrications is usually less rigid and long-lasting than the unyielding belief observed in delusional individuals (Hirstein 2005, 19).

In the context of national narratives, confabulation is a more fitting concept than delusion. However, it is crucial here to distinguish between confabulation and the spread of "fake news." While both phenomena influence national narratives and collective memory, their origins and intents diverge significantly. Collective confabulation emerges unconsciously from cognitive errors, without any intentional deceit. It represents a psychological coping mechanism in response to the uncertainties and complexities of modern life, leading to the inadvertent creation and reinforcement of distorted narratives. In contrast, fake news is a product of intentional fabrication, strategically crafted and disseminated with the explicit aim of manipulating public perception and behavior for political gain. This kind of misinformation is designed to exploit cognitive biases and create a controlled narrative that serves specific interests. Thus, the spread of "fake news" in media might initially influence public opinion but could unravel when confronted with verifiable facts. Unlike delusions, national confabulations, though initially convincing, may not withstand prolonged scrutiny or shifts in social values. They are not held with the inflexible conviction characteristic of delusions; rather, they may change as the collective consciousness of a nation evolves. Additionally, while delusions are fundamentally disconnected from reality, national confabulations often include elements of historical truth, albeit distorted or misinterpreted, making them plausible and more easily accepted within the imagined community (Anderson 1991). Yet, in the context of the digital era, particularly within Western modernity, the lines between these two processes can sometimes blur. The rapid dissemination of information online allows for a symbiotic, even phantasmatic relationship between fake news and collective confabulation. Deliberate misinformation can seed narratives that, once rooted, are confabulated by collective memory into a form of "truth" that aligns with existing biases or fears, further complicating the distinction between reality and perception. This blurring of lines is exemplified in the case study of the Capitol Hill insurrection in January 2021, which I will discuss later in the chapter. This symbiosis challenges the understanding of how national identities and collective consciousness are constructed and manipulated. It raises critical questions about the stability and integrity of the shared narratives that nations rely upon and the potential consequences when these narratives are built not just on confabulated memories but also on strategically implanted falsehoods.

The relationship between memory and knowledge is complex, with a substantial fragment of our understanding anchored in our memory (Hirstein 2005, 38). Confabulations, however, throw a shadow of uncertainty over various kinds of accounts, particularly those pertaining to recollections and bodily states (Hirstein 2005, 38). Remembering is not simply a matter of retrieving data from the recesses of our minds into conscious awareness. It is, rather, a complex reconstructive procedure susceptible to a spectrum of distortions (Hirstein 2005, 43). Most adults can, with considerable accuracy, discern factual information from falsehoods, a skill that appears to be acquired or honed over time (Hirstein 2005, 45). In contrast, young children frequently struggle to separate fact from fiction, pointing to the developmental nature of this critical faculty (Hirstein 2005, 45). Extrapolating this to a national context recalls Renan's (2018) insights into the collective memory and forgetting foundational to the concept of a nation. His insights, pertinent in an era marked by burgeoning nationalism and state-building, underscore that just as individual memory is reconstructive and not merely reproductive, collective memory is similarly curated. This curation, essential in his time, involved the deliberate commemoration of certain historical events while concurrently omitting others, effectively engaging in a form of collective amnesia to forge a coherent national story (Renan 2018, 251).

Expanding on Renan's concept, the phenomenon of confabulation adds a new dimension to national narratives. These narratives, even if they diverge from factual accuracy, are often expressed with profound conviction, without the emotional strain typically linked to deceit (Hirstein 2005, 74). Renan (2018) speaks to the deliberate cultivation of collective memory and the strategic forgetting that crafts a nation's identity. However, confabulation introduces an involuntary aspect to this process. This is starkly illustrated when considering the historical narrative of Gallipoli, which over time has become a foundational story of valor for Australia and New Zealand. The campaign, originally marked by military failures and significant casualties, has undergone a remarkable transformation in the collective memory of these nations. The recontextualization of Gallipoli's narrative within the national consciousness is a testament to the fluid nature of collective memory, which can shift and evolve, not through deliberate revisionism, but as part of an organic, psychological drive for a narrative that confers unity and pride. This transition—from a tale of a tragic military episode to one of heroic sacrifice—underscores the dynamic nature of confabulation in shaping national identity. The "Anzac legend," as it developed, not only glossed over the grim realities of the Gallipoli campaign but also imbued the Australian and New Zealand Army Corps with qualities central to national identity: heroism, resilience, and mateship (Nelson 1997; Haltof 2010). Following Billig's (1995) concept of "banal nationalism," this narrative integration can be viewed as part of the subtle, often unnoticed ways national identity is embedded and reinforced in people's daily lives. Hirstein might suggest that this national story, recast through the years with unwavering belief, exemplifies communal confabulation, persisting despite discrepancies with the historical record (2005, 74). As the narrative evolves, it takes on new meanings and emphasis, adapting to contemporary needs and perspectives. Gallipoli's story has thus transcended factual accuracy, becoming a collective emotional truth. Confabulated narratives occupy an important position in the epistemology of a nation's history, underscoring the inherent instability of collective memory and cultural self-perception, and thereby demanding scholarly consideration equal to that afforded to more objective historical data. But how does this dynamic operate in the digital age, with its constant flow of information and the communal nature of online spaces? First, I will explore the new dynamics introduced by the digital era and how they have reshaped the processes of national identity formation, before proceeding to discuss how these dynamics might contribute to an increase in the instances of confabulation within national narratives.

NATIONAL CONFABULATIONS IN THE DIGITAL ERA

The digital era has not so much upended as intensified certain trends in the evolution of national identity, introducing a nuanced "digital crisis ambientality" that subtly but powerfully modulates how communities perceive and define themselves. National identities have never been static but rather complex and contested entities, historically shaped by an array of regional, ethnic, political, religious, and linguistic narratives. However, the advent of digital communication channels extends this inherent diversity, encouraging identities to adapt with unprecedented speed to the ebbs and flows of digital discourse. As Han (2022) observes, digital platforms create a dynamic environment where historical continuity is fragmented into impactful snapshots, altering the collective story with unprecedented speed. The careful curation of shared history now occurs alongside the spontaneous construction of identity amid the fervor of online engagement and the immediate impact of viral content. In the richly interconnected digital ecosystem, no longer is the construction of national memory solely in the hands of cultural, academic, or political custodians. Every participant has the potential to influence or challenge the national narrative, broadening narrative agency and cultivating a more polyphonic national story that incorporates a multitude of voices and perspectives. This does not suggest a collapse of the perceived coherence of national identity; instead, it injects increased variability and invites more widespread engagement, mirroring the dynamics of the digital era. Symbols and stories of the past now exist in tandem with the symbols and memes of the digital age, in a continuously renegotiated balance. This transformation suggests a conception of national identity that is more fluid, open to real-time reinterpretation, and capable of transcending the more fixed narratives of a pre-digital world, thereby crafting a global network of interconnected but diverse communal identities. This reveals the evolution in the mechanisms by which national identities are constructed, debated, and redefined—highlighting that while the contestation of national identity is not new, what has markedly changed is the scale, speed, and breadth of these contestations, signaling a departure from Renan's concept of deliberate, top-down curation of collective memory to a process that is now far more decentralized and pervasive.

On the one hand, the power of social media and online platforms to preserve and shape national identity can yield positive outcomes. For example, social media platforms emerge as contemporary spaces for collective remembrance and identity construction, offering strategic tools for individuals and communities to commemorate historical events, thus playing an active role in the shaping and reinforcing of national identities (Hoskins 2018; Davidjants & Tiidenberg 2022). The digital sphere thus becomes a space where the past is actively engaged with and where communal narratives are both constructed and contested (Wüstenberg & Sierp 2020). An example of this phenomenon is the centennial commemoration of the Armenian Genocide in 2015. The use of the hashtag #Remember1915 was not just a means of honoring the lives lost but also a crucial instrument in solidifying a unified Armenian identity. The hashtag allowed Armenians across the globe, as well as supporters, to exchange narratives, document history, and share personal reflections, effectively challenging Türkiye's persistent denial of the genocide. This worldwide, digitally-driven campaign served to counteract enforced forgetfulness by the Turkish state and reinforced a shared Armenian identity through the communal remembrance of historical atrocities.

On the other hand, digital platforms facilitate the rapid dissemination of narratives that can alter collective memory and obscure the distinction between historical accuracy and ideological agendas. The "Unite the Right"

(UtR) rally in Charlottesville, Virginia, in 2017, serves as a case study of how such platforms can amplify particular interpretations of national history. Supporters of the rally, which included white supremacists and neo-Nazis, convened to oppose the removal of a Confederate statue, an act that they perceived as a disavowal of their historical and cultural identity. The tragic escalation of events at the rally, leading to violent clashes and the death of a counter-protester, Heather Heyer, cast a stark light on the impact of digital mobilization (Blout & Burkart 2021, 1625). In their digital strategy, UtR organizers employed promotional tactics typical of benign social events, utilizing visually compelling imagery that obscured the gathering's underlying ideological motives (Blout & Burkart 2021, 1635). This demonstrates the facility with which digital spaces can be leveraged to not only bring together individuals with shared views but also to recontextualize historical symbols in alignment with current ideological positions, regardless of broader social values of inclusivity and equality. The aftermath of the rally saw the use of digital tools to create and spread disinformation campaigns targeting local authorities and critics, showing the versatile nature of digital expression in national identity construction (Blout & Burkart 2021, 1643). Specifically, a spurious conspiracy theory emerged against the Mayor of Charlottesville, falsely accusing him of directing police inaction during the rally—a narrative that misrepresented municipal authority and had no basis in fact. Yet, through its viral spread on platforms like Fox News and "Seeking the Truth," this narrative gained traction and added an inflammatory and divisive anti-Semitic slant to the discourse, reframing the rally as a strategically planned event to spark racial tensions for the benefit of a clandestine global power (Blout & Burkart 2021, 1644). The spread of these distorted, ideologically driven stories through digital channels illustrates the distinct effect such platforms can have on shaping and expressing national identity.

How do we, then, philosophically grapple with this transformation in national identity formation under the pervasive influence of digital crisis ambientality? Extant theories have largely concentrated on experiences anchored in material expressions of identity, such as cultural rituals, historical monuments, and symbolic artifacts confined within geographical boundaries. Yet, the digital era has ushered in a paradigm shift. Digital platforms now serve as arenas where national identity is both contested and reconstituted, transcending the confines of physical space and traditional identity markers. In these spaces, information is not merely relayed; it becomes a transformative force, fostering real-time collective ideation and action. Social media platforms in these spaces serve a dual role: they connect individuals and also offer a framework where national consciousness is actively engaged with, reinterpreted, and affirmed. This phenomenon in digital spaces aligns with Billig's (1995) idea of "banal nationalism" observed in traditional media.

However, unlike traditional media, daily and often subtle activities on digital platforms play a continuous role in shaping and reinforcing national identity. This influence in digital spaces is not just an online version of offline dynamics but rather a significant evolution driven by the immediacy and widespread reach of digital technology. As such, digital platforms are the new "print media," radically amplifying Benedict Anderson's (1991) concept of imagined communities. If print-capitalism once gave rise to national consciousness, today's digital immediacy and accessibility are redefining national narratives in real-time, shaping how national identity is perceived and articulated.

Movements like BLM offer a vivid illustration of how activism, grounded in historical trajectories like the Civil Rights Movement, can employ contemporary digital tools to recalibrate national narratives (Campbell 2018; Liebermann 2021). The movement challenges the United States' professed values of equality, justice, and freedom, exposing gaps between these ideals and lived realities. The viral video of George Floyd's death in May 2020 became a tipping point, demonstrating the movement's capacity to convert individual tragedies via digital engagements into catalysts for worldwide conversation on racial justice. The decentralized nature of digital technologies ensures that BLM does not project a singular, consolidated narrative. Rather, it presents a mosaic of individual testimonies and visual documentation, each augmenting the overarching narrative. In this decentralized space, every contributor becomes a narrator, underscoring the fluid and contested nature of national identity in the digital age. The BLM movement, deeply entrenched in the United States' long-standing history of racial injustice, thus gains significant traction in its digital form. This digitized immediacy accentuates individual episodes, making each event simultaneously a microcosm and part of a broader political conversation. Furthermore, BLM demonstrates the potential for digital platforms to dissolve national boundaries by resonating with global and diasporic communities, thereby transforming national identity into a more expansive, shared experience.

The digital age has not merely altered the mechanics of narrative dissemination but has fundamentally reshaped the way narratives are constructed, encountered, and retained in collective memory. Digital infrastructure lays the groundwork for unconscious narrative alterations to reshape national identity. This analysis does not aim to supersede but rather to complement and extend the analyses of national identity construction laid out by thinkers such as Renan, Gellner, Hobsbawm, Anderson, and Bhabha, among others. These foundational theories, which address the socio-historical and psychological aspects of nation-building, are enriched by considering the role of collective memory errors—confabulations—in the formation of national identities. Hirstein's exploration into the minds of confabulators reveals that these individuals do not consciously reject the truth; rather, they remain oblivious to their own ignorance (2005, 134). In digital spaces, this lack of self-awareness becomes part of a larger pattern of collective engagement, where the seamless integration of personal beliefs with communal discourse generates a distorted historical consciousness that masquerades as shared truth. The digital age, with its continuous streams of content and the potent algorithms that govern visibility and virality, can rapidly entrench certain narratives at the expense of others. These narratives, though not always aligned with empirical truth, do not emerge from intentional deceit but from an earnest—if at times misguided—search for identity. Consequently, the collective memory of a nation becomes more than a repository of factual history; it transforms into a living, breathing entity within the digital ecosystem. It is susceptible to the same cognitive biases and shortcuts as individual memory. The digital era amplifies these biases to a global scale, allowing them to crystallize rapidly into what can be seen as national confabulations—collectively held beliefs that, despite their detachment from historical accuracy, are believed with conviction by those who share them. This is not to say that all national narratives in the digital age are confabulations; rather, it highlights the increased potential for such narratives to emerge and disseminate. The interaction between individual cognitive processes and digital technology fosters these phenomena, allowing them to flourish in the fertile ground of national consciousness.

The shift of confabulation from a concept in individual psychology to a broader mechanism in the digital age highlights its evolving role in the formation of national identities. While confabulation has been evident in past eras, the significant increase in the speed and intensity with which these narratives are now disseminated represents a major transformation, exacerbating the nature of confabulation in the current era. The historical "Lost Cause" narrative, which arose in the post-Civil War era in the United States, represents a poignant example of national confabulation. This narrative recasts the Confederate struggle during the American Civil War not as a fight to preserve slavery but rather as a valiant and noble effort to uphold states' rights. It portrays the leaders and soldiers of the Confederacy with honor and valor, suggesting that their cause, though ultimately unsuccessful, was a just and dignified endeavor (Nolan 2000, 15). This revisionist history became a cornerstone of Southern identity, subtly distorting the factual basis of the conflict in favor of a more palatable and prideful regional narrative. Such a perspective was less a calculated deception and more a byproduct of a desire to find solace and dignity amid the rubble of defeat and the moral repercussions of slavery. This form of historical confabulation finds its contemporary equivalent in the digital age with phenomena like the QAnon conspiracy theory. Its ascent is a testament to the digital era's impact on public perception, demonstrating how unverified and even bizarre claims can rapidly gain traction and form committed communities of believers. QAnon, emerging from the shadowy corners of internet forums, propounds a conspiracy of a global elite engaged in nefarious activities such as child trafficking (Forberg 2023). The digital architecture's ability to disseminate information swiftly has enabled a narrative as fantastical as QAnon to be embraced by significant numbers of people, who adhere to its assertions with a conviction similar to those who held onto the "Lost Cause" narrative. Just as the "Lost Cause" was not solely about deliberate deceit but also reflected a sincere, though misguided, adherence to a reimagined past, QAnon represents not just a collective confabulation but a profound desire to make sense of a complex and often opaque political environment. The significant difference lies in the speed and scale with which digital confabulations take root. Consequently, whereas the "Lost Cause" narrative took decades to firmly embed itself in the collective memory, a digital-era confabulation like QAnon can achieve a similar level of entrenchment in a fraction of the time. These digitally fueled narratives, however inaccurate, are not mere fabrications but are indicative of the genuine efforts by communities to make sense of their realities. As Hirstein explains, the challenge with confabulations lies in their inherently self-deceptive nature; adherents are often blind to their misconceptions, "they do not know that they do not know," which leads to a susceptibility to disregard conflicting factual information (2005, 209). This phenomenon underscores the difficulty in counteracting such beliefs once they have taken hold, highlighting the distinctive challenges that confabulations present in the age of digital communication.

The idea that confabulators "do not know that they do not know" strangely resonates with former U.S. Secretary of Defense Donald Rumsfeld's notorious remarks about "unknown unknowns" during a 2002 news briefing concerning the Iraq War. Amid the geopolitical fervor following the 9/11 attacks, the U.S. administration under President George W. Bush was vehemently advocating for military action against Iraq, alleging the country's possession of weapons of mass destruction (WMDs) and its supposed links to terrorism. However, the evidence supporting these assertions was, at best, murky. In this contentious discursive environment, Rumsfeld made an attempt to elucidate the military intelligence and the challenges of decision-making under uncertainty. He famously stated: "There are things we know we know . . . But there are also unknown unknowns—the ones we don't know we don't know." This enigmatic statement was made in response to the absence of concrete evidence linking the government of Iraq to the supposed stockpile of WMDs. His words, rather than clarifying the rationale behind the push for war, confounded the public and critics, earning a mixture of ridicule and bemusement. The phrase "unknown unknowns" was perceived by many as a convoluted way of admitting there was no clear evidence while still maintaining a posture of certainty and control. However, Rumsfeld's remarks, which might have been dismissed as mere political doublespeak, found resonance among certain thinkers, including Žižek, who interpreted Rumsfeld's "unknown unknowns" as an accidental brush with deeper philosophical truth. Even more, Žižek reformulates it as "unknown knowns—things we unknowingly know—the beliefs and biases we are not consciously aware of but that nonetheless drive our actions and perceptions" (2004, 9). This reformulation, he suggests, reflects the Freudian unconscious, the aspects of our mind that influence our behavior despite being beyond our conscious recognition.

Given confabulation's digital and psychological dynamics, how do contemporary crisis cultures heighten the need for nations to actively shape their narratives? The ubiquity of crisis cultures in today's digital age necessitates a reevaluation of how national narratives are constructed and perpetuated. When faced with incessant crises, amplified by instantaneous digital communication and complex global linkages, nations are propelled into a relentless state of urgency. This urgency hinders the possibility of *Erfahrung*—deep, lived, and meaningful interactions with events—in favor of *Erlebnis*, a more direct, but often superficial, experience of reality. In this context, confabulation thus becomes a crucial mechanism for the ongoing shaping of national identity, serving as a means to create coherence in the face of relentless disruption. The German response to the 2015 migrant crisis illustrates this dynamic (Jäckle & König 2017; Funk 2018). The rise of *"Willkommenskultur"* (welcome culture) was less a deliberate narrative strategy and more an instinctual confabulation—a psychological reflex triggered to preserve a unified national narrative amid a deluge of "unknown unknowns." The immediacy of this crisis, paired with the ceaseless flow of digital information, barely allowed the German citizenry and their leaders the depth to engage—to truly experience the event's broad implications as *Erfahrung*. Consequently, the nation found itself navigating through uncertainties without the anchoring of deep, reflective introspection. The resulting confabulation, portraying Germany as a humanitarian leader, acted as a narrative bridge. It linked Germany's inherent need to reconcile with its traumatic past and its modern identity as a European leader. However, this narrative encountered resistance, fueled by counter-confabulations that anchored themselves in "known unknowns." Factions like the Alternative for Germany (AfD) raised alarms about potential strains on resources and German values, while Pegida rallies articulated fears of the West's Islamization (Rommel 2017). In an era defined by ongoing crisis and a lack of *Erfahrung*, confabulation thus becomes a vital tool for nations. It acts as both a method for reclaiming narrative coherence and a strategic means of navigating a reality where change is constant, and uncertainty is the only certainty. This underlines that nation-building, especially in times of ongoing crisis, is less about conscious narrative creation and more about subconscious confabulation—a reactive effort to maintain narrative coherence and bridge the unsettling gaps that "unknowns," both known and unknown, introduce into the national consciousness.

The confabulatory tendencies that I have explored in this chapter do not operate in isolation, nor are they all-encompassing; rather, they represent a nuanced facet of the post-truth era. This era is characterized not just by the widespread presence of misinformation but by a profound shift in public opinion, where emotional appeal and personal beliefs increasingly overshadow objective facts (Lewandowsky et al. 2017, 351). Lewandowsky et al. attribute this "elevation of belief" over factual accuracy to a multifaceted mix of cognitive biases, the echo-chamber effect, and the widespread dissemination of false information (2017, 352–354). In this environment, misinformation becomes a potent force, interweaving with human psychology, social networks, and political ideologies, creating communities that are often insulated from factual correction and alternative viewpoints. While the initial spread of fake news and false information may be deliberate, orchestrated by elites or driven by ideological pressures, these narratives often take on a life of their own. As they permeate through society, they can transform into confabulations by those who internalize and propagate them. This phenomenon presents a substantial challenge, especially within democratic frameworks where effective operation hinges on a citizenry's ability to engage in critical reasoning and to agree on a common set of facts (Lewandowsky et al. 2017, 370). When segments of society inhabit a "mirror world," as described by Naomi Klein (2023)—not due to divergent opinions, interpretations, or values, but because of fundamental discrepancies in perceived reality—it jeopardizes the foundations of democratic engagement. This is not a theoretical concern but a material obstacle to the proper functioning of societies.

This situation becomes clear through a striking example involving an unnamed official from the Bush Administration, who, during a conversation with journalist Ron Suskind, derisively referred to Suskind and others as belonging to the "reality-based community." The term was used to mockingly describe individuals who believe that "solutions arise from careful analysis of observable reality," implying that such an approach is naive or misguided. The official's rationalization was telling:

> That's not the way the world works anymore . . . we're an empire now and when we act, we create our own reality. And while you're studying that reality—judiciously as you will—we'll act again, creating new realities, which you can study too, and that's how things will sort out. We're history's actors . . . and you, all of you, will be left to study what we do. (quoted in Leicht & Fennell 2023, 43)

In the context of today's digital world, this dismissive attitude toward objective reality is not only evident but exacerbated, as digital spaces contribute to both the deliberate and unintentional shaping of perceived realities. These platforms are more than information exchange venues; they foster an environment where the distinction between intentional misinformation and accidental propagation of false narratives is increasingly blurred. While deliberate manipulation by political elites often initiates these distorted narratives, they can quickly evolve into confabulations as they are absorbed and propagated by the public. The challenge lies not just in the existence of these distorted narratives but in the overwhelming volume and speed at which digital information circulates. The continuous feedback loop in digital spaces means that confabulated stories can be perpetually reinforced in real-time, rendering them more resistant to correction. As narratives unfold, get reiterated, or are unknowingly adopted online, they have the potential to polarize societies. The resultant divisions are not merely based on diverse opinions or interpretations of facts; they are founded on entirely different sets of perceived realities, each buttressed by its own set of confabulated narratives, and each impervious to contradicting evidence. Thus, in this digital age, we find ourselves navigating a confabulatory era where the lines between reality and fabrication have become dangerously blurred, not only by those who wish to manipulate public opinion for strategic ends but also by our own unintentional yet innate tendencies toward narrative construction.

In this polarized environment, the phantasmatic relationship between deliberate misinformation and unconscious confabulation emerges as a key factor by which individuals and groups construct narratives that often eschew objective reality in favor of emotionally resonant, yet conflicting, versions of truth. These narratives, whether they lean toward utopian idealism or dystopian fatalism, are influenced by the underlying crisis culture, widening the gap between where we find ourselves and where we fear or hope we are heading. Confabulations, in this sense, serve as anchors, however illusory, allowing individuals and groups to reconcile the discrepancies between their lived experiences, their hopes for the future, and their interpretations of the past. However, while these fabricated narratives provide solace, they also entrench divisions, as they are crafted from selective memories and subjective experiences that often conflict dramatically with those of others. In the ensuing section, I will provide an analysis of the January 6, 2021, Capitol Hill insurrection in the United States as a concrete example of national confabulation. Through this examination, I aim to demonstrate the material impact that confabulated narratives can have on major national events and the collective mindset of a nation.

INSURRECTION AT CAPITOL HILL

This section considers how deeply ingrained national narratives and longstanding confabulations shape individual and group actions during pivotal moments of national crisis. The insurrection at Capitol Hill on January 6, 2021, stands as a significant point of analysis, demonstrating a dramatic convergence of confabulated narratives and their tangible repercussions. The goal is to clearly understand the collective forces that led to the events of January 6, 2021, by using the Capitol Hill insurrection as a paradigmatic example of how a nation can construct a shared yet flawed narrative in times of ongoing crisis. This involves examining how a subset of the citizenry came to internalize a narrative profoundly disconnected from objective reality and assessing the subsequent ramifications of such distortions on the fortitude of democratic institutions and social cohesion.

To understand how ingrained misconceptions influence key historical events, it is essential to examine the role and dynamics of rage. On January 6, 2021, fueled by unfounded claims of electoral fraud by outgoing President Donald Trump against President-elect Joe Biden, Capitol Hill became a focal point of rage, demonstrating how distorted narratives can drive mass behavior in national crises. That day, thousands of protesters, propelled by baseless claims of electoral fraud, forcefully entered the U.S. Capitol to challenge the presidential election results, marking a stark deviation from standard political processes and disrupting the long-established democratic tradition of confirming electoral outcomes. Historically, rage has been a powerful unifier, driving communities toward shared goals and often leading to significant social change (Han 2015, 22). Rage, in such contexts, arises as a visceral response to perceived injustices, pivotal in challenging and transforming the status quo, as seen in movements like the 1960s Civil Rights Movement in the United States (2015, 22–23). This movement, fueled by collective rage against racial discrimination, led to impactful legislation like the Civil Rights Act of 1964 and the Voting Rights Act of 1965. Other historical examples, such as the May 68 protests in France (Ross 2002) and the Occupy Wall Street movement in 2011 (van Gelder 2011), show how rage can effectively mobilize people against systemic injustices, raising awareness and challenging prevailing narratives that sustain economic and social systems.

Han (2015) notes a significant shift in the nature of public rage in the contemporary, digital era. Historically, rage was a unifying force that drove social change. However, today's rage is often fragmented into fleeting, individual expressions with minimal collective impact. Han describes this as part of a "burnout society," characterized by a rapid pace and information overload, which reduces rage's potential as a catalyst for substantial action (2015, 22–23). Contemporary expressions of rage are more of an immediate, superficial reaction (*Erlebnis*), lacking the depth and transformative quality (*Erfahrung*) that historically empowered long-lasting change and reshaped collective values. The previously unifying force of rage is now diluted by the constant distractions of modern life, where the future merges into an ever-present now, leading to transient annoyance or grievance rather than the sustained emotional energy necessary for decisive change (Han 2015, 23). This evolution in the nature of rage, Han argues, signifies a profound alteration in the dynamics of public dissent, prompting a reevaluation of how this emotion is mobilized and directed in a world increasingly influenced by digital media and ongoing crisis cultures.

The intense rage witnessed during the COVID-19 lockdowns in many global contexts and the Capitol Hill insurrection may seem, on the surface, to counter Han's (2015) thesis of a contemporary society marked by weakened and dispersed rage. Yet, a closer examination reveals that these instances align with Han's perspective. These instances of rage, although intense, draw heavily on confabulated narratives and manipulated truths, differentiating them from the constructive, society-changing rage of the past. My analysis suggests that the rage driving the Capitol Hill insurrection did not seek to challenge and reshape social structures but was instead a product of entanglement in a web of distorted realities. How, then, can society acknowledge and effectively channel its rage in an era rife with confabulated narratives and crisis cultures? What are the consequences when this rage, instead of being understood and constructively addressed, turns into misdirected hostility and division? The insurrection serves as a key example, showing how rage can be both intense and misguided—genuine in its emotional force, yet confused in its foundations. This is not the rage that induces contemplation, reflection, and demands a new inception. It is a rage that erupts, fueled by perceived injustices. In its disorientation, this rage is at risk of becoming a tool for destruction rather than a catalyst for transformation.

There is a paradox at the heart of crisis events: despite their extensive mediated coverage, achieving a full grasp of their true nature often remains elusive (Nünning 2012, 60–64). The United States Capitol insurrection is a prime example of this paradox. On one hand, the extensive media coverage provided an unparalleled view of the event as it unfolded, allowing viewers worldwide to experience the crisis together, irrespective of geographical location (Bushwick 2021). On the other hand, this same coverage also highlighted the inherent ambiguity of crisis events. Various perspectives and narratives, each with its biases and distortions, competed for attention. This is not merely a postmodern condition, where multiple perspectives circulate without a singular, divine source; rather, it is the relentless white noise of crisis cultures that muddles our perception and makes any real, profound experience of the event and the rage associated with it exceedingly difficult. As a result, the Capitol insurrection, despite its visibility and the vastness of its audience, maintained an aura of mystery, its fundamental components veiled in layers of contradiction. This historic episode thus necessitates a detailed analysis of the confabulations that escalated during the Trump presidency, especially postelection. Such distortions, I argue, significantly influenced the January 6 events by embedding falsehoods into the collective consciousness and driving the subsequent crisis events.

Donald Trump, throughout his tenure in politics, strategically positioned himself as a rebellious outsider, vehemently challenging what he portrayed as a fundamentally corrupt system. His rallying cry, "Drain the Swamp," resonated with a considerable segment of the U.S. electorate, capturing a widespread sentiment of disenchantment with the prevailing order (Bowden & Teague 2022, 1). Trump's depiction of the "Swamp" was ambiguous, at times seemingly encompassing the entire established order. He painted a picture of a deep-seated conspiracy, intricately woven into various sectors of U.S. society, surreptitiously working against the interests of the common citizen (Bowden & Teague 2022, 1). His utilization of the "Drain the Swamp" narrative transcended a mere campaign slogan; it was a sophisticated strategy of political branding, positioning him as the quintessential anti-hero in a purported battle against an obscure establishment (Green 2017). The term "Deep State" subsequently entered public discourse, with Trump employing it to denote career government officials and bureaucrats, whom he depicted as part of a covert network attempting to subvert his administration (Bowden & Teague 2022, 1). His denunciation of the "Swamp" was extensive, targeting the Democratic Party, which he depicted as an intrinsic component of the corrupt system, as well as any politicians he perceived as insincere or self-serving. The mainstream media, accused of disseminating fake news, and the tech giants that control online platforms were also implicated—even though Trump himself extensively utilized these platforms for direct communication with his followers (Bowden & Teague 2022, 1). Trump's politics were fragmented into tweets, reflecting a politics driven by viral information rather than a coherent vision (Han 2022, 19), and he did not hesitate to criticize members of his own party who disagreed with him. This strategic vilification of a wide array of individuals and institutions served dual purposes (Bowden & Teague 2022, 1). First, it enabled Trump to solidify his support base, providing a common adversary for his followers to unite against. Second, the ambiguous and indistinct nature of the "Swamp" narrative facilitated a space in which individuals could project their personal grievances and discontent, irrespective of their specific origins. Ultimately, "Drain the Swamp" transcended its status as a political slogan, evolving into a potent cultural meme, capturing a zeitgeist of anti-establishment fervor. Trump's rhetoric, infused with populism, consequently cultivated a unique form of political unity, rallying his supporters under a common banner of grievance and opposition. This gave rise to a charged political atmosphere, where the boundaries between objective reality and subjective perception became increasingly blurred, subtly laying the groundwork for national confabulation. The systematic erosion of trust in established institutions and the media, coupled with the emotive intensity of the populist movement, created a conducive environment for the acceptance of alternative realities. This situation mirrors wider cultural shifts toward relativism and the democratization of truth (Harsin 2015; Marwick & Lewis 2017). It could therefore be argued that the manipulation of public perception during the Trump presidency was deliberate and strategic, designed to weaken the collective grasp on truth and pave the way for widespread acceptance of baseless claims and conspiracy theories. Conversely, if this manipulation was unintentional, it would require acknowledging a deeply troubling level of societal vulnerability to misleading narratives. Regardless of the intention, this fostering of skepticism and discord effectively laid the groundwork for widespread confabulation. Within this narrative entanglement, a substantial segment of the U.S. population became predisposed to embrace and propagate falsehoods that aligned with their ideological leanings.

In *The Steal* (2022), Bowden and Teague examine the manner in which the term "patriotism" was co-opted and reconstituted by various factions within the U.S. population. They underscore the changing nature of patriotism during this period, illustrating its capacity to conform to the ideologies of diverse groups, all laying claim to the title of "patriot" (2022, 7). A broad spectrum of individuals and groups adopted the patriot label, ranging from those opposing racism and championing social justice, to those celebrating the country's diverse history while simultaneously supporting stricter immigration policies. This spectrum further included individuals advocating for reduced international engagement by the United States, yet paradoxically calling for an increased global military presence, as well as Christian fundamentalists, conspiracy theorists, and the archetypal "God-fearing, gun-carrying" demographic (Bowden & Teague 2022, 7). These groups, although ideologically varied, were united by a shared commitment to protecting what they perceived as a threatened "America." They perceived themselves as bulwarks against threats such as government overreach, the encroachment of multiculturalism, and affirmative action policies, which they saw as assaults on their traditional values and freedoms (Bowden & Teague 2022, 7). Bowden and Teague observe that the common bond among these patriots was more emotional than ideological: "It was less an ideology than a feeling" (Bowden & Teague 2022, 8). A key aspect of their collective identity was unanimous support for Donald Trump, whom they saw as embodying their values and defending their version of America. Trump was perceived as a leader capable of combating the threats they feared, fostering a connection based as much on shared identification and emotional resonance as on political support (Hochschild, 2016). The Trump era was thus marked not just by widespread skepticism toward established institutions but also by a significant reimagining and reframing of patriotism. This reimagined form of patriotism, serving as symbolic capital, coalesced individuals with varied emotional and ideological beliefs into a unified narrative of nationalistic fervor and defensive vigilance (Bourdieu 1986).

In the distinct sociopolitical landscape of the 2020 elections, compounded by the unprecedented challenges posed by the COVID-19 pandemic, established voting norms underwent significant transformation. Bowden and Teague explain this critical moment, underscoring the contrast between the Democratic Party's advocacy for mail-in voting as a secure and accessible option, and Donald Trump's strong condemnation of this method as inherently susceptible to fraud—a significant departure from the position of his party, which had actively promoted mail-in voting in many states (2022, 28, 37). Via platforms such as FOX News and Twitter, Trump claimed that mail-in voting possessed the potential to "rig" the election. He even postulated that it could lead to the "most CORRUPT ELECTION" in the history of the United States (Bowden & Teague 2022, 37). But the realities of COVID-19 had positioned mail-in voting as an indispensable alternative that balanced voter participation with the imperative to minimize viral transmission risks. Consequently, Republican uptake of mail-in voting was markedly lower in comparison to Democratic uptake (Bowden & Teague 2022, 28). The surge in mail-in ballots necessitated a thorough and prolonged counting process. This resulted in these particular votes being tabulated last—a procedural detail that saw initial leads for Trump in various jurisdictions diminish and subsequently reverse as the mail-in votes were counted, ultimately resulting in a Democratic majority in those areas (Bowden & Teague 2022, 28–29). For Trump's supporters, these events appeared to validate his prior warnings, seemingly materializing their deepest apprehensions of a manipulated election—a perception that would eventually solidify into the narrative commonly referred to as "The Steal" (Bowden & Teague 2022, 29). This environment was conducive to the widespread propagation of allegations pertaining to electoral fraud and engendered a pervasive atmosphere of skepticism regarding the integrity of the democratic process.

The Trump presidency was characterized by a widespread atmosphere of doubt and mistrust among his supporters, effectively encapsulated by the phrase "there's something funny going on here" (Bowden & Teague 2022, 22). This skepticism led many into the "mirror world" of confabulation—where distorted narratives supported claims of electoral fraud (Klein 2023). In this environment, the phenomenon of confabulation gained traction, with some voters constructing narratives to fill gaps in their understanding. For instance, the shift from pens to sharpies in certain counties and speculative theories about hidden rooms filled with fake ballots were perceived as proof of a vast conspiracy to undermine legitimate votes (Bowden & Teague 2022,

80). Bowden and Teague contend with the difficulty of discerning truth within digital spaces, noting that "Fantasy and fact share footing online, and where all information is weightless, you can choose to believe what you wish" (2022, 43). This blurred boundary between reality and fabrication fostered a propensity for confabulation among Trump's supporters, prompting them to fill gaps in their understanding with invented narratives. This inclination was exacerbated by the echo-chamber effect, as people gravitated toward and interacted with groups sharing similar viewpoints. This phenomenon resulted in a self-perpetuating cycle of misinformation, solidifying their confabulated stories. Any reluctance or denial by others to acknowledge their version of "truth" regarding electoral fraud was interpreted as further confirmation of a covert conspiracy.

The post-election legal strategy employed by Trump's lawyer Rudy Giuliani and his team has been described as a "Blunderbuss Strategy," an approach characterized by its indiscriminate and haphazard nature (Bowden & Teague 2022, 95). The blunderbuss, an antiquated firearm with a wide muzzle known for discharging a wide spray of projectiles, serves as a fitting metaphor for this legal approach, which was marked by its lack of precision and careful targeting. Giuliani's team indiscriminately launched numerous legal theories and allegations, paying little attention to their accuracy, coherence, or consistency. Rather than building a solid, evidence-based case, their aim was to overwhelm and shape public perception through the volume and boldness of their claims. They mixed absurd allegations with somewhat plausible ones, half-truths with complete fabrications, and significant accusations with patently paranoid ones. The strategy was not about proving these claims but about inundating public discourse with them, disseminating these accusations through social media, legal actions, public hearings, and media outlets supportive of Trump (Bowden & Teague 2022, 95). Despite widespread dissemination, these allegations were consistently dismissed for lack of substance, with some even being withdrawn by the plaintiffs themselves after errors were exposed in preliminary hearings (Bowden & Teague 2022, 99). Nonetheless, each legal filing from Giuliani's team seeking to halt the election certification made headlines, fueling Trump's supporters, regardless of the arguments' baselessness (Bowden & Teague 2022, 100). Concurrently, media allies of Trump amplified the Blunderbuss Strategy, broadcasting every single fraud allegation, irrespective of its triviality or implausibility, without subjecting them to critical examination (Bowden & Teague 2022, 100). Rather than attempting to construct a coherent narrative from these claims—a task that would have been indispensable given the expansive nature of the purported fraud—these media outlets exploited the confusion generated by the constant accusations to further their own agendas. Tucker Carlson, a notable example, referenced numerous affidavits compiled by Trump's legal team alleging a variety of electoral misconducts on his show. He focused on the most sensational claims, including allegations of counterfeit ballots and votes allegedly cast by deceased individuals, boldly proclaiming, "All of this is real. We spent all weekend checking it" (Bowden & Teague 2022, 101). However, this assertion is a clear example of rhetorical misdirection. While these claims were indeed made, portraying them as verified is a gross distortion of reality. Bowden and Teague use this instance to underscore the deceptive nature of the rhetoric employed by Trump and his associates, drawing a parallel between their tactics and the absurdity of claiming the earth is flat simply because a few individuals assert it (2022, 101).

The "Blunderbuss Strategy" used by Giuliani and his team reflects a wider trend in the evolution of crisis cultures in Western societies. In these cultures, the abundance of narratives and a deep-rooted sense of distrust are now key features of the era. This period can be seen as an extension of postmodernity, but it markedly differs in its level of relativism and the degree to which consensus is fragmented. While postmodernity introduced skepticism toward universal truths, the current era takes this skepticism further, evolving into a more extreme relativism where truth is frequently viewed as a product of power dynamics or a concept in constant negotiation and redefinition. Whereas postmodern thought critiqued grand narratives (Lyotard 1984) and espoused the view that truth is contingent on cultural and social contexts, the current historical moment goes further by often disregarding the notion of stable contexts altogether. It characterizes an era where the very mechanisms of constructing reality are exposed and multiple truths coexist, clash, and collapse with such regularity that the idea of a cohesive consensus becomes an anachronism. In this emergent paradigm, the very construct of truth is in a perpetual state of assembly and reassembly, contested not only in academic and philosophical arenas but in the daily streams of digital and mass media. In this hyper *post*-postmodern condition, the contestation and reconstruction of realities are normalized features of public discourse.

Following the election, Trump's relentless stream of tweets, marked by emphatic statements such as "Georgia will be a big presidential win, as it was the night of the Election!" served to direct the world's focus to the vote counting in Georgia. This scrutiny, a hallmark of the crisis ambientality in the Blunderbuss Strategy, amplified even minor details into topics of international debate and speculation (Bowden & Teague 2022, 113). This digital crisis ambientality, where ordinary events are portrayed as extraordinary, highlights the crisis culture's tendency for constant renegotiation of established facts. The spread of various conspiracies, ranging from minor incidents at counting centers to grand claims of election fraud, exemplifies this era of ongoing dispute, reflecting a mentality encapsulated by the phrase "if you can imagine it, it might be true" (Bowden & Teague 2022, 113). Trump's refusal to concede and his claims of a rigged election due to compromised Dominion voting systems mirrored a broader cultural trend of challenging accepted truth. He skillfully tailored his rhetoric to align with the conspiracy-focused views of groups like the Christian Nationalists, stirring fears about religious freedom and gun rights under a Biden presidency. This manipulation of narratives not only perpetuated the crisis culture but also amplified the zeal of his supporters and, in turn, influenced his own rhetorical approach. Research conducted by Douglas, Sutton, and Cichocka (2017) reveals the appeal of conspiracy theories, demonstrating that they fulfill crucial psychological needs by providing individuals with a semblance of understanding, control, and enhanced social identity. Trump, ostensibly firm in his convictions, actively engaged with various conspiracy theories that proliferated across digital platforms, strongly advocating for audits and investigations based on claims of dubious veracity (Bowden & Teague 2022, 193). This behavior, whether genuinely held or strategically chosen, highlights his use of confirmation bias and cognitive dissonance, as he focused on information that supported his beliefs while disregarding contrary evidence. The "Steal" narrative thus capitalized on the general lack of in-depth understanding of electoral systems, substituting complex truths with simpler, more appealing stories. This created an "alternative version of reality" and a "community of knowledge" impervious to external facts or expert opinions (Bowden & Teague 2022, 127–128).

Despite Senate Majority Leader Mitch McConnell publicly recognizing Biden's victory on December 15, Trump steadfastly continued to challenge the election results. His efforts to overturn the election spanned legal, political, and public domains but ultimately were unsuccessful in all areas. Legally, the weakness of Trump's claims became evident as all sixty-three lawsuits filed by his team were dismissed by the courts, revealing a lack of substantial evidence or convincing arguments (Bowden & Teague 2022, 198). Politically, even with support from some Republican figures, the adherence to legal standards and procedures by states led to Biden winning the Electoral College with a 306–232 margin (Bowden & Teague 2022, 198). As a last resort, Trump embraced a radical legal theory suggested by his attorney, John Eastman, which proposed that Vice President Mike Pence had the extraordinary power to reject the Electoral College results (Bowden & Teague 2022, 198). However, this extreme and seditious proposal gained no support as Pence, committed to constitutional norms and historical precedent, rebuffed the entreaty.

The Republican Party's ideological shift, which played a critical role in the events surrounding the 2021 election aftermath, has roots that extend back to the 2016 presidential campaign. In that election, Donald Trump, an outsider to the traditional political establishment, secured the presidency.

This victory underscored a burgeoning divergence from established Republican conservatism—a pivot toward a new, more populist and nationalistic approach. The change was not simply about new leadership but represented a deeper reconfiguration of the party's core philosophy, a shift captured and amplified by an evolving media environment. During the interlude between the 2016 and 2020 elections, traditional conservative media such as Fox News underwent a notable transformation (Benkler et al 2018). Historically, Fox News had championed Republican tenets such as free trade and competitive markets. However, as Trump's influence within the party grew, Fox News and similar outlets found their editorial positions increasingly realigned with the President's rhetoric and policy positions. This realignment signaled a broader change in the party's identity, one that Benkler et al. describe as both mirrored in and magnified by the media landscape, leading to what they term "network propaganda"—the strategic use of media networks to promote particular narratives and bring fringe ideas into the mainstream (2018, 25). The altered media landscape, as well as the political reorientation it reflected, set the stage for the post-2020 election period. When President Trump's re-election bid was unsuccessful, he and his supporters did not readily accept the outcome. Instead, they launched a series of demonstrations and "Stop the Steal" marches across the country. This response was rooted in the same transformed ideological perspective that had been solidifying since 2016—a perspective that viewed the political system with increased skepticism and was quick to question the legitimacy of the electoral process. The contention over the 2020 election's integrity reflected the power of the "network propaganda" apparatus to shape beliefs and mobilize action, even in the face of judicial dismissals and lack of evidence for widespread electoral fraud (Benkler et al. 2018, 25). The digital technologies that facilitated the rapid spread of these claims played more than a passive role; they allowed for an unprecedented scale of misinformation dissemination, challenging traditional methods of fact-checking and narrative control.

Given the ideological transformation within the Republican Party since the 2016 election, it is perhaps unsurprising that previous high-ranking officials felt compelled to intervene publicly. On January 3, 2021, all ten living former defense secretaries, crossing party lines, co-authored an op-ed in *The Washington Post*. Their collective voice stressed the seriousness of President Trump's efforts to overturn the election results, emphasizing the potential consequences of his actions (Bowden & Teague 2022, 205). This rare, unified position from officials across multiple administrations reinforced the commitment to constitutional duties and the electoral process, defending democratic principles against perceived autocratic tendencies. Subsequently, on January 6, 2021, the world watched as unprecedented events unfolded at the U.S. Capitol. Earlier that day, at the "Save America" rally, President Trump continued to assert the election's unfairness, encouraging his supporters to protest at the Capitol (Duignan 2022). The crowd, spurred by the day's rhetoric, overran security measures and disrupted the Congressional session intended to certify the Electoral College tallies. Amid the disturbance, legislators were hurriedly escorted to safety. Trump, responding via social media, continued to challenge the election's legitimacy before calling for peace. Eventually, the National Guard and law enforcement restored order, but not before there were casualties and injuries. That evening, Congress reconvened and confirmed President-elect Biden's victory by a 306–232 vote, despite opposition from some Republican legislators (Bowden & Teague 2022, 208). In the aftermath, various unfounded narratives emerged, reflecting a clash of national stories and the impact of "network propaganda" as described by Benkler et al. (2018, 25). These narratives tried to reframe the Capitol breach, with some falsely blaming Antifa or downplaying the attackers as merely tourists, but these claims faltered against overwhelming contrary evidence. Trump's refusal to concede marked a departure from the American tradition of peaceful power transitions, casting the January 6 events as an "insurrection" (Bowden & Teague 2022, 209). Despite the chaos, including bizarre scenes like a person in Viking attire in the Senate Chamber, the U.S. government's continuity remained intact (Bowden & Teague 2022, 209). Nonetheless, Trump and his closest allies continued to question the electoral outcome, a call that still resonated with many due to its alignment with a broader, contested vision of the nation (Anderson & Coduto 2022, 2–3).

The Capitol insurrection on January 6, 2021, epitomizes the psychological dimensions explored by Earl Hopper (2009), specifically in terms of incohesion through aggregation and massification. This event, as analyzed by Rudden (2021), demonstrates a complex interaction between national narratives and identity construction, aligning with Hopper's theoretical framework and illustrating the nuances of confabulation within collective behaviors. At the forefront of this unrest stood two prominent groups: Christian Nationalists and various militia organizations, both distinct in their ideological underpinnings yet united in their quest for narrative coherence. Rudden (2021) draws upon Hopper's concepts to interpret how Christian Nationalists conflated American identity with Christian ideology, thereby implicitly casting non-Christian citizens as second-rate patriots. The Trump presidency provided a focal point for this sentiment, casting Trump in a Messiah-like role, akin to biblical figures such as King David—a narrative that wove religious fervor into the fabric of nationalist sentiment (Rudden 2021, 374). This massification, as Hopper (2009) would term it, created a monolithic group identity centered around a divinely ordained national destiny. The phenomenon of confabulation, as observed in these narratives, arises not from a conscious intention to deceive but rather from an instinctual drive to construct a coherent narrative that supports and confirms their deeply held beliefs. Meanwhile, militia groups such as the Proud Boys, Three Percenters and Oath Keepers demonstrated an aggregation as described by Hopper (2009), rallying around a shared perception of encroaching federal overreach and a commitment to preserving individual liberties at all costs (Rudden 2021, 378–80). Trump's confrontational posture against the establishment acted as a validating force for their narratives, resonating with their self-perceived role as guardians of American values. Confabulations thus serve to preserve their identity against the cognitive dissonance that arises when their worldview is challenged by reality. Such narratives are not simply errors in judgment but play an essential psychological role. They forge a sense of unity and solidify identity within a broader context of perceived crisis (Ford & Feinberg 2020; Anderson 2022). The violence and chaos of that day were rooted not only in a physical assault on democratic institutions but also in an ideological clash—a battle of competing narratives as these groups sought to assert their vision of America, however misaligned with democratic principles.

The Capitol insurrection can therefore be seen as a potent manifestation of the entangled crises that shape contemporary cultures, revealing the extent to which national narratives can be simultaneously reflected and refracted through the prism of national confabulation. This event signals more than a momentary lapse into chaos; it marks a critical inflection point where narratives are continually tested against the foundational truths they purport to represent. This tension is exacerbated by the rapid digital exchange, which fuels the polarization of ideologies and the contentious field of identity politics, elements that conspire to undermine the solidity of established national narratives. These dynamics underscore the central thesis of this book: that crisis should be understood not as a singular, catastrophic event, but as a constitutive state characterized by the absence of meaningful, stabilizing events, which in turn intensifies latent societal tensions. The Capitol insurrection is a prime example of this phenomenon. It illustrates how ongoing crises and the cultures they spawn—permeated by emotional volatility, fragmented narratives, and temporal dislocation—fundamentally disrupt traditional conceptions of historical continuity and futurity. The enduring theories of Anderson, Hobsbawm, and Renan on nation-building and collective memory are increasingly pertinent in an era dominated by digital culture. However, these theories now require reinterpretation to address the unique dynamics of digital crisis cultures, which reshape collective memories and narratives at unprecedented speeds. It is within this reinterpretation that Han's (2022, 44) notion of "new nihilism" becomes critically relevant, pinpointing a "crisis of truth" that fragments the collective quest for a shared reality. This "crisis of truth"—cast by Han as an erosion rather than a direct assault on truth—is characterized by a pernicious fusion of fact and fiction, challenging societies to preserve authentic narratives about themselves (2022, 46). As the insurrection casts a long shadow over the concept of national identity, traditionally buoyed by common history, language, and culture, these pillars seem to waver in the digital age, where competing narratives gain strength through algorithms that underscore their presence. The quest for a unified national narrative thus becomes increasingly complex in an era where truth is decentralized and the authenticity of narratives is in constant contention. Consequently, in this era of new nihilism, the objective transcends the mere pursuit of a unified national story (if ever there was such a thing). Instead, it necessitates the construction of a new paradigm of identity—one robust enough to withstand the forces of digital fragmentation, where the multiplicity of truths does not signal a descent into discord but becomes the foundation of a more complex unity.

CONCLUSION

The Capitol insurrection vividly illustrates how crisis functions as a constitutive state, characterized by a dearth of stabilizing events which, in turn, magnifies underlying societal tensions. The ongoing crises and the cultures they engender—marked by emotional volatility, fractured narratives, and disrupted temporalities—demonstrate how contemporary crisis cultures continually destabilize and reshape national identities. This is evident in three key tensions: the clash between hope and apprehension, where aspirations for democratic resilience conflict with fears of institutional collapse; the dynamics between utopia and dystopia, as idealized visions of national unity confront the stark realities of societal division; and the struggle between history and futurity, where traditional historical narratives are contested by urgent demands for a reimagined future. In this light, the insurrection is not an isolated incident but a manifestation of the broader, persistent state of crisis that permeates contemporary societies.

Were the rioters who stormed the Capitol truly the "basket of deplorables" that Clinton spoke of? National confabulations, while serving as mechanisms for coherence and stability within particular settings, can simultaneously generate intense frustration among those who find themselves on the outside of these narrative constructions. It is important to reiterate here that my analysis does not lend credence to the simplistic and reductive binary of elite versus non-elite; rather, I explore the narrative potency that such a dichotomy assumes in this discourse. For the so-called elites, witnessing the unfolding of the Capitol insurrection, driven by distorted narratives, might engender feelings of disbelief, rage, and a profound sense of disconnection from the broader national identity. This sense of exasperation is intensified by the understanding that these confabulations are not mere anomalies but are ingrained and resilient, impervious to simple interventions or corrections. The elites, equipped with resources, educational backgrounds, and influential platforms, might find themselves grappling with the challenge of reconciling their perception of reality with the confabulated narratives that motivated the rioters' actions. In their quest to bridge this formidable gap, they might inadvertently engage in their own form of confabulation, crafting narratives that seek to rationalize the irrational and make sense of the seemingly nonsensical, all in an effort to restore a semblance of coherence to a situation marred by crisis and disarray. In this scenario, a potential confabulation by the elites could manifest as an oversimplified narrative that attributes the insurrection solely to ignorance and manipulation, neglecting the underlying systemic factors and feelings of disenfranchisement that may have also played a significant part.

In this context, Han contends that our contemporary society, especially within the parameters of what he calls an "infocracy," or amid what I call a digital crisis ambientality, is fragmenting into "irreconcilable identities without alterity," effectively replacing discourse with "*belief*" and "*confession*," intensifying identity-based conflicts (2022, 33). Viewing the Capitol insurrection through this lens, it emerges as a poignant illustration of the divisive nature of national confabulations, spotlighting the difficulties encountered when disparate segments of society dwell in conflicting narrative ecologies. The so-called elites, in their exasperation, are confronted with the limits of rational discourse and the formidable task of navigating a terrain where confabulated narratives wield significant influence over individual and collective behavior. Yet, this exasperation, while understandable, also necessitates a critical reflection on the part of the elites themselves. It calls for an examination of their role in the broader political landscape and the ways in which their actions, attitudes, and discourse might contribute to the perpetuation of the very confabulations that they find so exasperating. The Capitol insurrection, in this context, becomes a crucial point of reflection, a moment that demands a reassessment of the ways in which national narratives are constructed, contested, and perpetuated. It challenges the so-called elites to move beyond exasperation and to engage in a proactive, empathetic, and critical dialogue with those ensnared in confabulated narratives, recognizing that they, too, are part of the complex narratives of national identity and narrative construction.

The "stolen election" narrative's influence extended beyond the United States, finding resonance globally and among supporters of politicians akin to Trump in different national settings, who interpreted it as a personal affront. In my own experience, this narrative seeped into my family, with relatives finding it inconceivable that Joe Biden could secure more votes than Trump, repeatedly asking—"*How do you know?*"—a question that lays bare the divide in epistemological positions. For me, positioned within an educated elite, the circumstances surrounding the election results represent a "known unknown"—I am aware of my lack of direct access to the vote counting, but I trust in the established systems of verification and the multitude of corroborating reports (see Bowden & Teague 2022). However, for those sympathetic to "The Steal" narrative, this situation is an "unknown unknown." They are not only unaware of the specific details of the electoral process, but they also lack trust in the systems of verification, creating a gap that is easily filled by confabulation. Their disbelief was not just a personal skepticism but was part of a wider, global echo of confabulation that infiltrated intimate spaces. This demonstrates the power of national confabulations to shape both collective and individual thought processes, even within the confines of familial relationships. In environments subsumed in crisis cultures, where it feels as though "unknown unknowns" are persistently intruding into public space, this skepticism and detachment from established systems of knowledge become even more pronounced.

The question of how to interpret the stark polarization and divergent narratives in crisis cultures can be approached through Jürgen Habermas's (1987) concept of the "lifeworld." Habermas presents the lifeworld as an almost subconscious foundation of shared cultural understanding, essential for communication between individuals (1987, 154). This shared space, described as having a "peculiar *half-transcendence*," is familiar to everyone within a community but resists full conscious examination or articulation (1987, 125). Habermas situates the lifeworld within everyday social interactions, like those in families or civil society, where language and communication are key to navigating social interactions. According to Habermas, the lifeworld is fundamental in shaping the pattern of social systems. He posits that systemic structures are dependent on and need to be anchored in this shared cultural knowledge (1987, 154). However, the stability and integrity of the lifeworld are vulnerable to external factors, especially under the influence of globalization and hyperculturalization. These forces can disrupt the lifeworld's seamless integration into our consciousness, which is critical for smooth communication (Han 2022, 31). In a world where global networks expand and phenomena such as "defacticization" (disregarding factual bases in discussions) and "decontextualization" (removing context from information) are increasingly prevalent, significant challenges arise for our collective understanding (Han 2022, 31). These trends create barriers to communication and impair our ability to engage in effective discourse, contributing to the polarization and divergence we observe in crisis cultures.

Habermas's concept of the lifeworld invites a deeper examination of the seemingly binary perspectives between Capitol rioters and their sympathizers, and those labeled as the "elites." The lifeworld, being a repository of cultural knowledge and pre-understanding, fundamentally shapes the reality in which various groups operate. Rioters and their supporters, through a lifeworld infused with skewed historical accounts, come to see themselves as actors in a narrative of disenfranchisement, prompting them to regard the insurrection as a legitimate form of rebellion against perceived oppression. The authentic phenomenological reality they inhabit validates their actions and fuels a desire for radical change—a change grounded in the rectification of what they believe to be a distortion of justice and order. Conversely, the so-called elites navigate a lifeworld that ostensibly values logical discourse and informed debate. However, navigating the expansive and complex information environment to maintain a coherent national narrative presents substantial challenges. The insurrection is thus seen as a disruption, a threat to the very democratic frameworks they seek to uphold. This juxtaposition of lifeworlds does not imply that individuals conform entirely to one worldview or another. Rather, it underscores the dominant narratives that influence collective interpretations of such events. Habermas's lifeworld concept reveals a social reality where each element—be it an interpretation, experience, or expectation—plays a role in shaping the collective understanding within a society. These elements, although they might seem divergent, collectively constitute the framework through which a society interprets itself and its actions. The challenge lies not in aligning with one lifeworld or another, but in bridging these divergent lifeworlds to foster a shared reality that can accommodate multiplicity without succumbing to fragmentation.

In concluding this chapter, revisiting Benedict Anderson's conceptualization of nations as "imagined communities" (1991) invites contemplation on the nature of communal becomings in an age profoundly shaped by digital narratives. While the insurrection at Capitol Hill momentarily united the nation in reflection, it failed to induce a lasting change in collective consciousness or effectively counter the prevailing narrative distortions—exposing a crisis in the storyline of American democracy. Consequently, the idea of "communal becoming" within these imagined communities is not static but a continuous, ever-evolving journey. This journey is directed by the dynamism of shared stories, requiring from the community a degree of flexibility and strength derived from a deep-rooted commitment to continuous dialogue—a commitment that necessitates consistent reevaluation and renegotiation of the community's shared values. The act of remapping is key to facilitating communal becomings. This remapping is conceived as a thoughtful re-narration and redirection of the community's stories, charting paths through the winding landscape of history and collective memory. It is within this act of remapping that imagined communities might cultivate a form of collective resilience—one that is sensitively attuned to the variegated narratives of historical events and their manifold interpretations.

Chapter 4

Queering Crisis

The Greek concept of "philoxenia" (*φιλοξενία*), which translates to "love of strangers," is rooted in the ethos of ancient Greek society and culture. According to Gregory Papanikos (2020, 238), the term is better understood as being a friend of "hospitality" rather than a friend of a foreigner or stranger. The etymology of philoxenia combines "philo" (*φίλος*), meaning "love" or "friend," with "xenia" (*ξενία*), signifying hospitality. This semantic nuance is crucial in understanding the cultural and mythological layers that underpin this tradition in Greek society. A pivotal aspect of this tradition is the concept of "theoxenia" (*θεοξενία*), or divine hospitality. The term theoxenia is derived from "theos" (*θεός*), meaning "god," and "xenia" (*ξενία*), again meaning hospitality. This concept links the everyday act of welcoming guests with the sacred. In Greek mythology, gods often disguised themselves as ordinary mortals to test human hospitality. These divine tests were a way for the gods to ensure that mortals were upholding the values of kindness, generosity, and respect toward strangers. Failure to demonstrate proper hospitality could result in divine punishment, while those who performed philoxenia could be rewarded or blessed. This reveals a dual nature in philoxenia: it not only confers upon the guest a quasi-divine status, underscoring the sanctified aspect of hospitality, but also intimates the potential for divine retribution should hospitality be inadequately provided. Thus, the practice of philoxenia, as suggested by these mythological stories, is likely driven as much by reverence for the divine as it is by apprehension of divine repercussions for failing in one's hospitality duties.

My immersion in the tradition of philoxenia, deeply embedded in my upbringing within a Greek family, served as a living example of these ancient customs. Under my parents' guidance, our home transformed into a space where the ethos of philoxenia was not merely observed but actively embodied and celebrated. Guests from all cultures were welcomed with warmth and openness, reflecting a deeply ingrained cultural practice. Central to this tradition were our shared meals, where the act of sharing food symbolized a deeper sharing of ourselves. The dining table was more than just a place to eat; it was where stories, experiences, and connections were shared, fostering a sense of community and belonging. This communal aspect of dining transcended the physical act of eating by creating a space of mutual respect and understanding. My childhood role in this ritual was pivotal. I learned to anticipate and cater to the needs of our guests, appreciating the unique value and significance of each individual's presence within our home. This role was a critical aspect of my formative years, cultivating in me a deep sense of empathy and respect for others, continually shaped and reshaped through each interaction, reinforcing the underlying values of generosity and communal solidarity. This experience of philoxenia taught me the importance of looking beyond superficial differences to find common ground. It was a lesson in the essential humanity that connects us all, a lesson that has deeply shaped my outlook and interactions.

Yet, despite being raised in a culture deeply rooted in philoxenia, characterized by a nurturing environment where strangers were welcomed with open hearts and minds, my personal experience also reveals a striking contradiction. Growing up gay in a society that highly valued hospitality, I noted a pronounced absence of this same warmth and acceptance extended toward my own identity. While the concept of theoxenia in Greek culture implied divine retribution for failing to provide hospitality to strangers, there was no parallel doctrine for failing to accept and embrace differences within one's family, such as a gay child. Emmanuel Levinas (1969), in his treatise on ethical philosophy, considers the face-to-face encounter with the Other as an imperative ethical demand, where the presence of the Other necessitates a response, a form of obligation. In my case, growing up gay entailed navigating a liminal space where my own identity—the Other within—was in constant confrontation with prevailing cultural norms and expectations. Instead of receiving the unconditional acceptance typical of philoxenia, this internal Other was often met with silence and internalized shame. The cultural embrace of outsiders rarely seemed to extend to my own multidimensional identity, revealing a disjunction between the celebrated virtues of hospitality and the genuine embracement of diverse identities.

My journey, which has included phases marked by the concealment of my sexuality, has therefore prompted me to contemplate the meaning of community and belonging. This introspection arises from a life that, particularly during my childhood and formative years, was positioned at the intersection of otherness and inclusion—underscoring a significant discrepancy between theoretical ideals and actual lived experiences. It raises questions about the boundaries of acceptance and the conditions under which inclusion is granted. This tension is akin to the critique offered by philosopher Jean-Luc Nancy on the often-romanticized notion of an "original community," a mythical construct that idealizes past communal coherence and unity, which in reality never existed without internal contradictions and exclusions (1991, 10). He challenges the assumption that there ever was a harmonious, unfragmented community in the past, reinforcing how this nostalgic ideal often overlooks the realities of individual lived experiences. The effort to cultivate a common identity or sense of belonging can thus inadvertently lead to the establishment of norms that marginalize those who do not conform to them. In my experience, this has manifested as a form of conditional inclusion, where acceptance within the community is contingent upon compliance with often-unspoken norms and expectations. The idea of community, while ostensibly presenting a facade of unity and cohesion, can simultaneously engender feelings of isolation and marginalization from within. A community can therefore be both a source of belonging and alienation, often simultaneously, for individuals with diverse identities and experiences.

Can a tradition like philoxenia, which fosters openness toward others, facilitate a deeper self-inquiry, akin to what Heidegger (1962) conceptualizes as the "open" (*das Offene*)? While this concept is not as foundational as his notions of "*Dasein*" (being-there), Heidegger's "open," as interpreted by Leland de la Durantaye (2009), is a significant element in his early existential philosophy, deeply intertwined with his examination of human perception and the revelation of truth. Heidegger's concept of the "open" suggests a state of being where individuals momentarily transcend their habitual, preoccupation-laden environments (de la Durantaye 2009, 327). This transcendence is not simply physical but philosophical, enabling a retreat from daily engagements typically dominated by practical concerns and immediate reactions. In this space of detachment, we are not confined to the narrow scope of our personal environment but are exposed to a larger "world"—a realm that is vast, complex, and often enigmatic. This "world" includes the full spectrum of human experience, understanding, and being (de la Durantaye 2009, 327). The "open" allows for the unfolding of *Dasein*, as it offers an opportunity to confront the full reality of our existence beyond what is immediate and apparent. It is a transformative space, where consciousness is expanded, facilitating a deeper and more comprehensive understanding of ourselves and our surroundings. In Heidegger's ontological framework, the "open" aligns with the original Greek concept of truth, or "alētheia" ($\dot{\alpha}\lambda\acute{\eta}\theta\varepsilon\iota\alpha$) meaning "unconcealment" or "disclosure" (de la Durantaye 2009, 328). This interpretation of truth as an active process of uncovering rather than a passive state of being uncovered underlines Heidegger's philosophical exploration of truth as dynamic and evolving, rather than fixed and predetermined. Therefore, the ability to experience and reflect in this "open" space, recognizing and confronting our own *Dasein*, is what Heidegger believes sets us apart as human beings. Within this expansive realm, we immerse ourselves fully in our existence, navigating the totality of our being.

Reflecting on Heidegger's concept of "the open," I find myself contemplating its practicality, particularly in the context of contemporary crisis cultures, where attachment to identity, not detachment, is the norm. As Susan Stryker puts it, identity is "where the rubber of larger social and cultural systems hits the road of lived experience" (Stryker 2008, 11). Stryker's articulation demonstrates the tangible impact of social and cultural constructs on our daily lives, revealing how these abstract systems become deeply personal and influential in shaping individual experiences. In this vein, my exploration of Heidegger's concept of the "open" is set against a backdrop of evolving contemporary understandings of identity. It is important to note, however, that Heidegger's philosophy on the "open" was not formulated with contemporary understandings of identity in mind. Instead, my reinterpretation of the "open" serves as a rhetorical device to bridge philosophical theory with the concrete realities of identity, particularly how markers like queerness entrench individuals in distinct experiential frameworks. The current era is indeed one in which the significance of identity is pervasive. What has become known as identity politics emphasizes the recognition and appreciation of diverse identities from various social groups as a countermeasure to historical marginalization. Consequently, identity for many becomes a "second skin," providing solace and a sense of foundation. Even David Harvey, a notable critic of postmodernity, acknowledges the importance of embracing this diversity, underscoring the acceptance of "Otherness" and the validity of diverse groups expressing their unique experiences (1989, 47–48). Today, the layered nature of our identities, encompassing elements such as sexuality, gender, culture, and history, influences not only how individuals perceive the world but also how individuals are perceived by it. The entrenched nature of such identities poses a significant challenge to Heidegger's concept of "the open," which seems to advocate for a certain level of detachment from these deeply ingrained elements of the self. For individuals with marginalized identities, where such facets are integral to their being and often a source of both strength and vulnerability, the idea of accessing the "open" is not merely challenging; it risks being perceived as an impractical, if not unattainable, endeavor. It requires a form of abstract thinking that transcends the immediacy and particularity of the self, a task that becomes increasingly complex when identity is deeply intertwined with one's subjectivity and social position. Thus, the philosophical detachment implied by the "open" raises a critical question: Who has the privilege to shed their identity to access this "open"? Can individuals who are continually defining themselves in opposition to sociocultural norms truly experience Heidegger's "open," or does this concept imply a level of privilege not universally accessible?

In contemplating my identity as a queer individual, it is crucial to acknowledge that this journey is deeply personal and far from a uniform experience within the queer community. The uniqueness of each person's journey in discovering and embracing their queerness is shaped by distinct backgrounds, cultures, and personal circumstances. Consequently, the diversity within the queer community indicates the absence of a singular, definitive narrative of what it means to be queer, a term that encapsulates inclusivity and fluidity, yet is replete with complexity (Halperin 1995, 62). Nonetheless, this approach, prioritizing personal and diverse experiences over a homogeneous understanding of queerness, has encountered resistance. It has been met with skepticism from various writers who challenge its expansive scope and, occasionally, the very definition of queerness itself. These critiques typically arise from a preference for more definitive categorizations, thereby conflicting with the inherently diverse and fluid nature of queer identities (Oakes 1995; Green 2002; Escudero-Alías 2022). Even within the broader discipline of queer studies, the term has also been rigorously interrogated, questioning the emancipatory potential of queer identity, and arguing that the promise of liberation often associated with the label "queer" frequently—or always—remains unrealized, thereby underscoring a prevailing dissatisfaction with these identity constructs (Duberman 2018; Ferguson 2018). The dynamics within queer politics are further entangled by Lisa Duggan's (2003) concept of homonormativity. This concept critiques the trend within some segments of the LGBT+ community toward assimilating into mainstream, heterosexual norms, particularly those that emphasize monogamy, domesticity, and adherence to traditional gender roles. Duggan argues that this trend toward homonormativity privileges certain identities—often those that are white, middle-class, and align with heterosexual standards—while marginalizing others within the queer community. This phenomenon of assimilation and its critiques, paralleled by commentators like Richard Dawkins (2023)—who compares identity politics to a form of religion—reveal the heterogeneous and contested nature of queer identity politics. Thus, while the queer community continues to evolve and redefine itself, it remains a contested space where diverse perspectives coexist, often leading to existential dialogues and debates about the nature, scope, and future of queer identities and politics.

In an era characterized by pervasive crisis cultures, the enthusiastic embrace of diverse identities during periods of instability and uncertainty may appear counterintuitive. Conventional wisdom might suggest that during heightened times of crisis, such as the Capitol Hill insurrection on January 6, 2021, there would be a tendency toward more traditional, homogeneous national identities, sought as sources of comfort and security, based on the belief that familiarity and uniformity provide stability in an unstable world. However, while there is some truth to the notion that people might seek solace in traditional, homogeneous identities during moments of crisis, this tendency is not limited to conventional identities. The fervent adoption of both conforming and diverging identities from traditional norms suggests that during crises, individuals are just as likely to gravitate toward any identity that offers a sense of belonging, purpose, and stability, regardless of its traditional or non-traditional character. For example, during such times, people might embrace identities rooted in ethnic heritage, LGBT+ communities, feminist movements, environmental activism, or digital subcultures. This suggests that in times of crisis, the anchoring in identities that feel authentic and empowering is crucial for maneuvering through crisis cultures because it provides individuals with a sense of stability and agency amid widespread uncertainty. However, focusing on lived experiences, particularly those of marginalized groups like queer communities, is not without its critics. Skeptics argue that emphasizing individual, subjective experiences could undermine the pursuit of universal truths and objective reasoning (Pluckrose & Lindsay 2020, 192). The concern is that the emphasis on personal stories could lead to a relativistic approach to truth and knowledge, challenging the foundational principles of logical discourse and consensus-building within a liberal democratic framework.

In modern philosophy, the term "lived experience" is derived from the German word *Erlebnis*, which generally connotes a more immediate, pre-reflective, and personal variant of experience than *Erfahrung* (Casey 2023, 284). It signifies something that is new and fresh, immediate, and attested by one's own experience, as opposed to something simply being handed down. As Patrick Casey notes:

> Talk of lived experience serves as a reminder of the unique 'what it's like' aspect of being human, which is inherently internal and personal. However, in common usage, lived experience is often perceived as granting a privileged epistemic status. This perception tends to dictate that others should defer unquestioningly to those who possess such experience.
>
> (Casey 2023, 283)

Expanding on this, Casey underlines the challenge inherent in interpreting these experiences: "We have experiences—this doesn't mean that we automatically understand those experiences. Meaning is something that must be found in the interrelation of the parts of our lives on the whole" (Casey 2023, 290). The interpretative nature of lived experience thus suggests that understanding one's own experiences is a process that involves piecing together various aspects of life, such as social interactions, cultural contexts, and historical influences. Hence, a fundamental philosophical tension emerges—how to reconcile the value of individual lived experiences with the pursuit of broader, more universal truths.

Contrary to these critiques, I perceive queerness as more than a mere identity attribute; it constitutes a "second skin" essential to my being. In *Saint Genet* (2012, 588), Jean-Paul Sartre posed a thought-provoking question: "Does a homosexual exist?" This question is not an inquiry into the existence of homosexuality, but rather an intriguing contemplation of identity as an act of human freedom (Chitty 2020, 186). Sartre writes: "If he does exist, everything changes: if homosexuality is the choice of a mind, it becomes a human possibility" (2012, 588). This resonates with my understanding that my homosexuality, while an inherent aspect of who I am, becomes a deliberate act of defining my existence and agency through the conscious choice to embrace it as part of my identity, a choice grounded in the possibilities it opens up. I thus find inspiration in José Esteban Muñoz's *Cruising Utopia: The Then and There of Queer Futurity* (2009) in which he conceptualizes queerness as a future-oriented ideality, advocating for what he terms a "queer futurity." In Muñoz's perspective, this futurity is not about arriving at a concrete utopia, but rather it is an ideal that motivates and guides action toward transformative possibilities (2009, 1). In envisioning queerness as a transformative agent, Muñoz elevates it from a static facet of identity to a dynamic process of communal becoming. However, in the context of my argument about living in perpetual crisis cultures, where ongoing crisis seemingly impedes regeneration, this perspective requires a nuanced approach. Rather than perceiving this second skin as an element to discard in pursuit of Heidegger's "open," I regard it as a vital and empowering component of my identity. It signifies recognizing the richness and depth of the queer experience and harnessing it as a force for both personal and collective transformation, even within the framework of continuous crisis (Muñoz 2009, 1). Hence, my queer identity, my second skin, goes beyond mere classification; it represents a hope-filled striving for the future, embodying "an insistence on potentiality or concrete possibility for another world" (Muñoz 2009, 1). As Franco Berardi suggests: "When society enters a phase of crisis or approaches collapse, we can glimpse the horizon of possibility" (2019, 28). This understanding of crisis as a gateway to new horizons of possibility resonates with my understanding of queerness; it is within the ongoing crisis that the true potential and transformative power of queer identity and community can be most vividly realized.

Queerness, then, with its inherent challenge to normative structures and its fluid, transformative nature, offers a hermeneutic lens to interpret how groups might live *through* and *within* crisis cultures. To *queer* crisis is thus not only the embrace of an epistemology that values ambiguity and multiplicity, but also the embrace of an adaptive methodology in which the continuous negotiation and renegotiation of identitarian boundaries are not static but are continuously shaped and reshaped by social, cultural, and political forces. Indeed, the queer experience has always been marked by a state of ongoing crisis, characterized by the perpetual negotiation of identity within social and political frameworks that are resistant to non-normative expressions. This ongoing crisis is deeply embedded in the everyday lived realities of queer individuals, reflecting the ongoing tension between personal authenticity and identity construction. For instance, the LGBT+ community's response to the AIDS crisis in the 1980s and 1990s epitomizes the praxis of queerness navigating crisis through radical solidarity and collective activism. This period of suffering and marginalization was transmuted into a potent sociopolitical movement that not only demanded health rights but also sparked broader sociocultural transformations. The queer condition thus provides a framework for the potential for creative reimagining and communal becoming, characterized by shared experiences, in which the fluidity and adaptability of queer identities serve as a model for fostering new forms of solidarity and collective identity. Thus, by framing queerness as potentiality, I perceive it not as a failed project but as an ongoing, hopeful endeavor of communal becoming, uniquely positioned within the context of crisis cultures.

However, the postmodern proclivity toward identity politics is also not without its critiques. David Harvey points out the inherent challenges of embracing such a fragmented landscape (1989, 49). He argues that while identity politics empowers diverse voices and acknowledges a spectrum of experiences, it simultaneously complicates communication and the dynamics of power within societies. Harvey describes a postmodern condition in which language is perceived as an evolving interaction between the conveyed message (signified) and its medium (signifier), constantly mutating and reassembling in novel configurations (1989, 49). This view suggests that our understanding of the world, much like our identities, is subject to continuous change and redefinition. As Han warns: "A world [. . .] suffers a total loss of sense if it becomes devoid of all reference. Language is itself a referential structure, and a word or sentence owes its sense to that structure" (2019, 22). Hence, in a context where representations are unstable and constantly shifting, forging collective action and maintaining a coherent, unified approach becomes difficult to establish and sustain, potentially hindering the very progress that identity politics seeks to achieve (Harvey 1989, 52). For example, the distinct terminologies and frameworks employed by movements focused on racial justice, LGBT+ rights, and gender equality can create barriers to forming a cohesive, unified front, despite each addressing critical issues. Additionally, the varying approaches to activism and advocacy among LGBT+ groups can lead to disagreements on strategies and goals. One group might prioritize legal reform, while another emphasizes grassroots community building, leading to potential conflicts or misalignments in their efforts. Moreover, the proliferation of social media as a platform for activism, while amplifying voices, can also exacerbate these divisions. To address this fragmentation, Habermas (1987) argues for the advancement of the Enlightenment project. He challenges the relativism and perceived defeatism inherent in postmodernism, advocating for a balanced approach that acknowledges the significance of diverse identities while striving for a unified framework. This framework would facilitate effective communication and cooperative action, aiming to integrate diverse perspectives into a cohesive social structure. While the adoption of a "second skin" may empower individuals, it paradoxically contributes to the fragmentation that Habermas seeks to counter. Consequently, the challenge resides in embracing individual identities while cultivating a collective strategy that recognizes and leverages the diversity within identity politics for comprehensive social and political transformation.

Yet, if we accept that we are living in a *post*-postmodern era, characterized by crisis cultures, the challenges identified by both Harvey's and Habermas's critique of postmodernism's focus on identity become even more pronounced. As I have argued throughout this book, crisis cultures are characterized by an overwhelming prevalence of crisis narratives that obscure clear understanding and make genuine, profound experiences of events (*Erfahrung*) and their associated emotions increasingly ephemeral and transient. This constant bombardment of fragmented perspectives leads to a scenario where understanding and meaning are not only elusive but often lost in the noise of perpetual crisis narratives. Byung-Chul Han's insight here is therefore pivotal:

> Something only makes sense if it is integrated into a net of relations, a continuum or horizon of sense, that lies beyond that thing, and that precedes the apprehension of a thing or event without, however, itself becoming an object of conscious perception. (2019, 22)

This statement underlines the idea that for any entity or event to be meaningful, it must be contextualized within a broader relational framework. This "net of relations" acts as a backdrop that gives events and experiences their depth and significance, which often remains unperceived at the conscious level. In terms of identity politics, this concept implies that individual and group identities derive their significance from their place within a larger, interconnected social network. However, in the *post*-postmodern digital era, this relational framework may become occluded. The overwhelming influx of information and the rapid dissemination of perspectives online can blur the lines that connect individual experiences to broader social narratives, making it challenging to perceive and appreciate these deeper connections. This phenomenon leads to a paradoxical situation. On one hand, the celebration and affirmation of diverse identities are integral to recognizing and respecting the multiplicity of human experiences. On the other, this diversification, particularly in digital spaces, has inadvertently heightened ideological polarization (Pariser 2011).

Consequently, identities today are not just numerous but even more fluid and transient than in earlier periods, often rapidly evolving in response to current events or ideological shifts. This fluidity has led to a situation in which identities once hailed as symbols of diversity are now, at times, pejoratively critiqued as exemplifying "wokeness," drawing unfavorable comparisons to Maoism or cultural Marxism (Jones & Smith 2022; Gonzalez & Gorka 2022; Cruz 2023). A significant debate in this context revolves around intersectionality, a theoretical framework that examines how various social and cultural identities overlap and interact, particularly in contexts of discrimination or oppression (Crenshaw 1989). Critics argue that intersectionality constructs a matrix of grievances, focusing excessively on group identity at the expense of individuality and personal agency (Pluckrose & Lindsay 2020, 124). This critique suggests that intersectionality, while aiming to acknowledge diverse experiences, risks obscuring the uniqueness of individual narratives under the weight of collective categories. It calls into question the delicate equilibrium between acknowledging unique personal experiences and addressing the broader systemic issues associated with these overarching group identities. Alongside these critiques, the evolution of digital environments has led to the proliferation of niche online communities and the rapid spread of information, which in turn has facilitated the expansion of existing identities, such as ecofeminism, into new digital spaces. Ecofeminism, which originally emerged in the 1970s and 1980s (Gaard 1993), has found renewed vigor in the digital age, creating distinct online identities that combine environmental concerns with feminist perspectives. This digital resurgence represents a holistic approach to environmental activism, interconnecting the struggle for gender equality with ecological preservation. Conversely, in more contentious spaces, identities such as "incels" (involuntary celibates) have emerged, representing a group primarily found in online forums, characterized by their inability to find romantic or sexual partners, often accompanied by a specific set of beliefs and attitudes toward society and gender dynamics (Sugiura 2021). These examples highlight how the diversification of identity in the digital age not only expands self-definition but also disrupts traditional language and identity structures, effectively eroding the clear referential frameworks that once anchored identity to more stable sociocultural contexts (Han 2019, 22). This erosion unfolds as digital communication reshapes the speed and scope at which identities are expressed and perceived, challenging the permanence and coherence of traditional identity constructs. As a result, traditional markers of identity are being recontextualized and reshaped, leading to a new understanding of identity politics that is more fragmented and diverse than ever before. Hence, while critics of identity politics in the postmodern era sought to challenge the fragmentation of identities, advocating for a return to a classical liberal focus on the individual, the advent of digital cultures has only served to proliferate an even broader array of identities, from environmental activism to cyber-feminism and beyond. This proliferation underscores the continual reshaping of identity in the contemporary era, where digital influences constantly redefine how we perceive ourselves and others.

In this chapter, my examination revolves around the dialectic between my queer identity and the concept of crisis. As a queer individual, I am "queering" the idea of crisis, employing my experiences and perspectives to both challenge and reshape it. Conversely, there is a notable inversion at play where tautological narratives in contemporary crisis cultures are queering my own queerness. These narratives, ubiquitous in current cultural discourse, warp the expression of group identities, culminating in a peculiar situation where queerness is out-queered by non-queer interpretations. By examining the intersection of queer identity and crisis, this chapter highlights how crisis cultures perpetuate a state of ongoing instability that challenges traditional understandings of identity, community, and belonging. This approach leverages queer perspectives to deconstruct and reinterpret crisis narratives, revealing how they can both disrupt and offer new avenues for understanding the underlying tensions of hope and apprehension (emotion), utopia and dystopia (narrative), and history and futurity (temporality). Particularly, it emphasizes how queer identities navigate and resist the tautological narratives prevalent in crisis cultures. In the analysis that follows, I contextualize this discussion within the broader framework of identity politics, examining the dynamics of power within and across various group identities. The emergence of what Naomi Klein terms a "Mirror World" is utilized as a metaphor to depict a reality where identity definitions and boundaries, including those of queerness, are not only blurred but also reflected back in diverse and sometimes contradictory ways. In the following section, I examine Jasbir K. Puar's (2007) concept of homonationalism, which argues that certain queer subjects are implicated in nationalistic agendas, thereby reshaping traditional views of both nationalism and queer resistance. By doing so, it underscores the necessity of reevaluating and reimagining identity politics in the context of perpetual crisis, reinforcing the book's central thesis that crisis today is *a constitutive state defined by a lack of meaningful events leading to the intensification of underlying tensions*. The case study on the evolving landscape of queer politics in contemporary Spain epitomizes this phenomenon. It reveals a context where each aspect appears as a reflection of itself, contributing to a scenario where established perceptions of marginalized identities are continuously reinterpreted and recontextualized. Moreover, it demonstrates, as Dimitra Kotouza argues, that crises can impact citizens (and non-citizens) differentially and that certain groups, such as the LGBT+ community, can become renewed targets in the context of a return to identification(s) with the nation (Kotouza 2019, 6). This dialectic of queerness being *out-queered* by non-queer interpretations not only highlights how the lack of definitive events heightens existing tensions and forces a reconsideration of identity boundaries but also opens up a space for reimagining the boundaries and possibilities of identity, potentially unveiling new pathways for communal becomings.

THE POWER OF THE MIRROR

"Behavior," suggests Goethe, "is the mirror in which everyone shows their image" (quoted in Cozolino 2010, 187). In psychoanalytic terms, the concept of mirroring is essential for understanding self-formation and development. This process, as conceptualized by Jacques Lacan (1977) in his mirror stage theory, refers to a critical phase in early childhood when a child first recognizes their reflection in a mirror. This moment marks the beginning of the ego's formation, where the child starts to develop a sense of self that is distinct from the world around them. Mirroring in this context is more than a physical reflection; it represents the child's initial encounter with their external image, leading to an identification that contributes to the construction of the "I" that forms the foundation of self-identity. However, Lacan's concept of mirroring extends beyond the literal reflection in a mirror. It symbolizes the child's first steps into the social world, where they begin to see themselves in relation to others. The mirror thus becomes a metaphor for how individuals perceive themselves through the gaze of others. This process is not static but dynamic, involving a constant negotiation between how one sees oneself and how one is perceived by the external world. Mirroring is thus a complex interaction of self-recognition, identity formation, and the ongoing influence of external perceptions. It reveals the tension between one's inner sense of self and the external world's reflections and expectations.

Naomi Klein in *Doppelganger: A Trip into the Mirror World* (2023) presents a thought-provoking adaptation of the mirroring concept into the space of digital technology. Unlike Lacan's framework, grounded in physical reality and developmental psychology, Klein transposes this paradigm into the digital sphere. The fundamental difference in Klein's approach is the nature of the reflection itself. In Klein's *Doppelganger*, the tangible mirror is replaced by digital interfaces, facilitating interactions with virtual renditions of reality and self. The Mirror World Klein describes refers to a digital sphere where disparate identitarian groups ranging from far-right MAGA (Make America Great Again), supporters to health and wellness influencers, and new-age adherents converge, a space in which narratives are continuously constructed and deconstructed, often blurring the distinction between reality and fiction. Confronting the full scope of the Mirror World's impact, particularly on real-world events like election outcomes, COVID-19 restriction responses, and the Capitol Hill insurrection, poses significant challenges. These include discerning the real influence of digital interactions on individual perceptions and actions, separating genuine self-representation from digitally constructed personas, and understanding the role of digital engagement in shaping collective consciousness and propagating polarizing narratives. While these issues remain largely unexplored in academic discourse, it is plausible to suggest that the Mirror World, in its undefined boundaries, serves as a fertile ground for the growth and dissemination of the confabulations discussed in the previous chapter. Even so, it would be overly simplistic to claim that large portions of Western societies are completely immersed in this digital phenomenon. The mirror metaphor, however, is a useful rhetorical tool for understanding the development of emerging identities and their often-distorted reflection in identity politics.

Callison and Slobodian's (2021) concept of diagonalism offers a useful framework for understanding the evolving nature of identities in the post-COVID era. Diagonalism represents more than a mere amalgamation of left and right ideologies; it signifies a complex evolution from recent populist trends. This approach involves multidirectional political engagement and global interactions, moving beyond populism's linear appeal to mass sentiments. Diagonalists advocate an ideology that foregrounds individual liberty while harboring a critical, often conspiratorial attitude toward public authority, which is perceived as inherently suspect. This ideology merges diverse elements to create a distinct, frequently contrarian political identity that emphasizes disruptive decentralization and has a tendency toward right-wing radicalization. Klein (2023) also acknowledges the impact of diagonalism on contemporary political and social discourse, citing the wellness movement as a prime example of a diagonal identity. The wellness movement initially aligned with left-wing ideologies, focusing on holistic health and challenging mainstream medical practices. However, it has increasingly shifted toward right-wing ideologies, especially regarding bodily autonomy and health-related personal choices. This shift is particularly evident in the anti-vaccination movement and opposition to government health mandates during the COVID-19 pandemic (Klein 2023, 158–191). In digital spaces, this movement promotes narratives that claim exclusive, "truthful" insights into health, often contradicting established scientific consensus. Conventional medical knowledge is scrutinized, with adherents seeing themselves as having awakened to hidden realities against a perceived mainstream health discourse of "groupthink." This sense of possessing the "truth" illustrates how, in the digital era, these ideologies blend, reshape, and form new identities based on the conviction of having awakened to a hidden reality.

In the Mirror World, diagonalism significantly impacts identity politics, reshaping how identities are formed and expressed through digital interactions. However, Han offers a critical perspective against the common belief that the fragmentation of the public sphere is mainly caused by digital phenomena like filter bubbles and echo chambers. He argues that a more significant trend—growing atomization and narcissism—is the primary driver of this fragmentation and individualization in modern public discourse. According to Han, these underlying issues contribute more to the breakdown of collective communication and empathy than digital factors alone:

> the disintegration of the public sphere is *not a purely technical problem*. The personalization of searches and newsfeeds makes only a small contribution to this process of disintegration. Self-indoctrination or auto-propagandizing begins *offline*.

> We are becoming deaf to the *voice* because society is increasingly atomized and narcissistic. This also leads to a *loss of empathy*. Today, everyone buys into the cult of the self. Everyone stages and produces themselves. It is the *disappearance of the other*, the *inability to listen*, and not the algorithmic personalization of the internet that is responsible for the crisis of democracy.

(Han 2022, 29–30, original emphasis)

What Han terms the "disappearance of the other" underlines a decline in regard for the viewpoints and experiences of others. As society becomes more self-centered, people are less likely to listen to or empathize with others, leading to a breakdown in communication and understanding. In the context of identity politics, this shift indicates a move from collective activism and solidarity to a form of identity politics focused increasingly on individual expression and personal validation. Recent scholarship, such as *#HashtagActivism* (Jackson et al. 2020), underscores the positive impacts of this trend, showing how digital platforms empower marginalized groups to voice their experiences and concerns. However, while hashtag campaigns can be powerful tools for social change, they risk being co-opted for self-promotion, diverting focus from collective goals to individual narratives. This trend reveals a complex dynamic in digital cultures: while it appears to increase opportunities for individual expression, it can also lead to greater political fragmentation as the original collective message becomes diluted by personal branding efforts. This development results in a form of individualism that is not merely a continuation of classical liberalism but an inverted version of it. In this refracted view, the classical liberal principle of balanced individual autonomy transforms into hyper-focused self-absorption, disregarding the essential interconnectedness and interdependence needed for a functioning democratic society. It turns the focus inward to such an extent that it disrupts the potentiality for collective action and communal becoming.

As societies gravitate toward a narcissistic ethos, focusing on the individual rather than the collective, identity politics as a broad category becomes more fraught and contentious. This shift is notably illustrated by the rising trend of critiquing what has come to be labeled as "wokeism," a term now often used to challenge or dismiss progressive approaches to social issues. Wokeism, a label frequently used pejoratively, is closely associated with the concept of virtue signaling, which has gained substantial prominence in contemporary discourse since the advent of social media (Davies & MacRae 2022). Virtue signaling, traditionally defined as the act of publicly expressing opinions or sentiments to assert moral character or rectitude, is not a new social phenomenon (Westra 2021, 156). However, its impact and visibility are notably amplified in the digital era. Digital platforms, with their extensive reach and instantaneous nature, have become fertile ground for individuals to align themselves with moral or ethical positions, sometimes driven by a desire to enhance personal image or social standing. For instance, the tendency to share posts on social justice issues on platforms such as Instagram or TikTok, without accompanying concrete actions, can be perceived as a form of virtue signaling. The mechanics of social media, which reward user engagement, propel this trend, incentivizing the projection of moral superiority. Yet, it is vital to distinguish between authentic moral expressions and mere virtue signaling in online discourse. Critiques of virtue signaling often fail to recognize genuine engagement on these platforms. Nonetheless, the emphasis on personal branding and performative interactions online has unquestionably expanded the scope of virtue signaling, transforming it from a nuanced social dynamic to a pronounced and sometimes divisive element of online discourse.

Drawing on Foucault's (1979) theories of power, both the practice of virtue signaling and its subsequent critique can be understood as manifestations of disciplinary power. Foucault argued that power is not just exercised through repression but also through the creation and dissemination of discourse and knowledge. In this context, virtue signaling goes beyond the mere assertion of moral norms; it becomes a mechanism through which individuals and groups exert influence and power. This influence is often exerted through social media platforms, where likes, shares, and comments can quickly amplify certain moral positions while marginalizing others. The phenomenon of cancel culture emerges as the ultimate expression of this disciplinary power. It leverages public opinion to enforce certain moral standards through collective actions like social media boycotts or public shaming, regulating behavior and speech to align with dominant ethical codes. This tool enforces conformity to prevailing moral and ethical standards, often leading to the ostracization or silencing of those who deviate (Ronson 2015). Conversely, the critique of virtue signaling itself becomes a form of disciplinary power, shaping and controlling expressions of solidarity or ethical positions in the digital public sphere. These critiques often manifest as counternarratives challenging the authenticity or motives behind public displays of virtue, thus influencing perceptions of genuine versus performative activism. The backlash against corporate brands adopting social causes—also known as woke capitalism—often scrutinized for authenticity, illustrates this dynamic. In woke capitalism, power operates by challenging the alignment between a brand's public statements and its actual practices, thereby influencing consumer perceptions and brand reputations (Rhodes 2022). Such critiques effectively establish norms for what is considered legitimate engagement, shaping individual behavior and self-representation online. This phenomenon underlines how digital platforms have become arenas of constant power negotiation and contestation, where both the act of signaling virtue and the critique thereof shape the discourse on morality and ethics in the digital age.

In the context of these digital culture wars, the discourse surrounding identity politics, especially for marginalized groups like the queer community, is experiencing a notable transformation. While the pursuit of group rights by such communities has always been fraught with contention, the advent of digital platforms has amplified these debates, leading to a perceived reversal in power dynamics. Historically, the queer community's fight for visibility and equal rights was primarily seen as a struggle against discrimination. However, in the Mirror World, these same efforts are increasingly perceived as assertive, or even aggressive, grabs for power. For instance, initiatives like "Drag Queen Story Hour" in libraries across various Western nations, originally designed as inclusive educational programs, have ignited significant controversy (Davis & Hensman Kettrey 2022). Critics perceive these events as forceful endorsements of gender ideology, thereby challenging established gender norms and family values. This reframes historical actions aimed at combating discrimination and advocating for equity into something contentious and polarizing. Similarly, the increased inclusion of books addressing queer themes or supporting LGBT+ rights in schools, previously recognized as educational tools for promoting understanding, now faces opposition and book-banning campaigns (Pickering 2023). These campaigns, driven by concerns over an excessive queer influence in education, mirror a wider anti-woke sentiment, contributing to the acceleration of polarization. Consequently, the queer community, once predominantly seen as marginalized, has become central in the cultural debate on power and representation. The change in perception has led to a situation where individuals or groups previously perceived as victims of oppression may be perceived as oppressors. This transition is indicative of a broader trend in identity politics, where power dynamics are not just about who possesses power but also about how it is perceived and portrayed. As the queer community gains visibility and influence, it encounters new challenges, balancing between asserting its identity and being perceived as imposing its ideology on others.

Slavoj Žižek's (2017) reflections on the Vancouver Pride Parade, which he watched from a hotel room while visiting Canada, underscore this dilemma. Pride parades historically function as platforms for both resistance and visibility, thereby capturing the queer community's aspiration to assert their presence publicly while celebrating their unique identity away from conventional norms. Yet, Žižek admits that the parade "left a bitter taste in [his] mouth" (2017, 190). Part of his distaste, it seems, emerges from what he perceives as a fundamental contradiction in the queer community's historical narrative: a tension between seeking legitimacy in public spaces on the one hand, and relishing the transgressive excitement of existing outside social norms, on the other (Žižek 2017, 188–189). This tension, this liminal existence, is itself a form of mirroring—reflecting both a desire for integration into the mainstream and a simultaneous celebration of difference. This duality encapsulates the queer community's ongoing struggle: to be recognized and accepted within the broader society while maintaining a distinct, often countercultural identity. But mostly, his distaste stems from the media portrayal of the event, which, he contends, was characterized by an all-inclusive "oceanic feeling" of love (2017, 187–188). This, he suggests, is not "authentic" love but rather a feeling that is "ideology embodied" and "a feeling that obliterates all struggle and antagonism" (2017, 188). He perceives this portrayal of queer love as paradoxically creating a hierarchy that subtly favors non-heterosexual orientations, presenting them as less prone to ideological capture and more inherently subversive (2017, 188). In Žižek's analysis, Pride parades are thus no longer viewed as expressions of resistance against a heteronormative society and a celebration of queer identity. Instead, they are now seen as challenging the normative status of heterosexuality, which, in contrast, is increasingly viewed as conformist. This change in perception suggests that the dynamic and varied nature of queer identities is setting new cultural standards, positioning heterosexuality as less progressive, marking what Žižek implicitly interprets as a reversal in the conventional hierarchy of sexual norms. Essentially, what was once considered mainstream and normative (heterosexuality) is now seen as mundane, while queer identities, once marginalized, are perceived as more avant-garde or trendsetting. In my interpretation of Žižek's argument, the queer community's dominant influence in crafting narratives of inclusivity, particularly through its slogan "we are all queer," is a form of mirroring, where once fringe identities are now at the forefront of cultural discourse. However, when he compares the Vancouver Pride Parade to the state parades of communist Yugoslavia he used to attend as a child, observing similarities in tone and rhetoric, Žižek inadvertently engages in a kind of double mirroring through his own critique (2017, 190). This second layer of mirroring is not just about the queer community's cultural evolution but also reflects on the nature of critical discourse itself. Does the symbolic power Žižek attributes to queer communities through their public pride events truly signify a shift in power dynamics, or might it represent a paradoxical scenario where increased visibility and symbolic power of queer communities inadvertently leads to heightened resistance and backlash against them?

Žižek's critique, intriguing as it is, seems to overstate the symbolic power held by queer communities, potentially overlooking the underlying and often challenging realities of their lived experiences and oversimplifying the dynamics within social structures and the nuanced roles that queer communities play within them. Han's theorization of power suggests that genuine power arises when the oppressed align with the desires of the oppressor, indicating that what Žižek perceives as a power reversal could be an internalization of dominant narratives, not a true subversion of them (2019, 2). Such an interpretation implies that the perceived shift in power dynamics, as suggested by Žižek, might not be as straightforward as a transition from marginalization to dominance. Instead, it could represent a more subtle process whereby queer communities, in their quest for acceptance and visibility, may inadvertently adopt some aspects of the dominant cultural narratives. Such an adoption, while seemingly empowering, might not necessarily disrupt the existing power structures but rather might work within them. Furthermore, Žižek's comparison of Pride parades to state parades in communist Yugoslavia, though provocative, could be viewed as a reductive analogy that fails to capture the heterogeneity and historical significance of Pride events. While he points out similarities in the public display of unity and strength, this comparison neglects the grassroots origins of Pride as a movement that arose in response to oppression and marginalization, notwithstanding its recent commercialization. His interpretation fails to recognize that many Pride events originated from violent confrontations, as seen in Madrid, Sydney, and other cities during the late 1970s and 1980s (Tomsen & Markwell 2009; Esteban 2023, 87). Moreover, Pride events continue to encounter hostility in places like Moscow and Belgrade, indicating ongoing struggles for LGBT+ rights and visibility (Mršević 2013; Stella 2013). By equating these parades to state-imposed ideological assertions, his analogy suggests an ideological uniformity within these parades that overlooks their historical context and grassroots origins. Žižek's critique, therefore, seems to trivialize the ongoing adversities faced by queer communities, suggesting an erroneous correlation between visibility and actual social and political influence. Ultimately, Žižek's critique constructs an alternate reality, a double mirror effect, where the queer community's quest for equality is misconstrued as a strategic accumulation of power. This perspective glosses over the ongoing struggles of the queer community, raising critical questions about the nature and impact of such perceived power reversals.

Han's (2019) conceptualization of a "continuum of sense" takes on critical importance when examining Žižek's critique and its potential to misrepresent the queer experience. This concept suggests a shared cognitive framework that forms the foundation of our collective interpretation of reality, subtly shaping public consensus and simplifying our interactions with the world (Han 2019, 35–37). Drawing from Heidegger's philosophy, Han posits that this continuum usually orients individuals within a pre-interpreted world, thus reducing the necessity for constant reinterpretation of their surroundings. In a stable continuum of sense, public consensus on events, actions, and identities is relatively consistent, guiding individual interpretations and responses. However, in the so-called Mirror World, as exemplified by Žižek's analysis, this continuum is dramatically disrupted. Marginalized identities, once solely viewed through a lens of struggle and pursuit of equality, are now perceived as wielding substantial power and influence, leading to a collision of different and conflicting "horizons of sense." This leads to a distorted reflection of reality, where the perceived image is not a true representation, but a significantly refracted version of it. As a result, the "horizon of sense," which should underpin our understanding of social dynamics, becomes skewed, leading to significant ambiguity and misconceptions about the power dynamics involving marginalized communities (Han 2019, 36). Thus, the crisis experienced by the queer community is not fully recognized as a meaningful event (*Erfahrung*) but is refracted through the lens of superficial events (*Erlebnis*), contributing to the polarization and misinterpretation of their identities and struggles. Consequently, Lee Edelman's assertion that "queerness can never define an identity; it can only ever disturb one" (2004, 17) becomes less evident as movements that originally sought rights and recognition are now, ironically, seen as embodiments of power and privilege, the new so-called "elite."

The phenomenon of mirroring is not only applicable to queer identities. Almost all group identities in this contemporary era of crisis cultures perceive a form of mirroring at play against their identities. Howard Jacobson (2023) perceives a significant shift in how the world views the Jewish community, especially in the aftermath of the Hamas attacks on Israel on October 7, 2023. He argues that Jews are now being charged with the very crime—genocide— that was historically inflicted upon them. He contends that this mirroring effect not only distorts historical realities but also inverts the roles of victim and perpetrator, thereby leading to a misreading of the current geopolitical situation and a fundamental misunderstanding of Jewish history and suffering. The charge of genocide against Jews, in his view, is not only a historical inversion but also a moral one, where the victims of one of history's most egregious crimes are now being portrayed as perpetrators of a similar crime. Men's rights groups are another revealing example of the mirroring phenomenon in the context of gender dynamics. These groups can be seen as a mirrored response to feminism, not only in their existence but also in their approach and rhetoric, adopting a language of empowerment and rights advocacy similar to that of feminist movements. They invert feminist arguments, highlighting perceived male disadvantages in areas historically dominated by discussions on women's issues. Where discourse once primarily addressed women's challenges and inequalities, men's rights groups reflect this narrative back onto men's experiences, advocating for the acknowledgment of male-specific issues in a society increasingly attentive to female empowerment (Galla 2023).

The mirroring phenomenon extends beyond these examples to encompass a wide range of group identities. Another compelling example is seen within certain feminist factions, particularly TERFs (Trans-Exclusionary Radical Feminists), who, while advocating for safe spaces for cisgender women, mirror this need by marginalizing trans women (Pearce et al. 2020). This reflects a straightforward inversion where the advocacy for the safety and rights of one group inadvertently leads to the exclusion and alienation of another, thus replicating the very dynamics of exclusion they often stand against. Similarly, within migrant communities, there is an intriguing mirroring of mainstream political discourse. Some established immigrant groups perceive new migrants as threats, echoing sentiments that were possibly once directed toward them (Ang et al. 2022). This mirroring effect reveals how group identities can shift over time, from being marginalized to adopting views that align with mainstream narratives about immigration and integration. Additionally, the dynamic of mirroring is prominently observed in politics. Each political faction tends to reflect and counter the ideologies of its opponents, viewing themselves as the correctors of the others' excesses or failures. This mirroring extends beyond mere opposition to policies; it often involves adopting a mirrored version of their rivals' rhetoric and strategies, thereby reinforcing a cycle where each side sees itself as rectifying or resisting the perceived missteps or extremities of the other. These examples underline how the mirroring phenomenon is not just a simple reflection of views but often involves a process of inverting and reframing narratives to articulate ideological perspectives, sometimes leading to the replication of the very biases and exclusions they seek to overcome. The continuous cycle of mirrored discourses reinforces the argument that crisis today is a constitutive state defined by a lack of meaningful events, where the saturation of refracted and mirrored narratives obscures genuine understanding and resolution (*Erfahrung*).

Critics of identity politics, spanning the political spectrum from left to right, argue that the increasing emphasis on identity-based issues has, perhaps unintentionally, led to the neglect of a crucial segment of society: the working class (Michaels & Reed 2023). This perspective posits that the concentration on issues such as race, gender, and sexuality, while undoubtedly important, seems to have eclipsed the pressing concerns rooted in class inequalities and economic disenfranchisement. This situation has been compounded in recent times as the left has increasingly adopted discourses of "social mobility" and "meritocracy," originally rooted in conservative thought (Moreno-Caballud 2015, 71), thus further distancing from working-class concerns. The working-class demographic, with its distinctive set of struggles and perspectives, finds itself marginalized in these identity-focused debates, leading to a perception of neglect and invisibility. Such an oversight is perceived as a fundamental flaw within the identity politics framework. As a result, a narrative has emerged that frames the current backlash against identity politics as predominantly a response from the working class, a group voicing its frustration over being culturally, economically, and politically marginalized. Berardi (2019, 47) argues that the working class, historically a significant political force, now primarily comprises precarious laborers in temporary employment, unable to form a cohesive community or advocate for their collective interests, a condition exacerbated by persistent deterritorialization. The backlash against the so-called "elites" and their diverse identities seems to be the only form of power left to them (Terman 2020). As an individual who identifies as both working class and queer, this narrative presents a paradox only if one assumes that queerness intrinsically bestows privilege and an elite status. However, this viewpoint has always seemed incongruent to me, as my queer identity is inextricably linked to my working-class background. The rise of diagonal identities (Callison & Slobodian 2021), traversing these conventional binaries, further complicates such straightforward categorizations. It is critical, therefore, to acknowledge the overlapping and sometimes conflicting aspects of personal identity, which challenge the prevailing notion that one identity aspect must invariably overshadow or negate another.

The phenomenon of backlash in identity politics, as discussed by Terman (2020), reveals a complex relationship involving power, influence and perceived status loss among different social groups. This idea underscores how the endeavors of marginalized communities to secure rights and recognition can inadvertently provoke counterreactions, resulting in the rise of polarizing figures and movements. Philosophically, this concept aligns with the idea that every action may provoke an equal and opposite reaction; thus, the efforts of one group to achieve equality are potentially seen as instigating a backlash from another. This dynamic is evident in phenomena such as the ascendancy of Donald Trump and the divisiveness surrounding Brexit, often interpreted as responses to the perceived overreach of identity politics. Critics of identity politics have thus conferred an immense amount of power onto minority identities, effectively shifting the onus onto these groups to resolve social divisions. They contend that identity politics, originally stemming from the left's intentions to foster inclusivity and equality, has evolved into a divisive element, fragmenting society and hindering collective progress (Chua 2018; Mounk 2023). However, while some criticisms of identity politics may hold merit, the primary issue lies in the disproportionate power and responsibility ascribed to marginalized identities. This critique prompts the question of whether the efforts of marginalized groups for rights and recognition should be seen as the root of political division, or if such division is an existing condition accentuated by these tensions. For example, by framing the queer community's fight for equality as a shift toward elitism and a trigger for backlash, this argument might overlook systemic inequalities and biases that predate these movements. Consequently, this approach of critiquing marginalized responses, rather than addressing the root causes of inequality, not only distorts the narrative but also exacerbates the existing power disparities. It does so by assigning the onus of social division to the very groups fighting systemic injustices.

In concluding this examination of the mirror's role in identity politics, it is important to position the homosexual, the queer, and other similar identities as epitomes of mirrored identities. Historically, the concept of the homosexual underwent significant transformations, reflecting social attitudes and understandings. The term "invert," for instance, was once commonly used, suggesting a kind of photographic negative or mirror image of conventional sexual and gender norms (Reed 2001). This historical context underpins the argument that queer identities have often functioned as a mirror, reflecting, refracting, and sometimes distorting broader social and political narratives. Homonationalism, a term introduced by Jasbir Puar (2007), is a quintessential example of this mirroring process. It describes how LGBT+ identities are assimilated into nationalist frameworks, essentially mirroring and aligning with dominant ideologies that may contradict the original intents of queer liberation movements. The ensuing discussion of homonationalism thus serves as a critical next step in understanding the complexities and contradictions inherent in the mirrored world of identity politics, where identities are not only reflected but also refracted and reconstituted in ways that align with broader political agendas.

THE SHADOW IN THE MIRROR

In the last few decades, the advancement of queer rights has seen significant global progress, albeit with varying degrees of acceptance and legal recognition across different regions. In Western contexts, particularly in North America, Europe and Australia, there have been landmark legal achievements, most notably the widespread legalization of same-sex marriage (Angelo & Bocci 2021). These achievements reflect a concerted effort of activism and advocacy within LGBT+ communities and their supporters. In contrast, in many parts of Africa, Asia and the Middle East, queer individuals continue to face formidable challenges, including criminalization, social stigma and limited legal protections. Nonetheless, these regions have witnessed some signs of gradual change, such as the decriminalization of homosexuality in India in 2018, a historic verdict overturning a colonial-era law (Kidangoor 2018). Moreover, in Latin America, a region historically influenced by conservative cultural and religious values, significant strides have been made in countries such as Argentina, Mexico and Uruguay, which have shown progressive attitudes toward LGBT+ rights (Encarnación 2016).

On the surface, this overall progress may seem to align with what Dagmar Herzog describes as the "liberalization paradigm," a concept that envisions a steady progression toward sexual freedom (2009, 1295). Herzog, however, contests this interpretation of linear historical progress, describing, for example, the developments in Western Europe's acceptance of sexual difference as having a "syncopated quality" (2009, 1297). This argument emphasizes the erratic and fluctuating nature of sexual politics, marked by both forward movements and regressions, aligning with Christopher Chitty's observation in *Sexual Hegemony* (2020, 48) that the liberalization paradigm fails to account for the recurring revival of conservative attitudes. Chitty critically examines the argument that positions moral or religious ideologies as the primary drivers of sexual intolerance and oppression (Chitty 2020, 42). Instead, he presents a compelling argument for a correlation between periods of crisis and increased enforcement against homosexuality and other non-normative sexualities. He states, "The achievement of gay rights only appears as a dramatic reversal when homophobia is misconstrued as a perennial force of social exclusion" (2020, 37). Crucially, Chitty argues that sexual and gender norms are dynamic, evolving in response to various social, political, or economic crises. He suggests that such crises can either weaken, destabilize, or reinforce existing norms and perceptions regarding sexuality and gender (2020, 41). From this standpoint, it becomes clear that the progress of the LGBT+ movement is not a simple linear progression toward acceptance. Rather, these achievements are intimately connected to the broader oscillations of social and economic changes. The path toward equality and recognition for non-normative sexualities should therefore be understood as a complex, iterative process marked not by linearity but by ongoing negotiation, reevaluation, and the possibility of reversals.

Chitty's analysis extends to examining the evolution of LGBT+ rights within the framework of socioeconomic transformations that have unfolded since the 1970s. Key among these are the emergence of flexible employment practices, the decline in real wages, an increase in debt-driven consumerism, and the growth of asset bubbles (2020, 37–38). In affluent societies, these shifts have led to significant changes in the way social dynamics are organized and experienced. A pivotal outcome of these socioeconomic changes is the disintegration of traditional family structures. Economic challenges and changing employment patterns have redefined intimate relationships, thereby influencing social attitudes toward sexual diversity. Consequently, there has been a reduction in moral objections to sexual differences, culminating in a more inclusive environment. This evolution is reflected in the legal and social recognition, particularly in extending marriage and family rights to gay and lesbian couples in certain regions (Chitty 2020, 38). Further, Chitty notes a transformation in the perception of same-sex couples. Once marginalized, these couples are now increasingly perceived as models of neoliberal citizenship in high-income nations, characterized by consumerism, individualism, and economic behaviors aligned with neoliberal (and heteronormative) values (2020, 38). However, Chitty cautions against interpreting this transformation as universally applicable, or even positive. He emphasizes the varying experiences across different societies and stresses the influence of cultural, economic, and social factors on these transformations. Therefore, understanding these changes requires considering the intersection of economic factors and sexual identity politics. This argument underscores that these shifts are not merely cultural phenomena but are linked to wider socioeconomic trends (2020, 38). Looking ahead, Chitty speculates about the future role of sexual orientation in identity formation, particularly in high-income countries. He suggests that the significance of sexual orientation as a central aspect of identity might wane, evolving into a spectrum of consumer preferences influenced by various sociopolitical factors (2020, 234).

Yet, as Tavia Nyong'o (2017) observes: "The terrain of the political is far from one in which gay rights is settled common sense . . . we are not all of us folded into the nation just yet!" (2017, xiv). This statement points to the ongoing struggle for inclusion and recognition of some LGBT+ individuals within national narratives, despite legal and social advancements in certain areas. In this context, Jasbir K. Puar's *Terrorist Assemblages: Homonationalism in Queer Times* (2007), offers an essential framework for understanding the dichotomous nature of assimilation and marginalization of queer identities. Puar introduces the term "homonationalism" to interrogate how the

Queering Crisis 167

acceptance and tolerance of gay and lesbian individuals are often utilized to reinforce a nation's legitimacy (2007, 227). As Puar notes:

> as the [. . .] nation-state produces narratives of exception through the war on terror, it must temporarily suspend its heteronormative imagined community to consolidate national sentiment and consensus through the recognition and incorporation of some, though not all or most, homosexual subjects. (2007, 3)

This observation marks a significant shift from the historical association of queer identities with death, particularly during the AIDS epidemic, to their current association with life and productivity, as evidenced by developments such as the legalization of same-sex marriage and the recognition of queer families (2007, xx). However, Puar emphasizes that this transition is selective, reflecting complex political negotiations around queer lives, and she critiques the conditional inclusion of certain queer identities within these national frameworks, which often depends on the exclusion of other racial and sexual groups, such as Muslims. Within this dynamic, queerness serves a dual purpose: it is both a tool for creating disciplined subjects and a means of controlling and identifying specific populations, notably in the context of anti-terrorism efforts. This tool creates a dichotomy between "civilization" and "barbarism" and is used to marginalize the Muslim population, contrasting "acceptable" homosexuals with Muslims, and accentuating racial and cultural divisions. Her critique underscores that this binary framework often neglects important socioeconomic factors, such as class and immigration status. Consequently, both conservative and liberal movements have strategically employed Islamophobic sentiments to enhance the visibility of gay and lesbian individuals in various national contexts (2007, 4). This approach integrates LGBT+ rights into broader political and cultural narratives, often portraying these rights as opposed to Islamic cultures, which are framed as inherently oppressive. The phenomenon of gay tourism accentuates this dichotomy, where destinations marketing themselves as LGBT+ friendly are often perceived as more progressive and open (Puar 2007, xxii). Puar thus challenges the common perception that homosexual subjects are inherently excluded from heterosexual nationalist formations. She asserts that in a state of exception, what is exceptional becomes normalized, losing its distinctiveness as it is incorporated into the standard regulatory framework (2007, 9). Homonationalism thus demonstrates how many Western nation-states embrace aspects of queer culture to project an image of liberalism and modernity while sidelining those who do not align with these prescribed standards. This concept thus evokes a poignant parallel to the conditional inclusion I experienced under the guise of philoxenia during my childhood. As a member of the LGBT+ community, I occupy a distinctive and somewhat paradoxical role, benefiting from a system that resembles the very one that previously imposed barriers to my acceptance.

The concept of homonationalism, originally contextualized during the War on Terror, has since found relevance in various political environments, notably during the Trump administration in the United States. In the postscript of the second edition of her book, released a decade after its initial publication, Puar offers an incisive analysis of a 2017 LGBT+ rally at Stonewall Inn. She notes that this rally, ostensibly supporting LGBT+ rights, primarily attracted a white audience and failed to address critical issues of white supremacy and the Trump administration's travel ban affecting predominantly Muslim nations (2017, 223–224). This omission, according to Puar, inadvertently mirrored Trump's rhetoric following the Orlando massacre in June 2016, when a gunman killed forty-nine people at the Pulse nightclub, a venue popular with the largely Latinx local LGBT+ community. In the wake of this tragedy, Trump cast the LGBT+ communities as victims needing protection from Muslim groups, crafting a narrative that interlinked terrorism, sexuality, and race. This situation underlines the precarious and fluctuating nature of homonationalism under Trump's regime, which demonstrated a dualistic approach to LGBT+ rights: promoting them as indicators of social advancement in global governance on one hand, while simultaneously hinting at the revocation of these rights—such as marriage equality—domestically, on the other. However, the relevance of homonationalism is not limited to populist regimes alone. The Obama administration also propagated paradoxical political rhetoric, marked by the advancement of progressive LGBT+ policies domestically amid escalating military actions in the Middle East and tying international aid to homonationalist benchmarks (Puar 2017, 225). This contrast reveals the sophisticated integration of homonationalism in U.S. political strategies, emphasizing how LGBT+ rights are intimately aligned with broader geopolitical objectives and strategies.

While there might be differing views on Puar's advocacy for a more inclusive coalition of progressive causes, the prominence and undeniable relevance of homonationalism within crisis cultures is unmistakably evident. Representing a pivotal historical transition, homonationalism marks a key evolution in the interpretation and application of liberalism, becoming central to contemporary discussions on identity and nationalism (2017, 230–231). In her analysis, Puar thus dubs the contemporary period as the homonational era, an era distinguished by confining individuals to specific sexual identity categories and employing a rigid form of liberalism to categorize and differentiate the Other (Puar 2017, 230). This period signifies a significant shift from a previous focus on heteronormativity to gradually embracing and normalizing homosexual identities, a process Puar describes as the assimilation of homonormativity (2017, 231). In this context, homonormativity refers to the process by which homosexual identities are progressively integrated into the mainstream, aligning with a liberal framework that simultaneously supports and delimits these identities within certain acceptable boundaries. Homonationalism thus enables nation-states to leverage sexual identity as a tool for biopolitical control, forming persuasive national narratives around freedom and rights. In this context, the legalization of same-sex marriage and the enhanced visibility of LGBT+ individuals in media and politics are not simply indicators of progress. Rather, they function as instruments through which nation-states negotiate and reshape their identities. For many in the LGBT+ community, embracing homonationalist discourse offers a reprieve from the long-standing polarization and debates over their identities. This alignment with homonationalism grants a sense of inclusion and recognition within the national narrative. However, it also requires an acceptance of participating in a system that racializes others, remaining confined within a framework that continues to define and negotiate the boundaries of acceptable sexual identity norms.

In Western Europe, particularly France and the Netherlands, right-wing parties have increasingly adopted homonationalist discourse. In the Netherlands, Pim Fortuyn's political legacy is a prime example, as he used LGBT+ rights to contrast Dutch liberal values with what he perceived as the less liberal values associated with Islam (Puar 2007, 19–20). Similarly, in France, the National Rally, previously known as the National Front, incorporates LGBT+ rights into its narrative, framing these rights as a hallmark of French secular liberalism and in opposition to what they deem the illiberal values of Islamic culture (Möser & Reimers 2022). While in Western Europe, as seen in France and the Netherlands, homonationalism is often used to assert a national identity in opposition to Islam, Eastern European discourse around LGBT+ rights, as evidenced in Poland and Hungary, tends to focus more on resisting Western cultural norms and protecting traditional values. In Poland, there has been a notable resistance to LGBT+ rights, with the Law and Justice party often framing these rights as a threat to traditional Polish values and a form of Western cultural imperialism (Cornejo-Valle & Ramme 2022). In Hungary, under the leadership of Viktor Orbán, LGBT+ rights have similarly become a site of contention, with the government promoting traditional family models and opposing what they view as Western liberal encroachments, including LGBT+ advocacy (Kalmar 2022). Hence, while Western European examples like France and the Netherlands demonstrate homonationalist tendencies, in the Eastern European context the focus is on protecting traditional values and national identity against perceived liberal and foreign influences, including those related to LGBT+ rights. This divergence in approaches underlines how the application and interpretation of homonationalism are deeply influenced by the unique historical, cultural, and political circumstances of individual nations.

How does homonationalism, then, shape the contours of crisis cultures and its encompassing digital crisis ambientality? Homonationalism, originally a mechanism for Western nation-states to establish civilizational distinctions against Muslim-majority countries, is now revealing deep-seated internal contradictions. The subsequent analysis in this chapter examines these inherent contradictions, particularly how they manifest as a discursive shift away from previously conditional acceptance of *some* queer subjects to an even more tenuous attitude toward *all* queer subjects under the influence of rising populist right parties. This "turn away" from a more comprehensive embrace of queer identities does not signify a total abandonment of homonationalism; rather, it underscores the deepening contradictions borne from the dynamics of digital crisis ambientality. Within this framework, the "shadow in the mirror" metaphor emerges as a poignant illustration. This metaphorical shadow, elusive yet persistent, symbolizes the perpetual challenge of reconciling national identity with evolving queer narratives within the context of crisis cultures.

THE QUEER POLITICS OF POLARIZATION IN CONTEMPORARY SPAIN

Spain is widely recognized as one of the most LGBT+ friendly countries in the world, boasting a rich history of LGBT+ rights activism. In 2005, Spain's progressive position on LGBT+ issues was further solidified when it became the third nation-state in the world to legalize same-sex marriage, succeeding the Netherlands and Belgium. A pivotal moment in Spain's LGBT+ rights history occurred in February 2023, when the left-wing coalition government enacted what became known as *La Ley Trans* (the Trans Law). This groundbreaking legislation bolsters rights for LGBT+ individuals, notably by allowing gender recognition based on self-identification and dispensing with the requirement for a medical diagnosis or treatment. The law is multifaceted, encompassing various areas including assisted reproduction, sexuality education, rights of intersex children, parental recognition for unmarried same-sex couples, and an extension of anti-discrimination measures (González Cabrera 2023). Madrid Pride, also known as Orgullo Madrid or MADO, stands out as one of the largest global Pride celebrations, drawing hundreds of thousands of visitors each year. According to a report by the UCLA Williams Institute, Spain holds the sixth position worldwide in social acceptance of LGBT+ people, only surpassed by nations such as Iceland, the Netherlands, Norway, Sweden, and Canada (Flores 2021, 34). For a nation-state that transitioned from nearly four decades of an ultra-Catholic military dictatorship in 1975, this dramatic shift, almost utopian in its nature, underscores a profound transformation in social attitudes toward LGBT+ rights and identities.

Yet, Spain's path toward embracing LGBT+ rights has been complex. Under the Franco regime (1936–1975), Spanish nationalism closely aligned with the Catholic Church, creating a highly repressive environment for LGBT+ individuals. During Franco's rule, any deviation from heteronormativity faced severe consequences, including persecution and execution (Pichardo Galán et al. 2009, 273). The regime's policies and rhetoric not only stigmatized homosexuality but also promoted the dominance of heterosexual marriage, reinforcing a cultural norm of heterosexual hegemony (Calvo & Trujillo 2011, 229). This era represented a significant regression from the more progressive laws and attitudes of the Second Republic (1931–1939), which had decriminalized homosexual acts except in military contexts with the repeal of Article 616 in 1931 (Esteban 2023, 40). The transition to Franco's regime marked a stark shift from these earlier, relatively more tolerant attitudes. Chitty (2020, 41) theorizes that the acceptance of homosexuality fluctuates with social, economic, and political crises, a pattern clearly evident during the Franco era. Following the Spanish Civil War, Spain experienced an economic crisis, leading to intensified repression against LGBT+ rights. This period of heightened oppression demonstrated a severe regression in attitudes toward sexual minorities, fostering a climate of fear and discrimination. A notable example of this repression was the 1954 re-enactment of laws criminalizing homosexuality, which resulted in harsh punitive measures, including the imprisonment of men in facilities derogatorily called "*galerías de invertidos*" (galleries for the deviant) (Martinez & Dodge 2010, 229). Legal judgments during the Franco regime were heavily influenced by religious dogma and lacked an empirical basis (Calvo & Trujillo 2011, 229). Franco's policies were not just suppressive; they deeply embedded homophobia and heteronormativity in Spanish society. The regime's oppressive policies engendered an atmosphere of fear and stigma surrounding homosexuality, effectively quelling public discourse and activism related to LGBT+ rights.

In the period following Franco's dictatorship, Spain experienced a rapid liberalization toward non-heteronormative relationships, a process closely linked with its economic growth and integration into the European Union. The burgeoning economic prosperity paralleled a broader evolution toward more liberal views on same-sex relationships (Calvo & Trujillo 2011, 563). Similar to trends in other Western nations, the advancement of LGBT+ rights in Spain has been predominantly aligned with left-of-center politics (Esteban 2023, 37). Significant milestones, such as the legalization of same-sex marriage and the Trans Law, were primarily championed by the Spanish Socialist Workers' Party (PSOE), often in collaboration with Unidas Podemos, a coalition formed from the 15-M Movement (*los indignados*) in 2014. This era of liberalization, particularly under José Luis Rodríguez Zapatero's government (2004–2011), marked substantial progress in acknowledging and addressing discrimination based on sexual orientation and gender identity. Key achievements included the Historical Memory Law of 2007, which offered redress to LGBT+ individuals affected by state policies, and the enactment of same-sex marriage legislation in 2005 (Esteban 2023, 47). However, despite these legislative successes, challenges to complete acceptance and equality for LGBT+ individuals persist. Data indicates that 54.4% of LGBT+ adults in Spain have faced harassment, with younger and transgender individuals being particularly affected (Devís-Devís et al. 2022, 11).

Spain's advancement in LGBT+ rights, though substantial, faced resistance, notably from the Roman Catholic Church, which staunchly opposed any departure from traditional family structures (Esteban 2023, 71–79). Historically, the conservative center-right Popular Party (PP) has been a traditional opponent of initiatives like same-sex marriage, advocating for the preservation of conventional marriage norms. This position led to legal challenges in Spain's Constitutional Court against same-sex marriage, arguing that it altered the fundamental nature of marriage (Lister & de Moura 2015). Former Prime Minister Mariano Rajoy, from the PP, preferred civil unions over same-sex marriage, deeming the latter offensive to Catholics (Lister & de Moura 2015). However, in the early 2000s, the PP began publicly portraying itself as a supporter of LGBT+ rights, despite often maintaining an ambiguous position on specific legislation and rights (Esteban 2023, 18–19). Nacho Esteban's detailed examination of the PP's historical track record on LGBT+ issues suggests that the party's shift has been limited, with few legal advances favoring LGBT+ rights under its leadership. Nonetheless, the Spanish Constitutional Court's 2012 decision to uphold the legality of same-sex marriage was recognized by Rajoy, ending the party's legal opposition to it (Guzmán 2012). Santiago Cervera, a PP member, acknowledged on a radio program that "gay marriage no longer shocks anyone in this country," reflecting a growing societal acceptance of homosexual unions (Guzmán 2012). Additionally, Rajoy's attendance at PP senator Javier Maroto's same-sex wedding in 2015 marked a significant shift in the party's discourse on LGBT+ issues (Lister & de Moura 2015). This change in the PP's approach was indicative of an adaptation to both the global homonationalist trend and the changing sociocultural dynamics in Spain, where queer identities are increasingly normalized, as seen in popular culture through the works of filmmakers like Pedro Almodóvar. Jasbir Puar's (2007) argument about the integration of homosexual subjects into nationalist narratives aligns with these shifts. Consequently, Spain's major political parties, including the PP, have increasingly adopted a more supportive and accepting language toward

LGBT+ communities, despite occasional homophobic remarks from some party members. This evolution, particularly for the PP, is notable as the party had, until recently, been averse to such measures. However, the PP's gradual shift toward a more liberal discourse on LGBT+ issues may not necessarily reflect a fundamental change in the party's core beliefs or policies regarding LGBT+ rights but rather a strategic response to the changing homonationalist terrain.

In the 2010s, leading up to around 2018 before the rise of the far right on the political scene, Spanish nationalist discourse aimed to capitalize on its progressive reputation, even if it did not explicitly mirror the stark terms of homonationalism as outlined by Puar. The transition from the ultra-conservative, Catholic-dominated society of the Franco regime to a liberal democracy paved the way for this evolution. Tavia Nyong'o's notion of "settled common sense" (2017, p. xiv) aptly characterizes Spain's advancement toward LGBT+ rights during this period, culminating in a bipartisan consensus that transcended political ideologies, despite residual resistance from traditional Catholic values. However, this shift toward inclusivity and liberalization occurred against the backdrop of Spain's complicated political landscape, marked by regional nationalism and internal conflicts, such as the quest for Catalan independence and the Basque Country's distinct identity and history of seeking autonomy. These regional aspirations for autonomy, alongside historical legacies of division, significantly influenced Spain's national discourse and policymaking, often intersecting with and complicating the nation's approach to LGBT+ rights and broader social issues. Notably, the pervasive anti-Islamic sentiment that emerged globally post-9/11 found comparatively less resonance in Spain, despite the Islamic terrorist attacks in Madrid on March 11, 2004, and Barcelona in 2017. This contrasts sharply with many other European nations, such as Poland, where anti-Islamic narratives gained substantial momentum (Möser & Ramme 2022). Spain's relative inattention to external threats allowed its political discourse to focus more intensively on internal matters, including debates on regional autonomy and national identity. This inward orientation prevented sexuality from becoming a prominent divisive issue, thereby distinguishing Spain's experience of homonationalism from that of most other European and Western nations.

The incorporation of LGBT+ rights into the European narrative, as Puar (2017, 20) observes, often resonates more with projecting European values than with a profound commitment to these rights. Significant milestones such as the legalization of same-sex marriage are frequently viewed not so much as authentic emancipation but rather as alignment with the prevailing image of European modernity. This alignment has elicited criticism from some queer activists, who argue that the campaign for same-sex marriage represents a deviation from the original objectives of the gay liberation movement. These activists contend that the pursuit of marriage equality symbolizes assimilation into heteronormative systems, diverging from the movement's initial goal of challenging and redefining conventional relationship norms (Schulman 2012; Conrad 2014; Nair 2023). Or, as Guy Hocquenghem (1993) might have critically observed, achievements such as same-sex marriage could represent the assimilation and domestication of homosexual identity within capitalist structures. Puar's concept of "upright homosexuals" thus comes into play, referring to those who adhere to "sanctioned kinship norms" and embody an LGBT+ identity congruent with the wider European modernity context (2017, 20). This paradox, wherein the progression of certain LGBT+ rights inadvertently reinforces nationalist and conservative structures historically opposed to these rights, illustrates how LGBT+ identities can be instrumentalized within political narratives, diverging from the original aims of LGBT+ rights activism. Consequently, the assumption that LGBT+ individuals predominantly align with leftist ideologies is increasingly being contested. In fact, a notable proportion of queer individuals, including those in Spain, either affiliate with or actively support right-wing and nationalist ideologies (Puar 2017, 4). A 2021 poll revealed that 16.5% of non-heterosexual voters in Spain supported a right-wing party (Esteban 2023, 37). This statistic reveals a significant shift in the traditional political affiliations of the LGBT+ community, unveiling a multifaceted political terrain where LGBT+ identities intersect with a spectrum of political ideologies, including those historically unsympathetic to LGBT+ interests. Such a shift indicates that for some, advocating for LGBT+ rights is not inherently antithetical to conservative values but can be integrated within these ideological frameworks. Milestones such as the legalization of same-sex marriage therefore become symbolic not only of liberation but also of adherence to a specific model of Western modernity.

Spain's distinct brand of homonationalism, particularly during the 2010s when the Popular Party (PP) accepted same-sex marriage, demonstrates how LGBT+ rights became intertwined with a broader vision of progress, albeit within a specific and limited consensus. However, this brief consensus was quickly disrupted due to two key factors: the rise of the populist right-wing party Vox, which shifted the narrative from celebrating Spain's progressive stance on LGBT+ rights to promoting a more conservative agenda, and the impact of crisis ambientality, magnified through digital platforms. Until 2017, Spain was regarded as a notable exception in Europe for its resistance to right-wing populism. This resistance was often attributed to the country's relatively weak national identity and the enduring legacy of the Franco regime (González-Enríquez 2017, 3). Both Spain and Portugal, with their histories of military dictatorships, appeared resilient to the allure of right-wing populism, including its xenophobic and anti-globalization tendencies. González-Enríquez even doubted the likelihood of such movements ever gaining substantial traction in Spain (2017, 37). This perception shifted dramatically with Vox's success in the 2018 regional Andalusian elections, where it secured twelve seats and later joined a coalition with center-right parties. By 2019, Vox had established itself as a major political force, securing 15.1% of the national vote and becoming Spain's third-largest political party. Alonso and Rovira Kaltwasser had previously noted the Great Recession's role in creating a conducive environment for a radical right party to emerge, positioning itself as a defender of "the people's" interests (2015, 39). Spanish politics, intertwined with nationalism, territorial integrity, traditional values, and economic challenges, provided fertile ground for Vox's ascendance.

The rise of Vox marks a significant shift in the Spanish political landscape. Initially, Vox echoed the anti-immigration and anti-European Union sentiments common to other European far-right parties, but it distinctively focused on Spanish-centric issues, like resisting regional nationalism in Catalonia and the Basque Country. Their emphasis on national unity and sovereignty, particularly amid concerns about Spain's potential "balkanization," resonated strongly in the post-2017 political environment (Arroyo 2019). The turmoil following Catalonia's 2017 independence referendum presented Vox with an opportunity to broaden its appeal by integrating law and order themes and critiques of gender violence legislation into its agenda (Pardo 2019). Under Santiago Abascal's leadership, Vox's influence grew, leveraging the global surge in right-wing populism and strategic digital campaigning. Depicting itself as a bastion of traditional values amid rapid social changes, Vox reflects the wider disarray in Spanish politics characterized by economic, political, and social crises. The party effectively uses both traditional and digital media to amplify the ideological divide, framing it as a critical crisis of values, paralleling global populist trends with slogans like "make Spain great again" (Pardo 2019). The ideological pivot represented by Vox underscores a broader shift in Spanish society, where nationalist and conservative sentiments have gained traction against a backdrop of economic instability. Vox's rhetoric, focusing on themes such as national identity, sovereignty, and traditional values, has found a receptive audience among those disillusioned with the status quo and concerned about the perceived erosion of Spanish cultural and national identity. Furthermore, Vox's rise has influenced other political parties in Spain, pushing them to adopt more conservative positions on certain issues to retain their voter base. This shift has had a ripple effect on the broader political spectrum, altering the nature of policy debates and legislative priorities. As a result, the conversation around LGBT+ rights, regional autonomy, and national identity has become increasingly charged, reflecting the deeper societal divisions that Vox has both exploited and exacerbated.

Vox's strategy not only mirrors and amplifies certain aspects of the PP's conservative ideology, particularly in reshaping the discourse on LGBT+

rights, but it also marks a clear deviation from Spain's previously more progressive trajectory in these areas. The party's position on traditional family values, evident in its resistance to gender quotas and advocacy for the "natural family" and the "parental PIN"—which is intended to control the content of school programs to counteract what they view as ideological indoctrination and erosion of traditional family values—marks a notable ideological departure in Spanish political discourse (Esteban 2023, 109). Being the sole party committed to repealing LGBT+ laws, gender violence laws, and the Historical Memory Law—a law intended to acknowledge and give reparations for the injustices of the Franco dictatorship—Vox's platform sharply contrasts the prior, albeit limited, bipartisan consensus on LGBT+ rights (Esteban 2023, 107). This development has heightened debates and made events like Madrid Pride a point of contention, with Vox criticizing them as ideological impositions on mainstream society (Esteban 2023, 116). Nonetheless, this shift does not represent a complete transformation of Spain's political landscape. The continued influence of left-leaning parties, which advocate for LGBT+ rights and progressive gender violence legislation, highlights a dynamic yet increasingly polarized political environment.

Homonationalism, once interpreted as the assimilation of LGBT+ rights into nationalist frameworks to delineate "liberal" societies from "illiberal" ones, usually against Islamic cultures, is now confronted with a significant ideological shift. Countries previously celebrated for their progressive approach to LGBT+ rights, such as Spain, are experiencing a subtle yet profound deviation from this established pattern. The rise of Vox, a party that utilizes homonationalist rhetoric while endorsing conservative nationalist policies, has been instrumental in this transformation. This emergence has prompted a transition from the previously conditional acceptance of *some* queer subjects to an increasingly tenuous attitude toward *all* queer subjects. This situation has led to the propagation of what I identify as "tautological narratives." These narratives represent a discursive technique where a position is simultaneously affirmed and negated, creating self-validating loops. This rhetorical strategy is designed to mask the genuine ideological foundations of political parties. In the context of Spain, both Vox and the PP adeptly utilize these narratives. They publicly advocate for LGBT+ rights, projecting an image of inclusivity, yet their actions often undermine these very rights. Such narratives are not merely rhetorical flourishes but serve a strategic purpose. By simultaneously embracing and retracting support for LGBT+ rights, Vox and the PP manage to appeal to a broader electorate, ranging from progressive liberals to conservative nationalists. This duality allows them to navigate the politically charged terrain of LGBT+ rights without committing fully to either advocacy or opposition. Hence, tautological narratives in Spain's political discourse serve as a tool for maintaining political ambiguity, ensuring electoral viability while avoiding ideological clarity. Ultimately, this shift points to the fragility of the progress made in LGBT+ rights and the ease with which it can be co-opted by conservative nationalist agendas. It challenges the notion of linear progress in social rights, revealing the contradictions inherent in contemporary political strategies.

In the case of Vox, the party frequently champions LGBT+ rights when it strategically seeks to redirect its antagonism toward other perceived threats, notably immigrants and Muslims (Esteban 2023, 108). In the tradition of classical homonationalist rhetoric Abascal in a promotional video stated: *"No queremos que desde la Giralda se arroje a los homosexuals o se les ahorque"* (We do not want homosexuals to be thrown from the Giralda or hanged); and a year later, he denounced the Daesh attack against a gay nightclub in Orlando, resulting in forty-nine deaths (Esteban 2023, 108). Additionally, he criticized Socialist Prime Minister Pedro Sánchez for the left's historical antagonism toward homosexuals (Esteban 2023, 108). This maneuvering illustrates a tautological approach, where the party's public endorsements of LGBT+ rights are juxtaposed with actions or statements that undermine these rights, revealing the duplicitous nature of their political strategy. Abascal's public statements, which oscillate between condemning violence against homosexuals and delineating "acceptable" LGBT+ individuals from those he categorizes as part of the "gay lobby," exemplify this tautological narrative. Such rhetoric serves to align with Vox's nationalistic and anti-immigrant agenda while simultaneously marginalizing parts of the LGBT+ community that do not align with these objectives (Esteban 2023, 108). This rhetoric is not merely opposing LGBT+ rights; it is a complex construction of a narrative that vacillates between support and opposition based on the party's broader political agenda. Furthermore, Abascal's expression of solidarity with the leaders of Hungary and Poland against the "progressive dictatorship" of Brussels underscores the transnational nature of this homonationalist narrative, aligning with a broader European populist right pattern of using LGBT+ rights as a rhetorical tool while implementing policies that fundamentally oppose those rights (Esteban 2023, 110).

As Esteban (2023, 262) notes, the right-wing in Spain has presented a façade of accepting and promoting LGBT+ rights while concurrently obstructing meaningful measures for the LGBT+ community. This duplicity illustrates a double mirroring effect: Vox not only revisits more regressive elements from Spain's political past but also finds its stringent discourse on LGBT+ rights reflected and perpetuated by the PP. Notably, Isabel Díaz Ayuso, a key figure in the PP and President of the Autonomous Community of Madrid, embodies this shift. Her administration's recent modifications to LGBT+ and trans laws in Madrid, originally implemented by the PP, mark a subtle yet substantial shift in the party's policy. These reforms, ostensibly designed to circumvent direct accusations of eroding rights, have effectively dismantled crucial protections and educational content related to gender identity and non-discrimination (Puentes 2023). Ayuso's public remarks have also reflected this shift. In a 2022 interview, she criticized Madrid's Pride festivities as "a lever to promote hatred against others," a "media hijacking" that "causes tremendous damage" and forces one to "endure it for a month," which, in a manner akin to Žižek's critique, leaves a bitter taste in her mouth (Esteban 2023, 236). Furthermore, José Luis Martínez-Almeida, the mayor of Madrid, exhibits more rigid conservatism than earlier PP mayors, evidenced by his collaboration with Vox in curtailing support for LGBT+ organizations. Alberto Núñez Feijóo, the PP's current leader, also contributes to this trend by proposing to repeal the Trans Law, trivializing the process as "easier than obtaining a driver's license" (Anarte 2023). Amid this background, the PP maintains a narrative of supporting LGBT+ rights, accentuated by references to its *"Nuevas Gayneraciones"* (New Gaynerations) and assertions of being a defender of these rights (Esteban 2023, 18, 254). This narrative strategy creates an environment of uncertainty and ambiguity, allowing for varying degrees of conservatism within the party, from Ayuso's rhetoric to Feijóo's attacks on the Trans Law. Hence, the PP's approach of rolling back some rights, refusing to fly the rainbow flag during Madrid Pride, while extolling its historical support for LGBT+ communities (Esteban 2023, 118), mirrors Vox's tautological narratives, characterized by simultaneous advocacy and opposition to LGBT+ rights. Thus, this development underlines the growing influence of the populist right in reshaping Spain's political landscape, posing a challenge to the established norms and consensus that have characterized the nation's post-dictatorial democratic era, particularly regarding LGBT+ rights.

The recent inclination of center-right parties, like the PP in Spain, toward anti-woke rhetoric and explicit criticism of what they deem gender ideology, mirrors a wider transnational trend indicative of a global conservative political realignment (Esteban 2023, 108). This trend is amplified by digital technologies that enable the swift propagation of such narratives beyond national boundaries, contributing to what may be described as an "imagined community" of digitally mediated populism (Anderson 1991). This digital environment serves as a conduit for conservative ideologies, which pose challenges to earlier progress in sexual and gender rights. This phenomenon reaffirms that the advancement of LGBT+ rights is not a straightforward journey but follows an iterative and syncopated pattern. It is not a linear progression but rather a trajectory marked by advancements, setbacks, and constant fluctuations (Herzog 2009, 1297). Consequently, in such polarized political environments, the LGBT+ community is compelled to navigate a precarious terrain characterized by tautological narratives.

These narratives construct a complex matrix where LGBT+ identities are ostensibly embraced as part of a nation's progressive image, yet simultaneously, they are politicized and exploited for broader, often contradictory, political ends. This dynamic underscores the fluid nature of homonationalism, illustrating how the inclusion of LGBT+ communities is subject to the caprices of political discourse and alliances. Such a situation demonstrates the precariousness of LGBT+ rights within crisis cultures, where they are often instrumentalized for varying political agendas, highlighting the need for a more steadfast and consistent approach to LGBT+ advocacy and policymaking.

Unsurprisingly, some within the LGBT+ community view assimilation into the nationalist narrative as a strategic move to mitigate the direct effects of these tautological narratives. Yet, this assimilation often demands a compromise, necessitating alignment with specific political agendas that might not fully represent their values or interests. Conversely, for those unable or unwilling to conform to these homonationalist frameworks, the response is distinctively different. They embrace their queer identity as a "second skin," a necessity for navigating a society in which their very existence becomes a focal point of contention. Serving as both a shield and a statement, this identity becomes a means of self-preservation and community solidarity in the face of external pressures and public debate. However, this situation presents its own tautological challenge: in defending their identity, LGBT+ individuals and communities might inadvertently reinforce the "us-versus-them" dichotomy that populist movements exploit. The act of asserting one's identity, which is ostensibly linked to the fight for recognition and rights, can inadvertently feed into the cycle of polarization that they strive to dismantle. This polarization, fueled by the very tautological narratives that seek to co-opt or marginalize LGBT+ identities, creates a self-reinforcing cycle where the defense against external threats inadvertently contributes to deeper social divisions. Therefore, the LGBT+ community's navigation of these tautological narratives in Spain—and in other national contexts—represents not just a political challenge but a philosophical and existential struggle. It entails a continual balancing act between asserting one's identity and not allowing that identity to be weaponized in the broader political game. For the LGBT+ community, this necessitates an ongoing reinterpretation of identity within political discourse. Reflecting on the underlying dilemma that LGBT+ communities face, the queer Spanish poet Luis Antonio de Villena wrote: "*Entre la pedrada y el gueto, me quedo con el gueto*" (Between the stone-throwing and the ghetto, I choose the ghetto) (quoted in Shangay Lily 2016, 13). Do we choose the raw truth of the ghetto, or the conditional acceptance of the stone-throwers? Must we choose at all?

CONCLUSION

In the case of contemporary Spain, crisis serves as a constitutive state defined by a lack of meaningful, transformative experiences (*Erfahrung*), which intensifies underlying tensions across various dimensions—emotional, narrative, and temporal. Without such experiences to solidify collective memory and identity, society remains incapable of consolidating progress or transcending cycles of tension and resolution. Emotionally, the polarization surrounding LGBT+ rights highlights a persistent tension between hope and apprehension. While progressive laws such as the legalization of same-sex marriage and the Trans Law represent significant advances, the rise of Vox and their conservative agenda fuels apprehension, creating an environment of uncertainty and fear among the LGBT+ community. Narratively, Spain's journey oscillates between utopian aspirations and dystopian realities. The initial liberalization and advancements in LGBT+ rights can be seen as a utopian moment, but the subsequent backlash and the propagation of tautological narratives by Vox and the PP represent a dystopian counternarrative, undermining these achievements. Temporally, the crisis in Spain disrupts the linear progression of social rights, intertwining history and futurity. The legacy of the Franco regime's repression resurfaces in contemporary political discourse, as conservative forces attempt to roll back progressive gains, demonstrating how historical injustices continue to influence present struggles and future aspirations. This cyclical pattern of tension and resolution reflects a broader crisis culture, where the lack of definitive, meaningful events leads to the perpetual intensification of these underlying tensions.

The polarization emerging from the defense of LGBT+ identities that I laid out above is indeed likely to embolden critics of identity politics. Notably, many of these critics are queer themselves, and they might interpret this feedback loop—a cycle where defending marginalized identities leads to further social division—as evidence supporting their skepticism. They might assert, with perceived vindication: "See? This is why identity politics does not work." This critique is rooted in the belief that focusing on group identities exacerbates social fractures rather than heals them (Pluckrose & Lindsay 2020; Doyle 2022). However, this perspective fails to consider a critical aspect: the psychological imperative for individuals, particularly for many of those from marginalized communities, to uphold their group identity. While it is true that we should not necessarily grant a privileged epistemic status to everyone's lived experience (Casey 2023, 283), there is a need for a remapping to reconcile the tension between valuing individual lived experiences and broader, more universal truths. The suggestion to abandon identity politics naively presumes that individual rights can be protected independently of the social and cultural contexts that define and often limit these rights. For the LGBT+ community, and indeed any identitarian group, disregarding the importance of collective struggle and solidarity is a fundamental misjudgment. Consequently, the psychological bond to one's group identity acts as both a defense mechanism and a means of affirming their existence in a society where acceptance is not a given but often contingent. While queer lives are entangled in webs of tautology, this entanglement is likely to lead to a preference for the ghetto over the stone-throwing. This is not about fostering grievance but rather an understandable retreat into safety. The phenomenon of attributing power to the marginalized group identity and labeling it as the new elite is thus a rhetorical strategy used to dismiss these underlying realities. This mirroring phenomenon, which casts marginalized groups as the new powerholders, is employed to undermine the legitimacy of their struggle, ignoring the complex dynamics of power and identity that shape their lived experiences.

Is the necessity to uphold group identity indeed the logical conclusion of living in crisis cultures? This question arises from the ways in which the deployment of tautological narratives exceeds the homonationalist frame. That is, these narratives replicate and surpass the homonationalist framework, leading to a paradox where non-queer political actors redefine queer identities, effectively *out-queering* the queer community themselves. Although this phenomenon is not entirely new, as arguably this has historically often been the case, what distinguishes the current era is the intensification of this dynamic within crisis cultures. These crisis cultures amplify and accelerate the co-optation and manipulation of queer identities by those wielding broader social, cultural, and political influence. This strategic co-optation, reflecting the *Erlebnis*-saturated environment of contemporary crisis cultures, transforms queer identity into something transient and superficial. In an *Erlebnis*-dominated world, the rapid and often sensationalized repurposing of queer narratives aligns with the ephemeral and immediate nature of today's political discourse. This dynamic risks overshadowing the authenticity and agency of queer identities with political strategies that might not reflect the interests of the LGBT+ community. As a result, queer identity becomes a contested terrain, a battleground not only for rights and recognition but also for the control of narrative and representation. Thus, the essence of queer identity is increasingly obscured by a mirrored version of itself, reduced to a mere performative tool in a broader political game. Paraphrasing Žižek, living in a crisis culture invariably leaves a bitter taste in one's mouth (2017, 190). However, the intensity of this bitterness varies across divergent lived experiences and identities. For the queer community, contending with these tautological narratives and their political manipulations poses a challenge not only to their rights but also to their very identity, continually vulnerable to reinterpretation and exploitation in a world where crisis is the norm.

Thus, contrary to José Esteban Muñoz's (2009, 118) idea that queer utopian practice is about "building" and "doing" in response to the status of "nothing" assigned to the queer by the heteronormative world, homonationalism assigns the queer a specific "something" to do. This assignment disrupts the traditional narrative of queer existence in the margins by offering a certain lightness, a tentative step into visibility and recognition. This is a welcome relief for many queers who have always lived as creatures of darkness, finding solace in the cover of night (Burkert & Marinatos 2010, xv). Yet, the queer is perhaps most comfortable in their mirrored state, straddling both realms—the darkness and the light. It is within this liminal space, between visibility and obscurity, acceptance and marginalization, that the potential for communal becomings may arise. Perhaps then, the queer can also reach "the Open" with the totality of all its being. In darkness and light. In light and darkness. In dark. In light.

Conclusion

In his essay "Create Dangerously," originally published in 1950, Albert Camus wrote: "we are living in an interesting era. . . . The writers of today know this. If they speak up, they are criticized and attacked. If they become modest and keep silent, they are vociferously blamed for their silence" (2018, 1). Camus articulates the perilous position of the creator in a time of crisis, emphasizing that to create today is to create dangerously. Any publication is an act, and that act exposes one to the passions of an age that forgives nothing (Camus 2018, 3). This argument is strikingly relevant to the current era of crisis cultures, where the act of creating remains fraught with risks and responsibilities. Much like in Camus' time, today's creators face a terrain where their work is relentlessly scrutinized and where silence can be as heavily criticized as outspoken commentary. The visibility of societal inequities has increased, driven by the interconnectedness and immediacy of digital media. The public's awareness of various crises—from economic disparity to environmental degradation—has therefore intensified, demanding constant engagement and response. Just as Camus noted the unforgiving nature of the age, the contemporary era similarly offers little forgiveness.

The perpetual oscillation between creation and critique in an age of heightened crisis evokes a sense of disorientation akin to madness. Franco Berardi (2019, 24) expands on this notion, dividing madness into two aspects: the external, chaotic reality of the world, and the internal, subjective experience of this chaos. The external aspect, described as "the factual meaninglessness of the world, the surrounding magma of matter, the uncontrollable proliferation of stimuli, the dazzling whirl of existence" (Berardi 2019, 24), captures a world inherently chaotic and devoid of intrinsic meaning. This external disarray not only shapes but is reciprocally shaped by internal experiences, which Berardi describes as "the painful sentiment that things are flying away, the feeling of being overwhelmed by speed and noise and violence, of anxiety, panic, mental chaos" (2019, 24). This mutual intensification between the external chaos and internal torment mirrors the experiences of individuals immersed in crisis cultures, where relentless pressures lead to a pervasive sense of disorientation and mental distress. This internalization of crisis impacts social cohesion and mental health, creating a cyclical effect where the response to crisis further intensifies the crisis itself.

The journey through these pages has not been a linear narrative, but rather a reflective journey through the crisis narratives that define our era. Crisis cultures disrupt not only the understanding of events but also distinctly shape our collective and individual consciousness. This disruption marks a fundamental shift in our perception and interpretation of past and future experiences, compelling a reevaluation of our "space of experience" (Koselleck 1985, 271–276). This reevaluation involves reassessing our historical narratives, national identities, and individual subjectivities, as these concepts are continuously reshaped by the crises we encounter. At the same time, crisis cultures exert a significant impact on our "horizon of expectation" (Koselleck 1985, 271–276). The omnipresence of crisis narratives, heightened by the reach and speed of digital media, fundamentally changes how we perceive and experience these crises. This environment envelops us in a relentless stream of information, emotions, and affective responses, shaping our expectations and projections for the future. The growing disparity between Koselleck's concepts of the "space of experience" and the "horizon of expectation" reveals a critical tension: our experiences are increasingly defined by a continuous state of crisis, while our expectations for the future are being reshaped, often in unpredictable ways. In the case studies presented in the preceding chapters, from the discursive reconstructions during the Greek economic crisis, the rapid return to "normal" in the aftermath of the COVID-19 pandemic, the ideological conflicts during the Capitol Hill riots, and the interrogation of identity within queering frameworks, it is clear that crises reconfigure the symbolic orders and narrative structures that underpin both individual lives and collective identities. These ongoing reconfigurations create tension between our understanding of the past and our aspirations for the future, a theme that is central to the discussions presented in this book.

In *Crisis Cultures*, I extend Koselleck's (2006 371–272) interpretative possibilities by proffering a fifth possibility for understanding crisis. This novel perspective, rather than superseding existing interpretative frameworks, introduces a fresh lens to understand the crisis ambientality of the present moment and its affective underpinnings. Within this new interpretative possibility, crisis is not only chronic and all-pervasive but also a constitutive state characterized by an absence of meaningful events, which in turn intensifies underlying tensions. This perspective, examined through various case studies in the preceding chapters, suggests that crisis cultures are defined not just by the presence of continuous crises but also by a void where significant, transformative events are expected but do not materialize. The fragmentation of experience is therefore significantly influenced by the distinction between the two German terms for experience: *Erfahrung* and *Erlebnis* (Casey 2023, 284). *Erfahrung*, symbolizing cumulative, transformative experiences that shape individual and collective wisdom over time, faces a diminution in its sense-making power within crisis cultures. Once indicative of a well-traveled path and a cultural roadmap, this term struggles to maintain relevance amid the relentless and multifaceted nature of modern crises. In contrast, *Erlebnis*, denoting immediate, personal experiences, becomes more prevalent in these crisis cultures. This shift indicates a move away from the conventional wisdom and long-term perspective associated with *Erfahrung*, toward a focus on the more ephemeral experiences typical of our historical moment. As a result, the traditional, deeper understanding of experiences that shape our long-term view of the world loses its grounding, leading, instead, to a "space of experience" defined by *Erlebnis*-saturation. This evolution leads to a fragmented perception of crises, diminishing the ability to utilize past experiences as a heuristic tool for future orientation. Consequently, the growing dependence on immediate, personal experiences to interpret and respond to crises becomes more pronounced, further contributing to the overall sense of fragmentation within these cultures.

Digital crisis ambientality, a concept integral to understanding contemporary crisis cultures, refers to the transformative impact of digital spaces on our experiences and perceptions of crises. This phenomenon is characterized by how digital technologies and media reformulate and intensify our interactions with crisis narratives. In these digital spaces, information is not just passively consumed; rather, it actively shapes our understanding of and responses to crises. A key aspect of digital crisis ambientality is the role of these technologies in exacerbating polarization and amplifying underlying social tensions. The echo chambers and filter bubbles prevalent in digital environments often reinforce existing biases and viewpoints, leading to increased divisiveness and a heightened sense of conflict. Yet, as Han observes, these digital phenomena only go so far in explaining the polarization of contemporary societies because, as he argues, "self-indoctrination or auto-propagandizing begins *offline*" (2022, 29–30). Nonetheless, the inherent characteristics of digital spaces, such as rapid information flow and potential for anonymity, frequently hinder authentic communal engagement. While these platforms have the potential to connect and unite, they often become sites for contention and discord. This "Mirror World," as described by Naomi Klein (2023), often presents a distorted reflection of society, where everything is a reflection of itself. The lines between constructive community building and divisive rhetoric are thus blurred, complicating efforts to foster genuine communal becomings.

Even so, the case studies presented in the preceding chapters seek, where possible, to locate the *possibilities* they open up—to search for means to "transform an *impasse* into an escape route" (Agamben 1999a, 68) and read crisis cultures as being full of potentiality. In that sense, the concept of communal becomings emerges as a critical element of my reading of crisis cultures, representing moments of collective creativity and resilience amid ongoing crises. These stories provide a counterpoint to the pervasive sense of despair and disorientation, suggesting that even as our "space of experience" is marked by crisis, our "horizon of expectation" can still, at times, be a space of hope and possibility. It is eminently understandable that in such a context of perpetual crisis, individuals might be enveloped in profound despair, and to some, my persistent advocacy for hope may seem not merely impractical but verging on the delusional—a potential confabulation of my own cultural logic. Nonetheless, we each must navigate our own trajectories, choosing paths illuminated by what we conceive to be both possible and imperative.

Communal becomings can be envisioned as embodying a shift from the self toward a more collective understanding and responsiveness, a process underpinned by justice. According to Han:

> The just person listens to the things rather than to *him- or herself*. To refrain from having convictions means at the same time to refrain from *oneself*. The aim is—for the benefit of the things—to hear more, to see more, to go beyond one's momentary convictions, which always contain a being-convinced-of-oneself. The just person reserves his or her judgement which would *always* be *too early*. A judgment would already be a betrayal of the other. . . . Justice is practised by suspending one's convictions, one's opinions about the other, by *hearing, listening*, by refraining from judgements, i.e. from *oneself*. For the self enters the scene *always too early* and to the disadvantage of the other. Such singular abstinence cannot originate from power as such. There is no *hesitation* to be found in power. Power as such never refuses to judge or to think about the other. Rather, it is made up of judgements and convictions. (2019, 92)

Han thus reformulates justice around the importance of fostering a critical capacity to prioritize *listening* to external realities over internal convictions. This approach requires a conscious withdrawal from personal beliefs, thus cultivating a deeper interaction with external perspectives. Han's recommendation to distance oneself from these beliefs is not aimed at their negation but rather at their elevation, in order to attain a more holistic understanding of the external world. This emphasizes the necessity of acknowledging and sidelining one's ego to genuinely comprehend the complexities of a given situation. By presenting judicial abstention as a counterpoint to the typical exercise of power, Han invites a critical reassessment of prevailing models of authority and decision-making. Power, as Han describes it, tends to rapidly formulate judgments and is anchored in pre-established convictions. This suggests that power operates within a self-validating framework, where decisions are made on the basis of pre-existing beliefs and biases, affording minimal space for hesitation or reconsideration. Han's analysis thus implies that genuine justice involves a willingness to delay immediate judgment, engage in active *listening*, and contemplate various perspectives before reaching a conclusion.

Herein lies the promise of a pedagogy of listening, which could potentially serve as a linchpin in this intellectual endeavor. This pedagogic framework bridges the gap between "communal becomings" and Foucault's articulations of "counter-memory" (Foucault 1977), advancing a methodological scaffolding that extends beyond critical observation into active, praxis-driven engagement. Counter-memory, as articulated by Foucault, refers to the act of remembering that opposes, questions, or subverts the prevailing historical narratives sanctioned by those in power. It demands a purposeful and mindful effort to unearth and magnify the voices and experiences often neglected in mainstream narratives. This uncovering can only be undertaken by following Han's advice: "to hear more, to see more, to go beyond one's momentary convictions" (Han 2019, 92). Albert Camus, too, eloquently captures the essence of this endeavor in his reflection:

> Perhaps then, if we listen attentively, we shall hear, amid the uproar of empires and nations, a faint flutter of wings, the gentle stirring of life and hope. Some will say that this hope lies in a nation; others, in a man. I believe rather that it is awakened, revived, nourished by millions of solitary individuals whose deeds and works every day negate frontiers and the crudest implications of history. (2018, 32–33)

After all, what escape route remains to us within a crisis culture besides *listening*? Listening is the only tool we have. It is a tool infused with, and responsive to, our own emotions as well as those of others. The act of listening requires more than mere reception; it entails interpretation, thereby conferring value on those being listened to (Rinaldi 2001, 2–3). A pedagogy of listening thus raises the crucial question: Who is listening? And more importantly, *how* are we listening? In this, it echoes a broader epistemological reorientation, emphasizing listening as a critical act that reinscribes our understanding of the social terrain in terms of relationality and community. A pedagogy of listening becomes a hermeneutic tool for reconstructing crisis cultures, transcending simplistic queries like "what went wrong?" (Roitman 2014, 11). By integrating listening as an active, emotional, and temporally expansive endeavor, this pedagogy turns the act of listening itself into a form of critical intervention.

A pedagogy of listening, at its core, necessitates empathy. As Naomi Klein (2023) argues, our efforts should be oriented toward dismantling systems rather than attributing blame to individuals. Empathy in this context is not just about understanding and sharing the feelings of others; it is about recognizing the broader systemic forces that shape individual experiences. Klein's argument implies that a myopic focus on individual accountability can detract from the larger systemic problems that often underlie personal actions and decisions. A pedagogy of listening, therefore, is not merely about acknowledging every personal narrative as inherently epistemically valid (Casey 2023, 283). Rather, it is about positioning these narratives within the larger context of systemic structures, understanding how these structures influence individual experiences and perspectives. Moreover, in line with Arno Gruen (2007), it requires an emotional authenticity in understanding and navigating social structures. This pedagogic approach thus calls for an ongoing remapping, where listening and empathy are central, constantly probing the "so what?" of situations (milton 2023, 36). Such a methodology shifts the sense-making priority from a narrow focus on "what is *wrong*" to a broader and more constructive perspective of "what is *right*" (my emphasis) (Tomaselli 2023, 126). By focusing on what is *right*, we encourage a shift from problem-centric to solution-oriented thinking. This shift fosters a culture of proactive engagement, where the emphasis is on identifying and building upon strengths, resources, and positive dynamics within communities and systems. In doing so, it aligns with Gruen's (1997) advocacy for emotional authenticity, as it requires recognizing and validating the complex emotional realities and strengths that individuals and communities possess. By constantly flipping the sense-making priority, this remapping keeps the discourse relevant and grounded in the realities of those affected by crises, ensuring that our responses are not only empathetic but also effective and forward-looking.

"How does one stage utopia?" José Esteban Muñoz (2009) asks. This question invokes the concept of utopia not as a static, unreachable ideal but as a dynamic process of transformation and possibility. As Muñoz argues, thinking of utopia is productive when it is seen "as a moment when the now is transcended by a *then* and a *there* that could be and indeed should be" (original emphasis) (2009, 97). Staging utopia is thus about "building" and "doing" (2009, 118), but also importantly about *becoming*. The concept of becoming sees the future as an active agent, pointing to the idea that the future *does things*. In this horizon, the focus is not solely on what the utopia will be, but on what we are *becoming* as we strive toward it. Thus, staging utopia requires us to engage with the present in a manner that constantly seeks out and moves toward that transformative *becoming*. According to Lauren Berlant, "History hurts, but not only" (2011, 122). Staging utopia is thus not a mere escape from the harsh realities of the present, but a critical engagement with them, where the pain and challenges of history become the very materials with which we construct alternative futures. A remapping that is also a project of becoming is one that insists on the second half of that axiom—*not only*. When we listen, it is a first step to formulating our response to that enigmatic gesture. We are immersed in crisis cultures. But not only.

Bibliography

Agamben, Giorgio. 1993. *Stanzas: Word and Phantasm in Western Culture*. Minneapolis: University of Minnesota Press.
Agamben, Giorgio. 1999a. *The Man Without Content*. Stanford: Stanford University Press.
Agamben, Giorgio. 1999b. *Potentialities: Collected Essays in Philosophy*. Stanford: Stanford University Press.
Agamben, Giorgio. 2005. *State of Exception*. Chicago: University of Chicago Press. https://doi.org/10.2307/j.ctv1134d6w.16.
Agamben, Giorgio. 2007. *Infancy and History: On the Destruction of Experience*. London and New York: Verso.
Agamben, Giorgio. 2013. "The Endless Crisis as an Instrument of Power: In Conversation with Giorgio Agamben." *Verso Blog*, Jun 4. https://www.versobooks.com/en-gb/blogs/news/1318-the-endless-crisis-as-an-instrument-of-power-in-conversation-with-giorgio-agamben.
Agamben, Giorgio. 2021. *Where Are We Now? The Epidemic as Politics*. Translated by Valeria Dani. London: ERIS.
Ahmed, Sara. 2004. *The Cultural Politics of Emotion*. Edinburgh: Edinburgh University Press.
Alonso, Sonia and Cristóbal Rovíra Kaltwasser. 2015. "Spain: No Country for the Populist Radical Right?" *South European Society & Politics* 20 (1): 21–45. https://doi.org/10.1080/13608746.2014.985448.
Anarte, Enrique. 2023. "Spain's Madrid Region Partially Revokes Trans, LGBTQ Rights Laws." *Reuters*, Jul 17, accessed 12 December, https://www.reuters.com/world/europe/are-lgbtq-rights-stake-spains-election-2023-07-17/.
Anderson, Ben. 2009. "Affective Atmospheres." *Emotion, Space and Society* 2 (2): 77–81. https://doi.org/10.1016/j.emospa.2009.08.005.
Anderson, Benedict. 1991. *Imagined Communities*. London: Verso.
Anderson, Jennifer and Kathryn D. Coduto. 2022. "Attitudinal and Emotional Reactions to the Insurrection at the U.S. Capitol on January 6, 2021." *The American Behavioral Scientist* (Nov 2). https://doi.org/10.1177/00027642221132796.

Anderson, Kevin B. 2022. "The January 6 Insurrection: Historical and Global Contexts." (Dec 14), accessed 9 September, 2023, https://escholarship.org/uc/item/0sd6k6zf.
Ang, Sylvia, Elaine Lynn-Ee Ho, and Brenda S. A. Yeoh. 2022. "Migration and New Racism Beyond Colour and the 'West': Co-Ethnicity, Intersectionality and Postcoloniality." *Ethnic and Racial Studies* 45 (4): 585–594. https://doi.org/10.1080/01419870.2021.1925321.
Angelo, Paul J. and Dominic Bocci. 2021. "The Changing Landscape of Global LGBTQ+ Rights." *Council on Foreign Relations*, Jan 29, accessed 15 November, 2023, https://www.cfr.org/article/changing-landscape-global-lgbtq-rights.
Appadurai, Arjun. 2006. *Fear of Small Numbers: An Essay on the Geography of Anger*. Durham and London: Duke University Press. https://doi.org/10.2307/j.ctv11smfkm.
Arendt, Hannah. 1968. *Men in Dark Times*. New York: Harcourt Brace & World.
Arroyo, Luis. 2020. "Vox: Disección del disparate sobre los homosexuales." *infoLibre*, May 8. https://www.infolibre.es/noticias/opinion/columnas/2020/05/08/vox_diseccion_del_disparate_sobre_los_homosexuales_106578_1023.html.
Arthur, Charles. 2012. "The History of Smartphones: Timeline." *The Guardian*, Jan 25. https://www.theguardian.com/technology/2012/jan/24/smartphones-timeline.
Atkins, J. Spencer. 2023. "Defining Wokeness." *Social Epistemology* 37 (3): 321–338. https://doi.org/10.1080/02691728.2022.2145857. https://www.tandfonline.com/doi/abs/10.1080/02691728.2022.2145857.
Avramidis, Alexandros and Alkis Konstandinidis. 2023. "Rescuers in Greece find 18 Burned Bodies as Wildfires Spread." *Reuters*, Aug 23. https://www.reuters.com/world/europe/dozens-patients-evacuated-greece-wildfires-burn-fourth-day-2023-08-22/.
Badiou, Alain. 2005. *Being and Event*. Translated by Oliver Feltham. London: Continuum. https://doi.org/10.5040/9781350252035.
Badiou, Alain and Tusa Giovanbattista. 2019. *The End: A Conversation*. Translated by Robin Mackay. Cambridge: Polity Press.
Bal, Mieke. 2002. *Travelling Concepts in the Humanities: A Rough Guide*. Toronto: University of Toronto Press.
Barley, Joshua. 2015. "Greece and the Poetics of Crisis." *The White Review*, Feb. https://www.thewhitereview.org/feature/greece-and-the-poetics-of-crisis/.
Bateman, Jessica. 2019. "How Greek Crisis Helped Removed Taboo on Mental Health." *BBC News*, May 5. https://www.bbc.com/news/world-europe-48069644.
Baudrillard, Jean. 1989. "The Anorexic Ruins." In *Looking Back on the End of the World*, edited by Dietmar Kamper and Christophe Wulf, 29–45. New York: Semiotext(e).
Baudrillard, Jean. 1992. *L' Illusion De La Fin*. Paris: Galilée.
Baudrillard, Jean. 1994. *Simulacra and Simulation*. Ann Arbor: University of Michigan Press. https://doi.org/10.3998/mpub.9904.
Bauman, Zygmunt. 2000. *Liquid Modernity*. Cambridge: Polity Press.
Bauman, Zygmunt. 2002. *Society Under Siege*. Reprint. ed. Cambridge: Polity Press.
Bauman, Zygmunt. 2006. *Liquid Fear*. Cambridge, UK: Polity Press.

Bauman, Zygmunt. 2017. *Retrotopia*. Cambridge: Polity Press.
Beck, Ulrich. 1992. *Risk Society – Towards a New Modernity*. Translated by Mark Ritter. New York: Sage.
Bejamin, Walter. 1968. *Illuminations*. Translated by Harry Zohn, edited by Hannah Arendt. New York: Schocken Books.
Benjamin, Walter. 1999. *The Arcades Project*. Translated by Howard Eiland and Kevin McLaughlin. Cambridge and London: Harvard University Press.
Benkler, Yochai, Robert Faris, and Hal Roberts. 2018. *Network Propaganda: Manipulation, Disinformation, and Radicalization in American Politics*. New York: Oxford University Press.
Berardi, Franco "Bifo". 2019. *Futurability: The Age of Impotence and the Horizon of Possibility*. London and New York: Verso.
Berger, John. 2016. *Confabulations*. London: Penguin Books.
Berlant, Lauren. 1991. *The Anatomy of National Fantasy Hawthorne, Utopia, and Everyday Life*. Chicago: Chicago University Press.
Berlant, Lauren. 2011. *Cruel Optimism*. Durham and London: Duke University Press. https://doi.org/10.1515/9780822394716.
Bhabha, Homi K. 1990. "Introduction: Narrating the Nation." In *Nation & Narration*, edited by Homi K. Bhabha, 1–7. London and New York: Routledge.
Billig, Michael. 1995. *Banal Nationalism*. 1st ed. London: SAGE Publications. https://doi.org/10.4135/9781446221648.
Bloch, Ernst. 1995. *The Principle of Hope, Volume 1*. Translated by Neville Plaice, Paul Knight, and Stephen Plaice. Cambridge, MA: MIT Press.
Blout, Emily and Patrick Burkart. 2023. "White Supremacist Terrorism in Charlottesville: Reconstructing 'Unite the Right'." *Studies in Conflict and Terrorism* 46 (9): 1624–1652. https://doi.org/10.1080/1057610X.2020.1862850.
Boletsi, Maria. 2018. *The Futurity of Things Past: Thinking Greece Beyond Crisis*. Amsterdam: Amsterdam University Press.
Boletsi, Maria, Janna Houwen, and Liesbeth Minnaard. 2020. "Introduction: From Crisis to Critique." In *Languages of Resistance, Transformation, and Futurity in Mediterranean Crisis-Scapes*, 1–24. Cham: Springer International Publishing. https://doi.org/10.1007/978-3-030-36415-1_1.
Boltanski, Luc and Ève Chiapello. 2000. *Le Nouvel Esprit Du Capitalisme*. Paris: Gallimard.
Botanova, Kateryna. 2017. "Archaeology of the Future." In *Culturescapes Greece/Griechenland—Archaeology of the Future/Archäologie Der Zukunft*, edited by Kateryna Botanova, Christos Chrissopoulos and Jurriaan Cooiman, 6–13. Basel: Christoph Merian Verlag.
Bourdieu, Pierre. 1984. *Distinction: A Social Critique of the Judgement of Taste*. Translated by Richard Nice. Cambridge, Massachusetts: Harvard University Press.
Bourdieu, Pierre. 1986. "The Forms of Capital." In *Handbook of Theory and Research for the Sociology of Education*, edited by J. Richardson, 241–258. Westport, CT: Greenwood.
Bowden, Mark and Matthew Teague. 2022. *The Steal: The Attempt to Overturn the 2020 US Election and the People Who Stopped It*. London: Grove Press UK.

Brown, Rebecca M. 2009. "Spinning without Touching the Wheel: Anticolonialism, Indian Nationalism, and the Deployment of Symbol." *Comparative Studies of South Asia, Africa, and the Middle East* 29 (2) (Jan 1): 230–245. https://doi.org/10.1215/1089201X-2009-006.

Brown, Rebecca. 2010. *Gandhi's Spinning Wheel and the Making of India*. Routledge Studies in South Asian History. 1st ed. Vol. 9. London: Routledge. https://doi.org/10.4324/9780203852705.

Browning, Reed. 1993. *The War of the Austrian Succession*. New York: St. Martin's Press.

Burkert, Walter and Nanno Marinatos. 2010. "Introduction." In *Light and Darkness in Ancient Greek Myth and Religion*, edited by Menelaos Christopoulos, Efimia D. Karakantza and Olga Levaniouk, xv–xx. Lanham: Lexington Books.

Bushwick, S. 2021. "What the Capitol Riot Data Download shows about Social Media Vulnerabilities." *Scientific American*, Jan 21. https://www-scientificamerican-com.ezproxy.lib.uts.edu.au/article/what-the-capitol-riot-data-download-shows-about-social-media-vulnerabilities/.

Callison, William and Quinn Slobodian. 2021. "Coronapolitics from the Reichstag to the Capitol." *Boston Review*, Jan 12. https://www.bostonreview.net/articles/quinn-slobodian-toxic-politics-coronakspeticism/.

Calvo, Kerman and Gracia Trujillo. 2011. "Fighting for Love Rights: Claims and Strategies of the LGBT Movement in Spain." *Sexualities* 14 (5): 562–579. https://doi.org/10.1177/1363460711415330.

Campbell, Perri. 2018. "Occupy, Black Lives Matter and Suspended Mediation: Young People's Battles for Recognition in/between Digital and Non-Digital Spaces." *Young* 26 (2) (Apr): 145–160. https://doi.org/10.1177/1103308817713584.

Camus, Albert. 2018. *Create Dangerously*. London: Penguin Books.

Carpentier, Nico. 2017. *The Discursive-Material Knot: Cyprus in Conflict and Community Media Participation*. New York: Peter Lang.

Casey, Patrick J. 2023. "Lived Experience: Defined and Critiqued." *Critical Horizons* 24 (3): 282–297. https://doi.org/10.1080/14409917.2023.2241058.

Castells, Manuel. 2010. *The Rise of the Network Society*. Vol. 1. Chichester: Wiley-Blackwell.

Chandhoke, Neera. 2022. *Nelson Mandela Peace through Reconciliation*. Abingdon, Oxon: Routledge.

Chitty, Christopher. 2020. *Sexual Hegemony: Statecraft, Sodomy, and Capital in the Rise of World System*. Edited by Max Fox. Durham and London: Duke University Press. https://doi.org/10.1215/9781478012238.

Chrissopoulos, Christos. 2017. "A Biography of the Parthenon." In *Culturescapes Greece/Griechenland—Archaeology of the Future/Archäologie Der Zukunft*, edited by Botanovam Kateryna, Christos Chrissopoulos and Jurriaan Cooiman, 52–65. Basel: Christoph Merian Verlag.

Chua, Amy. 2018. "How America's Identity Politics Went from Inclusion to Division." *The Guardian*, Mar 1. https://www.theguardian.com/society/2018/mar/01/how-americas-identity-politics-went-from-inclusion-to-division.

Clarke, Harold D., Matthew Goodwin, and Paul Whiteley. 2017. *Brexit: Why Britain Voted to Leave the European Union*. Cambridge: Cambridge University Press. https://doi.org/10.1017/9781316584408.

Clinton, Hillary Rodham. 2017. *What Happened?* New York: Simon & Schuster.

Coffey, Mary K. 2012. *How a Revolutionary Art Became Official Culture*. 1st ed. Durham: Duke University Press. https://doi.org/10.1515/9780822394273.

Conrad, Ryan, ed. 2014. *Against Equality: Queer Revolution, Not Mere Inclusion*. Edinburgh: AK Press.

Conversi, Daniele. 1997. *The Basques, the Catalans and Spain: Alternative Routes to Nationalist Mobilisation*. London: Hurst.

Cornejo-Valle, Monica and Jennifer Ramme. 2022. "'We Don't Want Rainbow Terror': Religious and Far-Right Sexual Politics in Poland and Spain." In *Paradoxical Right-Wing Sexual Politics in Europe*, edited by Cornelia Möser, Jennifer Ramme and Judit Takács, 25–60. Switzerland: Springer International Publishing.

Cox, Lisa and Helen Davidson. 2020. "Australia Fires: Celeste Barber Fundraiser Tops $20m as Celebrities Pink, Nicole Kidman make Huge Donations." *The Guardian*, 5 Jan. https://www.theguardian.com/australia-news/2020/jan/05/australia-fires-celeste-barber-fundraiser-reaches-20m-as-pink-nicole-kidman-make-huge-donations.

Cozolino, Louis. 2010. *The Neuroscience of Psychotherapy: Healing the Social Brain*. The Norton Series on Interpersonal Neurobiology. 3rd ed. New York and London: W.W. Norton & Company.

Crenshaw, Kimberley. 1989. "Demarginalizing the Intersection of Race and Sex: A Black Feminist Critique of Antidiscrimination Doctrine, Feminist Theory, and Antiracist Politics." In *Feminist Legal Theory*, edited by Katherine Bartlett. 1st ed., 57–80: London and New York: Routledge. https://doi.org/10.4324/9780429500480-5.

Croxton, Derek. 1999. "The Peace of Westphalia of 1648 and the Origins of Sovereignty." *The International History Review* 21 (3): 569–591. https://doi.org/10.1080/07075332.1999.9640869.

Cruz, Ted. 2023. *Unwoke: How to Defeat Cultural Marxism in America*. 1st ed. New York: Regnery Publishing.

Davidjants, Jaana and Katrin Tiidenberg. 2022. "Activist Memory Narration on Social Media: Armenian Genocide on Instagram." *New Media & Society* 24 (10) (Oct 1): 2191–2206. https://doi.org/10.1177/1461444821989634.

Davies, H. C. and S. E. MacRae. 2023. "An Anatomy of the British War on Woke." *Race & Class* 65 (2): 3–54. https://doi.org/10.1177/03063968231164905.

Davis, Alyssa J. and Heather Hensman Kettrey. 2022. "Clear and Omnipresent Danger: Digital Age Culture Wars and Reactions to Drag Queen Story Hour Across Diverse Subreddit Communities." *Social Currents* 9 (1): 25–44. https://doi.org/10.1177/23294965211050019.

Davis, Darien J., ed. 2018. *Avoiding the Dark Essays on Race and the Forging of National Culture in Modern Brazil*. New York: Routledge. https://doi.org/10.4324/9780429463266.

Dawkins, Richard. 2023. "Replying to Jordan Peterson." *The Poetry of Reality with Richard Dawkins*, 4 Aug. https://richarddawkins.substack.com/p/replying-to-jordan-peterson.

Dawson, Alexander S. 1998. "From Models for the Nation to Model Citizens: Indigenismo and the 'Revindication' of the Mexican Indian 1920–1940." *Journal of Latin American Studies* 30 (2) (May 1): 279–308. https://doi.org/10.1017/S0022216X98005057.

De Chavez, Jeremy and Asha Varadharajan. 2023. "'Been Down so Long it Looks Like Up to Me': Rethinking the Humanities (in Times of) Crisis." In *The Humanities Reloaded: Addressing Crisis*, edited by Keyan G. Tomaselli and Pier Paolo Frassinelli, 51–63. London and New York: Routledge. https://doi.org/10.4324/9781003359920-5.

De la Durantaye, Leland. 2009. *Giorgio Agamben: A Critical Introduction*. Stanford: Stanford University Press.

Debord, Guy. 2014. *The Society of the Spectacle*. Translated by Ken Knabb. Berkeley, CA: Bureau of Public Secrets.

Del Noce, Augusto. *The Crisis of Modernity*. Translated by Carlo Lancellotti. Montreal & Kingston: McGill-Queen's University Press.

Delgado, Luisa Elena. 2015. *La nación singular: Fantasías de la normalidad democrática española (1996–2011)*. Madrid: Siglo Veintiuno Editores.

Dennett, D. C. 1991. *Consciousness Explained*. 1st ed. Boston, MA: Little Brown and Co.

Derrida, Jacques. 1994. *Specters of Marx: The State of the Debt, the Work of Mourning and the New International*. London: Routledge.

Devís-Devís, José, Sofía Pereira-García, Alexandra Valencia-Peris, Anna Vilanova, and Javier Gil-Quintana. 2022. "Harassment Disparities and Risk Profile within Lesbian, Gay, Bisexual and Transgender Spanish Adult Population: Comparisons by Age, Gender Identity, Sexual Orientation, and Perpetration Context." *Frontiers in Public Health* 10: 1045714. https://doi.org/10.3389/fpubh.2022.1045714.

Dietrich, René. 2012. "'The Dead Shall Inherit the Dead' – After Life and Beyond Catastrophe in Mark Strand's Post-Apocalyptic Poetry." In *The Cultural Life of Catastrophes and Crises*, edited by Carsten Meiner and Kristin Veel, 203–212. Göttingen: DeGruyter. https://doi.org/10.1515/9783110282955.203.

Dole, Christopher, Robert Hayashi, Andrew Poe, Austin Sarat, and Austin D. Sarat. 2019. "When is Catastrophe?: An Introduction." In *The Time of Catastrophe*, edited by Christopher Dole, Robert Hayashi, Andrew Poe, and Austin Sarat, 1–18. United Kingdom: Routledge.

Douglas, Karen M., Robbie M. Sutton, and Aleksandra Cichocka. 2017. "The Psychology of Conspiracy Theories." *Current Directions in Psychological Science* 26 (6) (Dec 1): 538–542. https://doi.org/10.1177/0963721417718261.

Doukas, Yiannis. 2015. "Epitaph." In *Futures: Poetry of the Greeks in Crisis*, edited by Theodoros Chiotis, 139. London: Penned in the Margins.

Doyle, Andrew. 2022. *The New Puritans: How the Religion of Social Justice Captured the Western World*. London: Little, Brown Book Group.

Duberman, Martin. 2018. *Has the Gay Movement Failed?* 1st ed. Oakland, California: University of California Press.

Dubois, Laurent. 2012. *A Colony of Citizens: Revolution and Slave Emancipation in the French Caribbean, 1787–1804*. Chapel Hill: The University of North Carolina Press.

Duggan, Christopher. 2008. *The Force of Destiny: A History of Italy since 1796*. Boston and New York: Houghton Mifflin.

Duggan, Lisa. 2003. *The Twilight of Equality?: Neoliberalism, Cultural Politics, and the Attack on Democracy*. Boston, MA: Beacon Press.

Duignan, Brian. "January 6 U.S. Capitol Attack Riot, Washington, D.C., U.S. [2021]." *Britannica.*, accessed 31 October, 2023, https://www.britannica.com/event/January-6-U-S-Capitol-attack.

Eagleton, Terry. 2015. *Hope Without Optimism*. New York and London: Yale University Press.

Eakin, Marshall C. 2017. *Becoming Brazilians Race and National Identity in Twentieth-Century Brazil*. Cambridge: Cambridge University Press. https://doi.org/10.1017/9781316800058.

Edelman, Lee. 2004. *No Future: Queer Theory and the Death Drive*. Durham: Duke University Press. https://doi.org/10.1215/9780822385981.

Eliassen, Knut Ove. 2012. "Catastrophic Turns – from the Literary History of the Catastrophic." In *The Cultural Life of Catastrophes and Crisis*, edited by Carsten Meiner and Kristin Veel, 33–57. Berlin: De Gruyter. https://doi.org/10.1515/9783110282955.33.

Ellinas, Antonis A. 2013. "The Rise of Golden Dawn: The New Face of the Far Right in Greece." *South European Society & Politics* 18 (4) (Dec 1): 543–565. https://doi.org/10.1080/13608746.2013.782838.

Emmerich, Karen. 2020. "Dwelling in Noncrisis (Im)Possibility: Transmigrant Collective Action in Greece, 2016." In *Languages of Resistance, Transformation, and Futurity in Mediterranean Crisis-Scapes*, edited by Maria Boletsi, Janna Houwen and Liesbeth Minnaard, 27–42. Cham: Springer International Publishing. https://doi.org/10.1007/978-3-030-36415-1_2.

Encarnación, Omar G. 2016. *Out in the Periphery: Latin America's Gay Rights Revolution*. Oxford: Oxford University Press. https://doi.org/10.1093/acprof:oso/9780199356645.001.0001.

Erinakis, Nikos. 2015. "The New Symmetry." In *Futures: Poetry of the Greeks in Crisis*, edited by Theodoros Chiotis, 203. London: Penned in the Margins.

Escudero-Alías, Maite. 2022. "The Institutionalization of Queer Theory: Where has Lesbian Criticism Gone?" *Journal of Lesbian Studies* 26 (3): 253–268. https://doi.org/10.4324/9781003371236-4.

Esteban, Nacho. 2023. *Por rojos y maricones: Homofobia y transfobia en el Partido Popular y el resto de la derecha española*. Barcelona and Madrid: Egales Editorial.

Fanon, Frantz. 1961. *The Wretched of the Earth*. New York: Grove Press.

Ferguson, Iain and Michael Lavalette. 2014. "Racism, Anti-Racism and Social Work." *Critical and Radical Social Work* 2 (1): 3–6. https://doi.org/10.1332/204986014X14150969631164.

Ferguson, Roderick A. 2018. *One-Dimensional Queer*. Cambridge, UK: Polity.

Flores, Andrew R. *Social Acceptance of LGBTI People in 175 Countries and Locations, 1981 to 2020*. Los Angeles: The Williams Institute, November 2021. https://williamsinstitute.law.ucla.edu/wp-content/uploads/Global-Acceptance-Index-LGBTI-Nov-2021.pdf.

Forberg, Peter L. 2023. "'No Cult Tells You to Think for Yourself': Discursive Ideology and the Limits of Rationality in Conspiracy Theory QAnon." *The American Behavioral Scientist* 67 (5): 649–664. https://doi.org/10.1177/00027642221091199.

Ford, Brett Q. and Matthew Feinberg. 2020. "Coping with Politics: The Benefits and Costs of Emotion Regulation." *Current Opinion in Behavioral Sciences* 34 (Aug): 123–128. https://doi.org/10.1016/j.cobeha.2020.02.014.

Foucault, Michel. 1972. *The Archaeology of Knowledge*. Translated by A. M. Sheridan Smith. New York: Pantheon Books.

Foucault, Michel. 1977. *Language, Counter-Memory, Practice: Selected Essays and Interviews*. Translated by Donald F. Bouchard and Sherry Simon. Ithaca, NY: Cornell University Press.

Foucault, Michel. 1979. *Discipline and Punish*. Translated by Alan Sheridan. New York: Vintage Books.

Furedi, Frank. 2002. *Culture of Fear: Risk-Taking and the Morality of Low Expectation*. London: Continuum.

Fukuyama, Francis. 1992. *The End of History and the Last Man*. New York: Free Press.

Funk, Nanette. 2018. "A Spectre in Germany: Refugees, a 'Welcome Culture' and an 'Integration Politics'" In *Refugee Crisis: The Borders of Human Mobility*, edited by Melina Duarte, Kasper Lippert-Rasmussen, Serena Parekh and Annamari Vitikainen. 1st ed. Vol. 1, 44–54. London: Routledge. https://doi.org/10.4324/9781351207553-5.

Gaard, Greta. 2010. "Living Interconnections with Animals and Nature." In *Ecofeminism*, edited by Greta Gaard, 1–12. Philadelphia: Temple University Press.

Galla, Sean. "Mensgroup", accessed 22 December, 2023, https://mensgroup.com/mens-rights-groups/.

García Sebastiani, Marcela. 2020. "Spain on Show. Nationalism and Internationalism in the Presentation of the 12 October Holiday Under Post-War Francoism." *Journal of Iberian and Latin-American Studies* 26 (3) (Sep 1): 295–315. https://doi.org/10.1080/14701847.2020.1851918.

Gellner, Ernest. 1964. *Thought and Change*. London: Weidenfeld and Nicolson.

Gellner, Ernest. 1983. *Nations and Nationalism*. Ithaca, NY: Cornell University Press.

Giddens, Anthony. 1991. *Modernity and Self-Identity: Self and Society in the Late Modern Age*. Cambridge: Polity Press.

Giddens, Anthony. 1994. *Beyond Left and Right: The Future of Radical Politics*. Stanford, CA: Stanford University Press.

González Cabrera, Cristian. 2023. "Victory in Fight for Gender Recognition in Spain." *Human Rights Watch*, Feb 16. https://www.hrw.org/news/2023/02/16/victory-fight-gender-recognition-spain-0.

Gonzalez, Mike and Katharine Gorka. 2022. "How Cultural Marxism Threatens the United States: How Americans Can Fight It." *The Heritage*, Nov. 14. Foundation. https://www.heritage.org/progressivism/report/how-cultural-marxism-threatens-the-united-states-and-how-americans-can-fight.

González-Enríquez, Carmen. 2017. "The Spanish Exception: Unemployment, Inequality and Immigration, but no Right-Wing Populist Parties (Working Paper)." *Real Instituto Elcano*. https://www.realinstitutoelcano.org/en/work-document/the-spanish-exception-unemployment-inequality-and-immigration-but-no-right-wing-populist-parties/#:~:text=Very%20few%20European%20countries%20have,national%20elections%20in%20recent%20years.

Green, Adam Isaiah. 2002. "Gay but Not Queer: Toward a Post-Queer Study of Sexuality." *Theory and Society* 31 (4): 521–545. https://doi.org/10.1023/A:1020976902569.

Green, Joshua. 2017. *Devil's Bargain: Steve Bannon, Donald Trump, and the Nationalist Uprising*. New York: Penguin.

Grossberg, Lawrence. 2010. "Modernity and Commensuration: A Reading of a Contemporary (Economic) Crisis." *Cultural Studies* 24 (3): 295–332. https://doi.org/10.1080/09502381003750278.

Gruen, Arno. 2007. *The Betrayal of the Self: The Fear of Autonomy in Men and Women*. Translated by Hildegarde Hunter and Hannum Hunter. Berkeley, CA: Human Development Books.

Guelke, Adrian. 2005. *Rethinking the Rise and Fall of Apartheid*. 1st ed. London: Bloomsbury Publishing. https://doi.org/10.1007/978-0-230-80220-9_1.

Guibernau, Montserrat. 2004. *Catalan Nationalism*. Routledge/Canada Blanch Studies on Contemporary Spain. 1st ed. Vol. 9. Abingdon, Oxon: Routledge. https://doi.org/10.4324/9780203300251.

Guzmán, Cecilia. 2012. "Rajoy en 2005: 'A lo largo de la historia el matrimonio ha sido la unión de un hombre y una mujer." *El Plural*, Nov 6. https://www.elplural.com/politica/espana/rajoy-en-2005-a-lo-largo-de-la-historia-el-matrimonio-ha-sido-la-union-de-un-hombre-y-una-mujer_54544102.

Habermas, Jürgen. 1985. *The Philosophical Discourse of Modernity*. Translated by Frederick Lawrence. Cambridge: Polity Press.

Habermas, Jürgen. 1987. *The Theory of Communicative Action. Volume 2: Lifeworld and System: A Critique of Functionalist Reason*. Translated by Thomas McCarthy. Boston: Beacon Press.

Hall, Stuart. 1990. *The Hard Road to Renewal: Thatcherism and the Crisis of the Left*. London: Verso.

Hall, Stuart. 1991. "Old and New Identities, Old and New Ethnicities." In *Culture, Globalization and the World System*, edited by Anthony D. King, 41–68. Minneapolis: University of Minnesota Press. https://doi.org/10.1007/978-1-349-11902-8_3.

Hall, Stuart. 1992. "Cultural Studies and its Theoretical Legacies." In *Cultural Studies*, edited by Lawrence Grossberg, Cary Nelson, and Paula Treichler, 287–304. United Kingdom: Routledge.

Halperin, David M. 1995. *Saint Foucault: Towards a Gay Hagiography*. New York: Oxford University Press.

Haltof, Marek. 1993. "In Quest of Self-Identity: Gallipoli, Mateship, and the Construction of Australian National Identity." *Journal of Popular Film and Television* 21 (1): 27–36. https://doi.org/10.1080/01956051.1993.9943973.

Han, Byung-Chul. 2015. *The Burnout Society*. Translated by Erik Butler. Stanford: Stanford University Press.

Han, Byung-Chul. 2019. *What is Power?*. Translated by Daniel Steuer. 1st ed. Cambridge: Polity.

Han, Byung-Chul. 2022. *Infocracy*. Translated by Daniel Steuer. Cambridge: Polity Press.

Harsin, Jayson. 2015. "Regimes of Posttruth, Postpolitics, and Attention Economies." *Communication, Culture & Critique* 8 (2) (Jun): 327–333. https://doi.org/10.1111/cccr.12097.

Harvey, David. 2005. *A Brief History of Neoliberalism*. Oxford: Oxford University Press.

Harvey, David. 1989. *The Condition of Postmodernity: An Enquiry into the Origins of Cultural Change*. Cambridge and Oxford: Blackwell.

Hashimoto, Akiko. 2015. *The Long Defeat: Cultural Trauma, Memory, and Identity in Japan*. Oxford: Oxford University Press.

Hayward, Mark. 2010. "The Economic Crisis and After: Recovery, Reconstruction and the Promise of Cultural Studies." *Cultural Studies* 24 (3): 283–294. https://doi.org/10.1080/09502381003750260.

Hegel, Georg Wilhelm Friedrich. 1977. *Phenomenology of Spirit*. Translated by A.V. Miller. Oxford: Oxford University Press.

Heidegger, Martin. 1962. *Being and Time*. Translated by John Macquarie and Edward Robinson. Oxford: Blackwell.

Herzfeld, Michael. 2002. "The Absence Presence: Discourses of Crypto-Colonialism." *The South Atlantic Quarterly* 101 (4) (Oct 1): 899–926. https://doi.org/10.1215/00382876-101-4-899.

Herzfeld, Michael. 2016. *Cultural Intimacy Social Poetics and the Real Life of States, Societies, and Institutions*. Routledge Classic Texts in Anthropology. 3rd ed. London: Routledge. https://doi.org/10.4324/9781315647289.

Herzog, Dagmar. 2009. "Syncopated Sex: Transforming European Sexual Cultures." *The American Historical Review* 114 (5) (December): 1287–1308. https://doi.org/10.1086/ahr.114.5.1287.

Hill, Alexander. 2023. "Why Russians Still Support Vladimir Putin and the War in Ukraine." *The Conversation*, December 12. https://theconversation.com/why-russians-still-support-vladimir-putin-and-the-war-in-ukraine-219484.

Hirstein, William. 2005. *Brain Fiction Self-Deception and the Riddle of Confabulation*. Cambridge and London: The MIT Press. https://doi.org/10.7551/mitpress/1660.001.0001.

Hobolt, Sara B. 2016. "The Brexit Vote: A Divided Nation, a Divided Continent." *Journal of European Public Policy* 23 (9): 1259–1277. https://doi.org/10.1080/13501763.2016.1225785.

Hobsbawm, E. J. 1990. *Nations and Nationalism since 1780: Programme, Myth, Reality*. Cambridge: Cambridge University Press.

Hobsbawm, Eric. 1992. "Introduction: Inventing Traditions." In *The Invention of Tradition*, edited by Eric Hobsbawm and Terence Ranger, 1–14. Cambridge: Cambridge University Press. https://doi.org/10.1017/CBO9781107295636.001.

Hochschild, Arlie Russell. 2016. *Strangers in their Own Land: Anger and Mourning on the American Right*. New York and London: New Press.

Hocquenghem, Guy. *Homosexual Desire*. Translated by Daniella Dangoor. Durham and London: Duke University Press.

hooks, bell. 2000. *All About Love: New Visions*. New York: William Morrow.

Hopper, Earl. 2009. "The Theory of the Basic Assumption of Incohesion: Aggregation/Massification Or (Ba) i:A/M." *British Journal of Psychotherapy* 25 (2) (May): 214–229. https://doi.org/10.1111/j.1752-0118.2009.01116.x.

Hoskins, Andrew, ed. 2018. *Digital Memory Studies*. 1st ed. New York and Abingdon: Routledge.

Howard, Michael. 2013. *The Franco-Prussian War the German Invasion of France 1870–1871*. New York: Routledge. https://doi.org/10.4324/9780203820834.

Hunt, Lynn. 2004. *Politics, Culture, and Class in the French Revolution: Twentieth Anniversary Edition*. Berkeley, CA: University of California Press.

Hunter, Wendy and Timothy J. Power. 2019. "Bolsonaro and Brazil's Illiberal Backlash." *Journal of Democracy* 30 (1): 68–82. https://doi.org/10.1353/jod.2019.0005.

Illouz, Eva. 2008. *Saving the Modern Soul Therapy, Emotions, and the Culture of Self-Help*. 1st ed. Berkeley: University of California Press. https://doi.org/10.1525/california/9780520224469.003.0001.

Inglehart, Ronald F. 2018. *Cultural Evolution: People's Motivations are Changing, and Reshaping the World*. Cambridge: Cambridge University Press. https://doi.org/10.1017/9781108613880.

Jäckle, Sebastian and Pascal D. König. 2017. "The Dark Side of the German 'Welcome Culture': Investigating the Causes Behind Attacks on Refugees in 2015." *West European Politics* 40 (2) (Mar 4): 223–251. https://doi.org/10.1080/01402382.2016.1215614.

Jackson, Sarah J., Moya Bailey, and Brooke Foucault Welles. 2020. *#HashtagActivism: Networks of Race and Gender Justice*. Cambridge, Massachusetts; London, England: The MIT Press. https://doi.org/10.7551/mitpress/10858.001.0001.

Jacobson, Howard. 2023. "Charging Jews with Genocide is to Declare them Guilty of Precisely what was Done to Them." *The Guardian*, Dec 3. https://www.theguardian.com/commentisfree/2023/dec/03/charging-jews-with-genocide-declare-them-guilty-precisely-what-was-done-to-them-middle-east.

Jameson, Fredric. 1984. "Foreword." In *The Postmodern Condition: A Report on Knowledge*, edited by Jean-François Lyotard, vii–xxi. Minneapolis: University of Minnesota Press.

Jones, David Martin and M. L. R. Smith. 2022. *The Strategy of Maoism in the West: Rage and the Radical Left*. Cheltenham, UK; Northampton, MA, USA: Edward Elgar Publishing. https://doi.org/10.4337/9781802209464.

Kalfopoulou, Adrianne. 2015. "Ungodly." In *Futures: Poetry of the Greeks in Crisis*, edited by Theodoros Chiotis, 65. London: Penned in the Margins.

Kalmar, Ivan. 2022. *White But Not Quite: Central Europe's Illiberal Revolt*. Bristol: Bristol University Press. https://doi.org/10.56687/9781529213621.
Kant, Immanuel. 1998. *Critique of Pure Reason*. Translated by Paul Guyer and Allen W. Wood. Cambridge: Cambridge University Press. https://doi.org/10.1017/CBO9780511804649.
Khamis, Sahar and Katherine Vaughn. 2014. "Online Journalism in Africa: Trends, Practices and Emerging Cultures." In *Online Journalism in Africa: Trends, Practices and Emerging Cultures*, edited by Hayes Mawindi Mabweazara, Okoth Fred Mudhai and Jason Whittaker, 156–171. New York and London: Routledge.
Kidangoor, Abhishyant. 2018. "India's Supreme Court Decriminalizes Homosexuality in a Historic Ruling for the LGBTQ Community." *TIME Magazine*, Sep 6. https://time.com/5388231/india-decriminalizes-homosexuality-section-377/.
Kierkegaard, Søren. 1962. *The Present Age*. Translated by Alexander Dru. New York: Harper & Row.
Kim, Youna, ed. 2013. *The Korean Wave Korean Media Go Global*. Internationalizing Media Studies. London: Routledge.
Kim, Youna, ed. 2021. *The Soft Power of the Korean Wave*. Internationalizing Media Studies. Abingdon, Oxon: Routledge. https://doi.org/10.4324/9781315859064.
Kindleberger, Charles P. and Robert Z. Aliber. 2005. *Manias, Panics and Crashes: A History of Financial Crashes 5th Edition*. Hoboken, New Jersey: John Wiley & Sons. https://doi.org/10.1057/9780230628045.
Kingman, David. 2013. *Will Young People be Poorer than their Parents: 50 Economics Experts Give their Views*. London: The Intergenerational Foundation.
Klein, Naomi. 2023. *Doppelganger: A Trip into the Mirror World*. London: Penguin Books.
Kontos, Michael, Demetrios Moris, Spyridon Davakis, Dimitrios Schizas, Emmanouil Pikoulis, and Theodoros Liakakos. 2017. "Physical Abuse in the Era of Financial Crisis in Greece." *Annals of Translational Medicine* 5 (7) (Apr 1): 155. https://doi.org/10.21037/atm.2017.03.26.
Koselleck, Reinhart. 1985. *Futures Past: On the Semantics of Historical Time*. Translated by Keith Tribe. Cambridge, MA and London: MIT Press.
Koselleck, Reinhart. 1988. *Critique and Crisis: Enlightenment and the Pathogenesis of Modern Society*. Cambridge, MA: MIT Press.
Koselleck, Reinhart. 2006. "Crisis." *Journal of the History of Ideas* 67 (2): 357–400. https://doi.org/10.1353/jhi.2006.0013.
Kotouza, Dimitra. 2019. *Surplus Citizens: Struggle and Nationalism in the Greek Crisis*. London: Pluto Press. https://doi.org/10.2307/j.ctvjnrt95.
Kupferschmidt, Kai. 2020. "'Vaccine Nationalism' Threatens Global Plan to Distribute COVID-19 Shots Fairly." *Science*, Jul 28. https://doi.org/10.1126/science.abe0601.
Lacan, Jacques. 1977. "The Mirror Stage as Formative of the Function of the I as Revealed in Psychoanalytic Experience." In *Écrits: A Selection*. Translated by Alan Sheridan, 1–7. New York and London: W.W. Norton & Company. https://doi.org/10.4324/9781003209140-1.
Lambropoulos, Vassilis. 2016. "Left Melancholy in the Greek Poetry Generation of the 2000s." *Journal of Modern Greek Studies* Occasional Paper 10: 1–17.

Lanthimos, Yorgos. 2009. *Dogtooth*, edited by Katerina Kaskanioti, Yorgos Lanthimos, Iraklis Mavroidis, Vicky Miha, Athina Rachel Tasngari, Yorgos Tsourgiannis and Angelos Venetis Boo Productions.

Larraín, Pablo. 2023. *El Conde*. Netflix.

Leicht, Kevin T. and Mary L. Fennell. 2023. *Crisis in the Professions*. New York and London: Routledge. https://doi.org/10.4324/9781003225485.

Lemon, Michael C. 2003. "The Structure of Narrative." In *The History and Narrative Reader*, edited by Geoffrey Roberts, 107–129. London: Routledge.

Lesser, Jeffrey. 1999. *Negotiating National Identity Immigrants, Minorities, and the Struggle for Ethnicity in Brazil*. 1st ed. Durham: Duke University Press. https://doi.org/10.1515/9780822399292.

Levinas, Emmanuel. 1969. *Totality and Infinity: An Essay on Exteriority*. Pittsburgh: Duquesne University Press.

Lewandowsky, Stephen, Ullrich K. H. Ecker, and John Cook. "Beyond Misinformation: Understanding and Coping with the 'post-Truth' Era." *Journal of Applied Research in Memory and Cognition* 6 (4): 353–369. https://doi.org/10.1016/j.jarmac.2017.07.008.

Liebermann, Yvonne. 2021. "Born Digital: The Black Lives Matter Movement and Memory After the Digital Turn." *Memory Studies* 14 (4) (Aug 1): 713–732. https://doi.org/10.1177/1750698020959799.

Lindqvist, Sven. 2018. *'Exterminate all the Brutes'*. Granta Editions. Translated by Joan Tate. London: Granta.

Lipiński, Artur and Gabriella Szabo. 2023. "Heroisation and Victimisation: Populism, Commemorative Narratives and National Days in Hungary and Poland." *Journal of Contemporary European Studies* 31 (2): 345–362. https://doi.org/10.1080/14782804.2022.2130190.

Lister, Tim and Helena de Moura. 2015. "A Same-Sex Wedding Sparks a Political Furor in Spain." *CNN*, Sep 17. https://edition.cnn.com/2015/09/17/europe/spain-gay-wedding-rajoy/index.html.

Llobera, Josep R. 2005. *Foundations of National Identity: From Catalonia to Europe*. New Directions in Anthropology. New York: Berghahn Books. https://doi.org/10.2307/j.ctv287shmq.

Loomba, Ania. 1998. *Colonialism/Postcolonialism*. The New Critical Idiom. London: Routledge.

Lynch, John. 1986. *The Spanish American Revolutions, 1808–1826*. Revolutions in the Modern World. 2nd ed. New York: W.W. Norton.

Lynn, John A. 2013. *The Wars of Louis XIV, 1667–1714*. London and New York: Routledge. https://doi.org/10.4324/9781315845982.

Lyotard, Jean-François. 1984. *The Postmodern Condition: A Report on Knowledge*. Translated by Geoff Bennington and Brian Massumi. Minneapolis: University of Minnesota Press. https://doi.org/10.2307/1772278.

Maher, Henry. 2023. "The Free Market as Fantasy: A Lacanian Approach to the Problem of Neoliberal Resilience." *International Studies Quarterly* 67 (3). https://doi.org/10.1093/isq/sqad050.

Martín, Maria. 2019. "Who are the Young People Protesting in Barcelona?" *El País (English Edition)*, 28 Oct. https://elpais.com/elpais/2019/10/28/inenglish/1572261576_849925.html.

Martinez, Omar and Brian Dodge. 2010. "El Barrio De La Chueca of Madrid, Spain: An Emerging Epicenter of the Global LGBT Civil Rights Movement." *Journal of Homosexuality* 57 (2): 226–248. https://doi.org/10.1080/00918360903488913.

Marwick, Alice and Rebecca Lewis. 2017. *Media Manipulation and Disinformation Online*. Data & Society Research Institute.

Marx, Karl. 1992. *Capital*. Harmondsworth: Penguin Books.

McCormack, Jo. 2010. *Collective Memory France and the Algerian War (1954–62)*. Plymouth: Lexington Books.

Meiner, Carsten. 2012. "The Metaphysics of Catastrophe – Voltaire's Candide." In *The Cultural Life of Catastrophes and Crises*, edited by Carsten Meiner and Kristin Veel, 89–101. Göttingen: DeGruyter. https://doi.org/10.1515/9783110282955.89.

Meiner, Carsten and Kristin Veel. 2012. "Introduction." In *The Cultural Life of Catastrophes and Crises*, edited by Carsten Meiner and Kristin Veel, 1–12. Göttingen: DeGruyter. https://doi.org/10.1515/9783110282955.

Michaels, Walter Benn and Adolph Reed. 2023. *No Politics but Class Politics*. London: ERIS.

milton, viola candice. 2023. "*Kind of Blue*: Can Communication Research Matter?" In *The Humanities Reloaded: Addressing Crisis*, edited by Keyan Tomaselli G and Pier Paolo Frassinelli, 35–50. London and New York: Routledge. https://doi.org/10.4324/9781003359920-4.

Mishra, Pankaj. 2017. *Age of Anger: A History of the Present*. St. Ives: Allen Lane.

Misouridis, Giannis. 2017. "The Aleph of Athens." In *Culturescapes Greece/Griechenland—Archaeology of the Future/Archäologie Der Zukunft*, edited by Kateryna Botanova, Christos Chrissopoulos and Jurriaan Cooiman, 76–88. Basel: Christoph Merian Verlag.

Moreno Caballud, Luis. 2015. *Cultures of Anyone: Studies on Cultural Democratization in the Spanish Neoliberal Crisis*. Translated by Linda L. Grabner-Coronel. Liverpool: Liverpool University Press.

Morin, Edgar and Anne Brigitte Kern. 1999. *Homeland Earth: A Manifesto for the New Millennium*. Translated by Sean Kelly. Cresskill, NJ: Hampton Press.

Morris-Suzuki, Tessa. 1997. *Re-Inventing Japan: Time, Space, Nation*. Japan in the Modern World. London: M. E. Sharpe.

Morton, Timothy. 2013. *Hyperobjects: Philosophy and Ecology After the End of the World*. Minneapolis: University of Minnesota Press.

Möser, Cornelia and Reimers, Eva. 2022. "The Sexual Politics of National Secularisms in Sweden and France: A Cross-Confessional Comparison." *Paradoxical Right-Wing Sexual Politics in Europe*, edited by Jennifer Ramme and Judith Takács, 87–118. Switzerland: Springer International Publishing. https://doi.org/10.1007/978-3-030-81341-3_4.

Mounk, Yascha. 2023. "Where the New Identity Politics Went Wrong." *The Atlantic*, Sep. 26. https://www.theatlantic.com/ideas/archive/2023/09/woke-ideology-history-origins-flaws/675454/.

Mršević, Zorica. 2013. "Homophobia in Serbia and LGBT Rights." *Southeastern Europe* 37 (1): 60–87. https://doi.org/10.1163/18763332-03701004.

Muñoz, José Esteban. 2009. *Cruising Utopia: The then and there of Queer Futurity*. New York and London: New York University Press.

Nair, Yasmin. 2023. *Gay Marriage Ruined Everything*. Yasminnair.Com. Jul 6. https://yasminnair.com/gay-marriage-ruined-everything/.

Nancy, Jean-Luc. 1991. *The Inoperative Community*. Translated by Peter Connor, Lisa Garbus, Michael Holland and Simona Sawhney, edited by Peter Connor. Minneapolis and Oxford: University of Minnesota Press.

Nancy, Jean-Luc. 2007. *Listening*. Translated by Charlotte Mandell. New York: Fordham University Press.

Nelson, Hank. 1997. "Gallipoli, Kokoda and the Making of National Identity." *Journal of Australian Studies* 21 (53): 157–169. https://doi.org/10.1080/14443059709387325.

Nicas, Jack. 2023. "Javier Milei, a 'Mini-Trump,' could be Argentina's Next President." *The New York Times*, Oct 20. https://www.nytimes.com/2023/10/20/world/americas/javier-milei-argentina-election.html.

Nietzsche, Friedrich. 1968. *The Will to Power*. Translated by Walter Kaufmann and R. J. Hollingdale, edited by Walter Kaufmann. New York: Vintage Books.

Nietzsche, Friedrich. 2006. *Thus Spoke Zarathustra: A Book for all and None*. Translated by Adrian Del Caro, edited by Robert Pippin. Cambridge: Cambridge University Press.

Nolan, Alan, T. 2000. "The Anatomy of the Myth." In *The Myth of the Lose Cause and Civil War History*, edited by Gary W. Gallagher and Alan T. Nolan, 11–34. Bloomington and Indianapolis: Indiana University Press.

Norman, Heidi. 2023. "Coming to Terms with the Past is More Important than Ever. the Voice Referendum is a Vital First Step." *The Conversation*, Oct 13. https://theconversation.com/coming-to-terms-with-the-past-is-more-important-than-ever-the-voice-referendum-is-a-vital-first-step-215152.

Nünning, Ansgar. 2012. "Making Crises and Catastrophes – How Metaphors and Narratives Shape their Cultural Life." In *The Cultural Life of Catastrophes and Crises*, edited by Carsten Meiner and Kristin Veel. Vol. 3, 59–88. Berlin, Boston: De Gruyter. https://doi.org/10.1515/9783110282955.59.

Nussbaum, Martha. 2010. *Not for Profit: Why Democracy Needs the Humanities*. Princeton and Oxford: Princeton University Press.

Nussbaum, Martha Craven. 2013. *Political Emotions Why Love Matters for Justice*. Massachusetts: Harvard University Press. https://doi.org/10.2307/j.ctt6wpqm7.

Nye, Joseph and Youna Kim. 2013. "Soft Power and the Korean Wave." In *South Korean Popular Culture and North Korea*, edited by Youna Kim, 31–42. New York: Routledge.

N'yong'o, Tavia. 2017. "Foreword to 2017 Edition." In *Terrorist Assemblages: Homonationalism in Queer Times*, xi–xvi. Durham and London: Duke University Press.

Oakes, Guy. 1995. "Straight Thinking about Queer Theory." *International Journal of Politics, Culture, and Society* 8 (3): 379–388. https://doi.org/10.1007/BF02142891.

Orr, Gregory. 2002. *Poetry as Survival*. Athens and London: University of Georgia Press. https://doi.org/10.1353/book11409.
Orr, James J. 2001. *The Victim as Hero*. Honolulu: University of Hawaii Press.
Outram, Dorinda. 2013. *The Enlightenment: Third Edition*. Cambridge: Cambridge University Press.
Papacharissi, Zizi. 2015. *Affective Publics: Sentiment, Technology, and Politics*. Oxford and New York: Oxford University Press. https://doi.org/10.1093/acprof:oso/9780199999736.001.0001.
Papanikolaou, Dimitris. 2017. "Archive Trouble, 2017." In *Culturescapes Greece/Griechenland—Archaeology of the Future/Archäologie Der Zukunft*, edited by Botanova Kateryna, Christos Chrissopoulos and Jurriaan Cooiman, 38–51. Basel: Christoph Merian Verlag.
Papanikos, Gregory T. 2020. "Philoxenia and Xenophobia in Ancient Greece." *Athens Journal of Mediterranean Studies* 6 (3): 237–246. https://doi.org/10.30958/ajms.6-3-4.
Pardo, Pablo. 2019. "Make Spain Great Again." *Foreign Policy*, Apr. 27. https://foreignpolicy.com/2019/04/27/vox-spain-elections-trump-bannon/.
Pariser, Eli. 2011. *The Filter Bubble: How the New Personalized Web is Changing What We Read and How We Think*. New York: Penguin Publishing Group.
Pearce, Ruth, Sonja Erikainen, and Ben Vincent. 2020. "TERF Wars: An Introduction." *The Sociological Review* 68 (4): 677–698. https://doi.org/10.1177/0038026120934713.
Peterson, Anne Helen. 2021. *Can't Even: How Millennials Became the Burnout Generation*. New York: Random House.
Peterson, Jordan. 2019. "Postmodernism: Definition and Critique (with a Few Comments on its Relationship with Marxism)." jordanbpeterson.com., accessed 30 August, 2023. https://www.jordanbpeterson.com/philosophy/postmodernism-definition-and-critique-with-a-few-comments-on-its-relationship-with-marxism/.
Peukert, Detlev. 1991. *The Weimar Republic the Crisis of Classical Modernity*. London: Allan Lane.
Pichardo Galán, José Ignacio, Belén Molinuevo Puras, and Robin L. Riley. 2009. "Achieving Real Equality: A Work in Progress for LGBT Youth in Spain." *Journal of LGBT Youth* 6 (2–3): 272–287. https://doi.org/10.1080/19361650902897581.
Pickering, Grace. 2023. "'Harmful to Minors': How Book Bans Hurt Adolescent Development." *The Serials Librarian* 84 (1–4): 32–45. https://doi.org/10.1080/0361526X.2023.2245843.
Pickering, Michael. 2004. "Experience as Horizon: Koselleck, Expectation and Historical Time." *Cultural Studies* 18 (2–3). https://doi.org/10.1080/0950238042000201518.
Piketty, Thomas. 2017. *Capital in the Twenty-First Century*. Translated by Arthur Goldhammer. Cambridge, Massachusetts: Harvard University Press. https://doi.org/10.2307/j.ctvjnrvx9.
Pinker, Steven. 2018. *Enlightenment Now: The Case for Reason, Science, Humanism, and Progress*. New York: Viking.

Pluckrose, Helen and James Lindsay. 2020. *Cynical Theories: How Activist Scholarship Made Everything About Race, Gender, and Identity - And Why this Harms Everybody*. Durham: Pitchstone Publishing.

Przeworski, Adam. 2019. *Crises of Democracy*. Cambridge: Cambridge University Press. https://doi.org/10.1017/9781108671019.

Puar, Jasbir K. 2007. *Terrorist Assemblages: Homonationalism in Queer Times*. Durham: Duke University Press. https://doi.org/10.1215/9780822390442.

Puar, Jasbir, K. 2017. "Postscript: Homonationalism in Trump Times." In *Terrorist Assemblages: Homonationalism in Queer Times*. Durham and London: Duke University Press. https://doi.org/10.1215/9780822371755.

Puentes, Ana. 2024. "¿Qué cambia la nueva 'ley trans' de Ayuso? ¿Por qué la anterior era 'más avanzada'? Las claves de un retroceso, según los expertos." *El País*, December 23, accessed June 8, 2024. https://elpais.com/espana/madrid/2023-12-23/que-cambia-la-nueva-ley-trans-de-ayuso-por-que-la-norma-de-cifuentes-era-mas-progresista-las-claves-de-un-retroceso-segun-los-expertos.html.

Rancière, Jacques. 2010. *Dissensus: On Politics and Consensus*. London and New York: Continuum.

Read, Piers Paul. 2012. *The Dreyfus Affair the Scandal that Tore France in Two*. New York: Bloomsbury.

Reed, Matt T. 2001. "Historicizing Inversion: Or, how to make a Homosexual." *History of the Human Sciences* 14 (4): 1–29. https://doi.org/10.1177/095269510101400401.

Renan, Ernest. 2018. *What is a Nation? And Other Political Writings*. Translated by M. F. N. Giglioli. New York: Colombia University Press. https://doi.org/10.7312/rena17430.

Rhodes, Carl. 2022. *Woke Capitalism: How Corporate Morality is Sabotaging Democracy*. Bristol: Bristol University Press. https://doi.org/10.2307/j.ctv21zp20t.

Rinaldi, Carlina. 2001. "The Pedagogy of Listening: The Listening Perspective from Reggio Emilia." *Innovations in Early Education: The International Reggio Exchange* 8 (4): 1–4.

Roberts, Hannah. 2023. "Italy's Meloni Gets Tough on Migrants." *Politico*, Sep 18. https://www.politico.eu/article/italy-prime-minister-giorgia-meloni-immigration-crackdown/.

Roitman, Janet. 2014. *Anti-Crisis*. Durham and London: Duke University Press.

Rommel, Inken. 2017. "'We are the People.' Refugee–'Crisis,' and the Drag-Effects of Social Habitus in German Society." *Historical Social Research (Köln)* 42 (4) (Jan 1): 133–154.

Ronson, Jon. 2015. *So You've been Publicly Shamed*. London: Picador.

Rose, Jacqueline. 1996. *States of Fantasy*. Oxford: Clarendon Press.

Ross, Kristin. 2002. *May '68 and its Afterlives*. Chicago: University of Chicago Press. https://doi.org/10.7208/chicago/9780226728001.001.0001.

Rousseau, Jean-Jacques. 1979. *Emile, or On Education*. Translated by Allan Bloom. New York: Basic Books.

Roy, Arundhati. 2020. "The Pandemic is a Portal." *Financial Times*, Apr 4. https://www.ft.com/content/10d8f5e8-74eb-11ea-95fe-fcd274e920ca.

Roy, Srirupa. 2007. *Beyond Belief: India and the Politics of Postcolonial Nationalism*. Politics, History, and Culture. 1st ed. Durham: Duke University Press. https://doi.org/10.1215/9780822389910.
Rudden, Marie, G. 2021. "Insurrection in the U.S. Capitol: Understanding Psychotic, Projective and Introjective Group Processes." *International Journal of Applied Psychoanalytic Studies* 18 (4) (Dec): 372–384. https://doi.org/10.1002/aps.1733.
Ruipérez Núñez, Ana and Elias Dinas. 2023. "Mean Streets: Power, Ideology and the Politics of Memory." *Political Geography* 103 (May). https://doi.org/10.1016/j.polgeo.2023.102840.
Salade Grecque. 2023. Directed by Lola Doillon, Antoine Garceau and Cédric Klapisch. Amazon Studios.
Sandel, Michael J. 2020. *The Tyranny of Merit: What's Become of the Common Good?* London: Penguin Books.
Sartre, Jean-Paul. 2012. *Saint Genet*. Translated by Bernard Frechtman. Minneapolis: University of Minnesota Press.
Schulman, Sarah. 2012. *The Gentrification of the Mind: Witness to a Lost Imagination*. Berkeley, CA: University of California Press.
Shangay Lily. 2016. *Adiós Chueca. Memorias del gaypitalismo: la creación de la marca gay*. Madrid: Ediciones Akal.
Sharon, Jeremy, Carrie Keller-Lynn, and Amy Spiro. 2023. "After Days of Indecision, Netanyahu, Gantz Agree to Establish Emergency War Government." *The Times of Israel*, Oct 11. https://www.timesofisrael.com/after-days-of-indecision-netanyahu-gantz-agree-to-establish-emergency-war-government/.
Siani-Davies, Peter. 2017. *Crisis in Greece*. London: Hurst & Company.
Simantke, Elisa and Harald Schumann. 2015. "Varoufakis: Greece's Creditors have Turned Negotiations into a War." *Euractiv*, 10 Jun. https://www.euractiv.com/section/euro-finance/interview/varoufakis-greece-s-creditors-have-turned-negotiations-into-a-war/.
Siminski, Peter. 2021. "68% of Millennials Earn More than their Parents, but Boomers had it Better." *The Conversation*, Jun 1. https://theconversation.com/68-of-millennials-earn-more-than-their-parents-but-boomers-had-it-better-161647.
Smith, Anthony D. 1991. *National Identity*. Reno: University of Nevada Press.
Smith, Linda Tuhiwai. 2021. *Decolonizing Methodologies: Research and Indigenous Peoples*. Ireland: Zed Books.
Somers, Margaret R. and Gloria D. Gibson. 1995. "Reclaiming the Epistemological 'Other': Narrative and the Social Construction of Identity." In *Social Theory and the Politics of Identity*, edited by Craig Calhoun, 37–99. Oxford: Blackwell.
Spivak, G. C. 1988. "Can the Subaltern Speak?" In *Marxism and the Interpretation of Culture*, edited by C. Nelson and L. Grossberg, 271–313. Urbana: University of Illinois Press.
Stafylakis, Kostis. 2017. "Mythologies of the Collective: Togetherness After Greek Neo-Patriotism and how to Taint It." In *Culturescapes Greece/Griechenland— Archaeology of the Future/Archäologie Der Zukunft*, edited by Kateryna Botanova, Christos Chrissopoulos and Jurriaan Cooiman, 236–255. Basel: Christoph Merian Verlag.

Statista. 2023. "Number of Smartphone Mobile Network Subscriptions Worldwide from 2016 to 2022, with Forecasts from 2023 to 2028." *Statista*, accessed 27 September, 2023, https://www.statista.com/statistics/330695/number-of-smartphone-users-worldwide/.

Steinberg, Jonathan. 2011. *Bismarck: A Life*. Oxford: Oxford University Press.

Stella, Francesca. 2013. "Queer Space, Pride, and Shame in Moscow." *Slavic Review* 72 (3): 458–480. https://doi.org/10.5612/slavicreview.72.3.0458.

Storey, Benjamin and Jenna Silber Storey. 2021. *Why We Are Restless*. New Forum Books. Princeton: Princeton University Press. https://doi.org/10.1515/9780691211138.

Stryker, Susan. 2008. *Transgender History: The Roots of Today's Revolution*. Berkeley: Seal Press.

Suárez, Sandra L. 2006. "Mobile Democracy: Text Messages, Voter Turnout and the 2004 Spanish General Election." *Journal of Representative Democracy* 42 (2): 117–128. https://doi.org/10.1080/00344890600736358.

Sugiura, Lisa. 2021. *The Incel Rebellion: The Rise of the Manosphere and the Virtual War Against Women*. Emerald Studies in Digital Crime, Technology and Social Harms. Bingley: Emerald Publishing Limited. https://doi.org/10.1108/9781839822544.

Szabó, Jakub. 2020. "First as Tragedy, then as Farce: A Comparative Study of Right-Wing Populism in Hungary and Poland." *Journal of Comparative Politics* 13 (2): 24–42.

Terman, Rochelle. 2020. "The Positive Side of Negative Identity: Stigma and Deviance in Backlash Movements." *The British Journal of Politics and International Relations* 22 (4): 619–630. https://doi.org/10.1177/1369148120948485.

Theodossopoulos, Dimitrios. 2013. "Infuriated with the Infuriated? Blaming Tactics and Discontent about the Greek Financial Crisis." *Current Anthropology* 54 (2): 200–221. https://doi.org/10.1086/669855.

Tomaselli, Keyan, G. 2023. "Alter-Egos: Cultural and Media Studies." In *The Humanities Reloaded: Addressing Crisis*, edited by Keyan G. Tomaselli and Pier Paolo Frassinelli, 113–132. New York: Routledge. https://doi.org/10.4324/9781003359920-9.

Tomsen, Stephen and Kevin Markwell. 2009. "Violence, Cultural Display and the Suspension of Sexual Prejudice." *Sexuality & Culture* 13 (4) (Dec 1): 201–217.

Tribe, Keith. 1985. "Translator's Introduction." In *Futures Past: On the Semantics of Historical Time*, edited by Reinhart Koselleck, xii–xvii. Cambridge, MA and London: The MIT Press.

Tzirtzilakis, Yorgos. 2017. "Identities and Sub-Modernity: Tropes and Psychic Apparatus in Contemporary Greek Culture." In *Culturescapes Greece/Griechenland—Archaeology of the Future/Archäologie Der Zukunft*, edited by Kateryna Botanova, Christos Chrissopoulos and Jurriaan Cooiman, 106–127. Basel: Christoph Merian Verlag.

Vaiou, Dina. 2016. "Tracing Aspects of the Greek Crisis in Athens: Putting Women in the Picture." *European Urban and Regional Studies* 23 (3) (Jul): 220–230. https://doi.org/10.1177/0969776414523802.

van Gelder, Sarah. 2011. *This Changes Everything: Occupy Wall Street and the 99% Movement*. Williston, VT: Berrett-Koehler Publishers.

Vigh, Henrik. 2008. "Crisis and Chronicity: Anthropological Perspectives on Continuous Conflict and Decline." *Ethnos* 73 (1): 5–24. https://doi.org/10.1080/00141840801927509.

Wachs, Anthony M. and Jon D. Schaff. 2020. *Age of Anxiety: Meaning, Identity, and Politics in 21st-Century Film and Literature*. Lanham: Lexington Books.

Weitz, Eric D. 2007. *Weimar Germany: Promise and Tragedy*. Princeton and Oxford: Princeton University Press.

Westra, Evan. 2021. "Virtue Signaling and Moral Progress." *Philosophy & Public Affairs* 49 (2) (Spring): 156–178. https://doi.org/10.1111/papa.12187.

Whaley, Joachim. 2012. *Germany and the Holy Roman Empire: Volume I: Maximilian I to the Peace of Westphalia, 1493–1648*. Oxford: Oxford University Press. ttps://doi.org/10.1093/acprof:oso/9780198731016.001.0001.

Wilson, Peter H. 2016. *Heart of Europe: A History of the Holy Roman Empire*. Cambridge, MA: Belknap Press. https://doi.org/10.4159/9780674915909.

Wodak, Ruth. 2015. *The Politics of Fear: What Right-Wing Populist Discourses Mean*. London: Sage. https://doi.org/10.4135/9781446270073.

Wood, Gordon S. 2011. *The Radicalism of the American Revolution*. New York: Vintage Books.

Wüstenberg, Jenny and Aline Sierp. 2020. "Online Transnational Memory Activism and Commemoration: The Case of the White Armband Day." In *Agency in Transnational Memory Politics*, edited by Jenny Wüstenberg and Aline Sierp. Vol. 4, 68–91. New York and Oxford: Berghahn Books. https://doi.org/10.2307/j.ctv21hrgfv.8.

Žižek, Slavoj. 2004. *Iraq: The Borrowed Kettle*. London and New York: Verso.

Žižek, Slavoj. 2006. *The Universal Exception*. London: Continuum.

Žižek, Slavoj. 2017. *The Courage of Hopelessness: Chronicles of a Year of Acting Dangerously*. London: Penguin.

Žižek, Slavoj. 2018. *Like a Thief in Broad Daylight: Power in the Era of Post-Humanity*. London: Penguin Books.

Žižek, Slavoj. 2020. *Pandemic: COVID-19 Shakes the World*. New York: Polity Press. https://doi.org/10.2307/j.ctv16t6n4q.

Index

Abascal, Santiago, 175, 177
Aboriginal peoples (Australia), 10; voice to parliament referendum, 111–12
abstraction, 38. *See also* postmodernism
academic disobedience, milton's concept, 51
Adorno, Theodor, 25, 49
affective responses: Berlant's analysis, 49; influence on crisis perception, 49; shaped by digital media, 61–62. *See also* affect theory; Berlant
affect theory, 50
Agamben, Giorgio, 5–6, 12, 16, 64, 82, 85–87, 186–87; biosecurity and "new normal," 85–86; concept of "phantasmatic space," 37; concept of "potentiality," 50; crisis as an instrument of rule, 74; critique of modernity, 35–36; critique of the isolation of art and artist, 43; destruction of experience, 35–36; distinction between *Erlebnis* and *Erfahrung*, 6, 83–84; *Infancy and History: The Destruction of Experience*, 35; role in digital crisis ambientality, 186–87; state of exception, 70, 85–87; sterile archive, 79. *See also* crisis ambientality; state of exception

Age of Anger, 3
Age of Anxiety, 3; critique of individualism, 47
Ahmed, Sara: emotion and crisis, 2, 11
Alhambra, 6
Almodóvar, Pedro, 173
Alternative for Germany (AfD), 124
ambientality: of crisis, 18; of digital crisis, 19
American War of Independence, 40
anarchy: as a form of utopian desire in Greece, 56
Anderson, Benedict: imagined communities, 75, 105–6, 141, 178; imagined communities and digital spaces, 121, 141
anxiety: link to radical individualism, 47; role in shaping societal responses to crises, 58. *See also* individualism
apprehension, 9–11, 180; economic fragility and insecurity, 10–11; impact on youth and economic outlook, 11; populist narratives as responses to apprehension, 11
Archive Trouble: concept by Papanikolaou, 77–78, 82; Greek Weird Wave connection, 78; transformation of archives into resistance and resignification, 78, 82.

See also crisis ambientality; Greek Weird Wave; Papanikolaou
Arendt, Hannah, 43
Armenian Genocide, 119
Athens: community-based artistic practices, 77; cultural hub, 76–77; role in crisis ambientality, 76–78. *See also* communal becomings; crisis ambientality; Greek Weird Wave
austerity measures: impact on Spain and Greece, 56
Australia: voice to parliament referendum, 111–12
authoritarianism: global rise, 50; link to decline of democracy and humanities, 50
authoritarian reflex, 8
autonomy: definition by Arno Gruen, 37
Ayuso, Isabel Díaz, 177

Badiou, Alain: on poetry, 80; transformative events, 31. *See also* poetry
Bal, Mieke: traveling concept, 26
Barcelona: impact of economic instability, 53; reflections on city in crisis and national identity, 54
Baudrillard, Jean: concept of catastrophe, 44; hyperreality, 65; *la grève des événements* (the strike of events), 32
Bauman, Zygmunt: concept of "retrotopias," 14, 16; critique of modernity, 25, 88–90; emotional capacity of nations, 109; liquid modernity and liquid fear, 8, 108; nationalism and statecraft, 98, 100; nation-state as an "unfinished project," 97–98, 100–101. *See also* liquid modernity; nationalism
Beck, Ulrich, 8
Benjamin, Walter, 5, 18, 26; concept of "now-time," 33; distinction between *Erlebnis* and *Erfahrung*, 6, 83–84; historical accountability, 34; poverty of experience, 5–6
Berardi, Franco: crisis as new horizon of possibility, 149; definition of power, 15–16; madness in crisis, 183–84
Berger, John: confabulations, 112; horizons of past and future, 112; state of forgetfulness, 112–13
Berlant, Lauren: crisis ordinary, 5, 43, 49–51, 53, 88–89; critique of history, 189; cruel optimism, 49, 88–90, 110; narratives as performative constructs, 51; nations as fantasy, 110. *See also* Archive Trouble; crisis cultures; cruel optimism
Bhabha, Homi K.; nation as narration, 106–7
Billig, Michael: banal nationalism, 118; banal nationalism in digital spaces, 120–21
biosecurity, 85–87
Bismarck, Otto von: role in German unification, 101; use of orchestrated crises, 101
Black Lives Matter Movement: connection to global threads of dissent, 57; digital activism, 121
Bloch, Ernst: principle of hope, 13; role of utopian narratives in crisis cultures, 13
Blunderbuss Strategy, 132–34
Boletsi, Maria: Athens as a site of social and cultural transformation, 76–77; concept of "arrested temporality," 74–75
Bourdieu, Pierre: concept of "habitus" in relation to economic and social crises, 68
branding, 23–24; political branding and slogans, 129–30
Brexit, 13–14
Buenos Aires: impact of economic instability, 53
burnout, 23–24, 46

burnout society: concept and critiques, 23–26, 37, 63–64
Bush Administration: reality-based community critique, 125–26; role in shaping narratives post-9/11, 123–26

Camus, Albert, 183–84
capitalism: crises linked to economic disruptions, 40; Marx's critique, 40; neo-Marxist critique, 41. *See also* economic discontent; Global Financial Crisis; neoliberalism
Capitol Hill insurrection, 7, 19, 96–97; analysis of rage and its impact, 127–28; impact on national identity and democratic institutions, 127–28, 136–40; role of Christian Nationalists and militia groups, 136–37; role of confabulated narratives, 126–28, 137; role of Donald Trump, 127, 129–30; role of elites and their reactions, 139–40
Carpentier, Nico: discursive-material knot, 1, 3–4, 12, 36–38
cartography: metaphor for future possibilities, 32
Casey, Edward: distinctions between *Erlebnis* and *Erfahrung*, 35–36
Castells, Manuel: network society, 108
Catalonia (independence), 13; 2017 referendum and its aftermath, 54, 174; economic frustrations, 56; nationalism and independence movement, 54, 171, 174; protests post-Supreme Court verdict, 54–55
catastrophe: concept evolution, 27, 32–33; effect of, 32; Voltaire and Baudrillard's views, 32
Charlottesville, Virginia: Unite the Right rally, 120
Chitty, Christopher, 20
class: social, 10
climate change, 7, 29–30, 33, 44–46, 63

Clinton, Hillary: basket of deplorables comment, 91–93; representation of political establishment, 94
Cold War, 10
commodification: experiences as consumable spectacles, 61
communal becomings, 1–2, 4, 12, 14, 17, 34, 87; as counter to mainstream crisis narratives, 50; emergence in artistic expression, 76–78; reflections on communal actions during COVID-19, 86–87. *See also* Athens; crisis ambientality; Greek Weird Wave
confabulation: definition of, 114, 118–26; digital era impact, 124–26, 132–34; national confabulation, 113–14, 117–18, 136–39; relation to collective memory, 113–18; role in shaping national identity, 113–18, 126–30, 137–38
conjunctures, 30–31
conspiracy theories: appeal and psychological impact, 134; connection to Trump's "Steal" narrative, 131–34; QAnon, 13
cost of living, 15
counter-memory, concept by Foucault, 50
COVID-19 pandemic, 7, 13, 15, 19, 31, 82–88; communal responses, 86–87; influence on global economic structures, 82–86; national identity and response, 109–10; protests against government restrictions, 57; state of exception during the pandemic, 85–88; surveillance concerns, 59, 82–88. *See also* Agamben; digital crisis ambientality; Great Resignation; Klein; state of exception
crisis: ambientality, 18, 58, 60–69, 71–72, 75, 82–90, 118–19, 132–34, 139, 174–75, 185–86; cultural life of, 27–28; definition and characteristics,

1–2, 4–5, 7, 20, 27, 38, 41; discourse of, 7, 57; economic, 2, 7, 18, 40, 56, 65–66, 68–72; etymology of, 4, 18; financial, 2, 25; genealogy of, 4, 26–27, 38; Global Financial Crisis, 2–3, 7; historical evolution of the term, 38; impact on daily life, 42; interpretation of, 11–12, 21, 44–46, 50, 56, 138–39, 178–79; literature, 3, 6–7; mediation, 61; narrative device, 43; neoliberal, 7, 24; polycrisis, 3; queering of, 20; relationship to utopian aspirations, 55; temporal dynamics of, 25–26; ubiquity in modern discourse, 3–4; virtualization of, 59–61. *See also* crisis ambientality; economic crisis; Global Financial Crisis

crisis ambientality: comparison to Heidegger's *Dasein* and Debord's "society of the spectacle," 60–61; impact on collective identity and imagined communities, 75–78, 124–27; impact on Greek society, 68–69; influence on digital interactions, 82–88, 118–19, 132–34, 139, 185–86; influence on national identity, 118–19, 174–75; parallels with vampire metaphor, 88–89; perpetuation of systemic inequities, 71; persistence and adaptability of crises, 88–90, 185; role in Athens' social dynamics, 76–77; role in crisis experience, 58, 60–61; role in Greek political polarization, 71–72; smartphones' influence on crisis perception, 58, 60–67. *See also* COVID-19; digital crisis ambientality; pandemic digital; virtualization of crisis

crisis cultures: affective capacity of, 3; cultural life of, 27–28; definition, 1–3, 5, 14, 16–17, 21, 26, 32, 44; discursive contestation, 36–37, 43; engagement with historical moments, 34; epistemological tools, 35; evolution from postmodernism, 44–46; impact of, 23, 25, 128, 137–38; lack of meaningful events, 5–6, 9, 180; new interpretative possibility, 5, 9, 184–85; as part of Western modernity, 1, 7–9, 20, 28; pedagogical responses, 186–88; queer identities within, 144–54, 181–82; role of narratives within, 42–43, 46–47, 51–52, 180–81; role of national identity, 123–24; temporality of, 25, 27–29, 34, 180. *See also* anxiety; communal becomings; crisis ambientality; history (impasse)

crisis ordinary concept by Berlant, 49
cruel optimism, 49
crypto-colonialism, 69–70
cryptocurrency, 25
cultural backlash, 92
cultural intimacy: concept by Michael Herzfeld, applied to Greek crisis, 69. *See also* Greek crisis; Herzfeld
cultural neo-Marxism: critique by Peterson, 48
cultural relativism: critique of, 47–48; in political discourse, 130

Dasein: definition of Heidegger's concept of "being-in-the-world," 60; relation to crisis ambientality and smartphone usage, 60, 63, 65
Dawkins, Richard: critique of identity politics, 147
Debord, Guy: concept of the "society of the spectacle," 61, 63, 65, 73–74; relevance to digital crisis ambientality, 61
decolonization, 106
Delgado, Luisa Elena, 110
Del Noce, Augusto: *Crisis of Modernity*, 48
democracy: Przeworski's insights on democratic crises, 57; retreat of, 8
Dennett, Daniel, 114

Derrida, Jacques, 25; time is out of joint, 50, 52
desire: role in Berlant's concept of "cruel optimism," 49
detachment, existential, 63–67
de Tocqueville, Alexis: contradictions of emerging democracies, 40; paradox of "immanent contentment," 40
diagonalism, 154–55
dialectics, 9, 20, 25, 28, 50
Diderot, Denis, 39
digital: communication, 118–26; crisis ambientality, 18, 19, 58–60, 62–63, 82–86; distraction, 63–67; impact on confabulation, 117–18; impact on crisis narratives, 58–59, 61, 183; impact on identity formation, 154–57; influence on national identity, 113, 118–23; influence on virtue signaling, 157–58; infosphere, 24; media, 63–64, 124–25, 127–34; role in amplifying conservative ideologies, 178–79; role in fostering diagonalism, 154–55; technologies, 18, 58, 178. *See also* crisis ambientality; digital crisis ambientality; information regime; smartphones
digital crisis ambientality: critique by Agamben, 85–87; definition of, 82–88; impact during COVID-19, 82–88; impact on confabulation and misinformation, 117–18, 125, 132–34; impact on identity formation, 154–57; relationship with *Erlebnis* and *Erfahrung*, 83–85, 124, 185; role in amplifying polarization, 178–79, 185; role in conspiracy theories, 84–85. *See also* Agamben; conspiracy theories; COVID-19; *Erfahrung*; *Erlebnis*; infocracy; Klein; media; smartphones
discursive material knot (Carpentier's framework), 1, 3–4, 12, 36–38

Doukas, Yiannis, 79–81; poem "Epitaph" and reflections on loss, 80–81. *See also* crisis ambientality; poetry
Duggan, Lisa: homonormativity, 147
dystopias, 8, 11–14, 24, 29; influence on crisis cultures, 13–14; narrative counterpoints, 12–13, 180

Eagleton, Terry: concept of, 10–11; role of hope in post-war Western societies, 10
economic crisis: austerity and youth protests, 56; dissolution of relationships due to economic instability, 53; Greek crisis and systemic vulnerabilities, 18, 68–72; impact on marginalized groups, 71; impact on Mediterranean countries, 56; mid-nineteenth-century development, 40; Spanish, 2, 56. *See also* crisis
economic discontent: driving force behind global protests, 57; link to austerity and precarity, 56–57
economic insecurity: impact on generational expectations and youth, 11; role in apprehensive outlook on the future, 10–11; shift from post-war prosperity, 9–11
education: impact on democracy and social cohesion, 50; role of humanities in crisis, 50
El Conde (film), 88–89
elections: Clinton *vs.* Trump in 2016 U.S. election, 93–94; Trump's allegations of electoral fraud, 131–32, 134, 136–37
elite: elite *vs.* non-elite dichotomy, 139
el procés: public narrative of Catalan independence issue, 55
emotions, 9, 15–16; affective capacity in relation to crisis cultures, 3; hope and apprehension, 9; stickiness, 11. *See also* anxiety; hope; narrative(s)

Engels, Friedrich, 41
Enlightenment: achievements defended by Pinker, 46; challenge to monarchical and religious authority, 98; impact on modernity, 25–26, 28–29; influence on critical thinking and political crisis, 39; influence on national sovereignty, 98; transition to postmodernism, 39, 44
epistemology: for responding to crises, 50
Erfahrung: contrast with *Erlebnis*, 83–84, 124, 185; definition and philosophical meaning, 6, 9, 35–36, 61–62, 82–85, 180–81; in digital contexts, 61–62; Kant's use in Critique of Pure Reason, 35; loss in modern times, 36; transformative experience during the pandemic, 82–84. *See also* COVID-19; digital crisis ambientality; *Erlebnis*; Klein
Erinakis, Nikos, 80; poem "The New Symmetry," 80–81; themes of resilience, 80–81. *See also also*crisis ambientality; poetry
Erlebnis: contrast with *Erfahrung* in the context of COVID-19, 83–84, 124, 185; definition and philosophical meaning, 6, 9, 35–36, 61, 83–84, 185; impact on crisis perception and cultural responses, 83–85, 180–81, 185. *See also* digital crisis ambientality, *Erfahrung*, Klein
European Union, 10, 13; pressures leading to austerity measures in Greece and Spain, 56; role in Greek financial crisis, 69–70
events: lack of meaning, 5, 9; strike of, 32
existential crisis: influence of postmodernity and individualism, 47; link to modern discontent, 49–50. *See also* individualism
experience: authentic experience, 37; definition and use across disciplines, 6, 34; digital impact, 61–62; *Erlebnis vs. Erfahrung*, 61, 148–49; fragmentation of, 5–6, 18, 34, 36; lived, 15, 28, 34, 59; narrative, 12, 180; temporality, 14, 26
Extinction Rebellion, 13

Fanon, Frantz: influence on postcolonial thought, 106
fear: culture of, 8
financial crisis, 2; definition, 2; Greek, 7, 18; transformation, 25
Foucault, Michel: concept of counter-memory, 50, 187; crisis as opportunity, 30; critique of historical continuity, 30; critique of modernity, 25; disciplinary power in virtue signaling, 157–58; normalization, 15
Francoism: historical legacy in Catalonia, 54
French Revolution, 29, 98
Friedman, Thomas, 10–11
Fukuyama, Francis; "end of history" thesis, 108
Furedi, Frank, 8
futurity: crisis influence on, 31–32; horizon of expectation, 28–29; role in crisis cultures, 14–15

Gallipoli: Anzac legend, 118; recontextualization in Australian and New Zealand identity, 117–18
Gellner, Ernest: nations as deliberate constructions, 102; role of modernity and industrialization, 102–3
gender inequality, 71
genealogy, 9; of the concept of crisis, 38
Giddens, Anthony: critique of nation-state's capacity, 108; reflexive modernity, 8, 16
gig economy, 67
Global Financial Crisis, 2, 16, 31; Grossberg's analysis, 44–46; impact on youth, referred to as "the

lost generation," 53; influence on migration patterns among youth, 53; influence on the author's understanding of crisis, 2–3, 7, 18, 68–72. *See also* crisis; crisis ambientality

globalization, 10; impact on nation-state relevance, 108; influence on national identities, 108–9

Goethe, Johann Wolfgang von, 154

Golden Dawn: ethnonationalist agenda, 56, 72; Greek nationalist desire for a purified nation, 56; violence linked to, 72

Great Depression, 68

Great Recession, 2, 174; impact on European youth, 53. *See also* Global Financial Crisis

Great Resignation, 84

Greece, 2; crisis etymology, 4; economic crisis, 7, 18, 56, 68–72; *Oxi* Vote, Greek 2015 bailout referendum, 57; riots, 2–3; shaming in international media, 56

Greek Weird Wave: role in exploring crisis ambientality, 78–79. *See also* Archive Trouble; Lanthimos, Yorgos; Papanikolaou, Dimitris

Grossberg, Lawrence, 44–46

Gruen, Arno: definition of autonomy, 37; emotional cycles and authenticity, 64, 188; modernity's paradoxes, 50; psychoanalytical viewpoints, 34

Habermas, Jürgen: discourse on modernity and crisis, 24–26; lifeworlds, 140–41; modernity as inherently crisis-ridden, 49

Haitian Revolution, 99

Hall, Stuart, 30, 42, 51; challenge to "dominant codes" of representation and meaning, 50

Hamlet: reference to "the time is out of joint," 52

Han, Byung-Chul: atomization and narcissism in public discourse, 156; *Burnout Society*, 23–26, 37, 63–64; critique of hyper-individualism, 46; critique of public discourse fragmentation, 156–57; digital platforms and historical continuity, 118; infocracy, 60, 139; listening, 186–87; new nihilism, 137–38; polarization in societies, 185; psychopolitics, 59; relational frameworks and identity, 151–52, 161. *See also* digital crisis ambientality; infocracy; information regime; psychopolitics; surveillance; virtualization of crisis

Harvey, David: critique of identity politics, 150–51; critique of postmodernism, 44; diversity, 146; time-space compression, 30–31

Hegel, Georg Wilhelm Friedrich, 9, 25

Heidegger, Martin: alignment with Greek concept of truth (alētheia), 145–46; Concept of "the open" *(das Offene)*, 145–47; concept of *Dasein* or "being-in-the-world," 60–61, 63, 65; smartphones and extending *Dasein*, 60–61. *See also* crisis ambientality; *Dasein*

Herder, Johann Gottfried: crisis as a historiographical tool, 39

Herzfeld, Michael: crypto-colonialism, 69; cultural intimacy and crisis, 69–75

heteronormativity, 182

Hirstein, William: definition of confabulation, 114–16; distinction between confabulation and delusion, 116; psychological motivations for confabulation, 115–16

history: determinism, 31; historical impasse, 16, 33; historical time, 4; philosophy of, 28–29, 33; progress, 10

Hobsbawm, Eric: analysis of nationalism, 98; concept of "invented traditions," 103–4

Holy Roman Empire, 98
homonationalism, 20, 169–75, 179–82
homosexuality: historical perceptions, 149; mirroring in queer identities, 154–61. *See also* queer(ing)
Hong Kong, democracy protests, 57
hooks, bell, 110
hope: apprehension towards the future, 10–11, 180; influence on crisis cultures, 9–11, 180; as a motivator for social change, 9, 57; post-World War II era hope, 9–10; principle of, 13; relation to utopias and crisis, 9–10, 57. *See also* Berlant; crisis cultures; utopia
horizon of expectation: definition of, 28–29, 33; impact on individual worldviews, 46; link to the experiences of Catalan youth, 55
Horkheimer, Max, 25
hospitality: Greek concept of philoxenia, 143–44; theoxenia and divine hospitality, 143
humanities: critique by De Chavez and Varadharajan, 50; Nussbaum's view of humanities in crisis, 50; role in democracy, 50. *See also* authoritarianism; education; Nussbaum
hyper-individualism: critique by Han, 46
hyperobject: concept by Timothy Morton, 7, 63
hyperreality, 65

identity: Catalan nationalism and historical narrative, 54; critique of identity politics, 146–48, 150–51, 159–61; group, 12, 16, 18, 20, 144–49, 161–62, 178–81; individual, 16, 23–24; intersectionality and critiques, 152; national, 18–19; role of digital age in identity fluidity, 152; sexual, 12, 20, 170–82

identity politics: critiques and challenges, 48, 150–51; impact of diagonalism, 154–55; intersection virtue signaling, 157–58; Žižek's critique of, 159–61. *See also* identity; mirror(ing); virtue signaling
imagined communities: crisis context, 75–76, 141; definition of, 105–6, 141
immigration: fear of, 13
impasse (historical), 16; role in the perpetuation of crises, 58
India: post-independence national identity, 107
indignados movement (Spain), 56
individualism: critique by Wachs and Schaff, 47; demands for self-reinvention, 46; linked to anxiety and societal fragmentation, 47; neoliberal narrative, 65. *See also* anxiety; existential crisis; neoliberalism
individual subjectivity, 17, 19, 24
industrial revolution, 7
inequality, 7, 10, 47; gender, 71
Infancy and History (Agamben): critique of modernity, 35; destruction of experience, 35
infocracy, 60, 139
information overload, 63–64
information regime: defined by Byung-Chul Han, 59–60
intersectionality, 152

Jameson, Fredric: postmodernism and uncertainty of narrative purpose, 44
Japan: Meiji Restoration and national identity, 105; post-WWII identity recalibration, 106

Kalfopoulou, Adrianne: poem "Ungodly," 79–80; themes of belonging and exile in her poetry, 79–81. *See also* crisis ambientality; poetry
Kierkegaard, Søren: warning against intellectual abstraction, 37

Klein, Naomi: concept of mirror world, 125, 153–55; digital ecosystem's role in the pandemic, 84–85; systemic critique, 188. *See also* conspiracy theories; digital crisis ambientality
Korean Wave (*Hallyu*), 108
Koselleck, Reinhart, 25; crisis as a lens for history, 14, 28; *Critique and Crisis*, 39; economic disruptions and crisis, 40; Enlightenment and critical thinking, 39; experience in relation to time, 34; historical evolution of the term crisis, 38; interpretative possibilities of crisis, 4–5, 20–21; Rousseau's influence on crisis concept, 39; space of experience and horizon of expectation, 28–31, 33, 35, 46, 55, 57, 183–85; teleological view of history, 39. *See also* crisis cultures; *Erfahrung*; *Erlebnis*; temporality
Kotouza, Dimitra, 71–72; critique of universalizing crisis experience, 7

labor markets: impact of crisis on employment stability, 42
Lacan, Jacques: mirror stage theory, 154
language: experience of, 6
Lanthimos, Yorgos, 78. *See also* Greek Weird Wave
Last Judgment: association with the term crisis, 38
Levinas, Emmanuel, 144
LGBT+; identity, 20; impact of crisis on, 7
Lindqvist, Sven, 21
liquid fear, 8
liquid modernity, 8
listening, 186–88
lived experiences, 38; impact on communal becomings, 59. *See also* COVID-19 pandemic
Lost Cause narrative: parallel with QAnon conspiracy theory, 123; post-Civil War Southern identity, 122
Lyotard, Jean-François: *The Postmodern Condition*, 44

Marx, Karl, 30; crisis as a tool for social critique, 41; impact on neo-Marxist theories, 41
media: role in amplifying Blunderbuss Strategy, 132–33; role in amplifying perceptions of danger, 62; role in crisis spectacle, 60–61; role in perpetuating misinformation, 135–36; role in transforming the concept of crisis, 41, 133–34. *See also* crisis ambientality; information regime
Mediterranean region: diverse forms of protest and dissent, 56
memory, 28; collective memory and national identity, 112–18, 180; role of confabulation in memory, 114–18
men's rights groups, 162
meritocracy: critique by Michael J. Sandel, 40; critique of equality of opportunity, 10
Milei, Javier, 94
mirror(ing), 20; phenomenon across group identities, 161–62, 181
Mishra, Pankaj, 13, 47; *Age of Anger*, 64; critique of neoliberal individualism, 46
misinformation: distinction from confabulation, 116, 125; role in confabulation, 125
modernity: acceleration of historical time, 24–26, 29; crisis as a defining aspect, 39; critique by Del Noce, 48; critique by Han, 46; critique by Nietzsche, 31; critique by Žižek, 66.; critiques in Western societies, 4, 8–9, 20–21; redefinition of history, 35–36; skepticism of linear progression, 46; transition toward postmodernism, 44; utopian vision of, 46–47. *See also* utopia
modernization, 30
moral relativism, 48
Moreton, Timothy: hyperobjects and large-scale crises, 7

Muñoz, José Esteban: queer futurity, 149, 182; staging utopia, 188–89; temporal dimensions as performative, 14, 16. *See also* identity politics; queer(ing); narrative(s); utopias

Nancy, Jean-Luc, 145
narrative(s): crisis as a narrative device, 43; crisis of grand narratives, 44; definition of, 11–12, 43, 51; dominant narratives, 36; influence on national identity, 105–7; new normal, 15–17, 19; of progress, 8; role in crisis cultures, 45–46, 51, 59, 65–67, 180–81; role in shaping national identity, 104–6; storytelling, 6, 11–12; tautological, 178–82; utopia and dystopia, 8, 11–14, 24. *See also* Berlant; crisis ambientiality; digital; narrative device; utopias
national identity: continuous negotiation of, 101; emotional capacity and resilience of, 109; formation and maintenance through confabulation, 113–18; influence of digital age, 113, 118–23; influence of globalization, 108–10; influence of regional identities, 102; negotiation through narrative and crisis, 104–7; postcolonial contexts, 106; role of collective memory, 112–23
nationalism, 15; Christian, 135; populist nationalisms and Catalan independence, 54; varying expressions in Greece, including Golden Dawn, 56
nation-building: historical evolution from Westphalia to modern times, 96; narrative construction during crises, 96–98, 100–101; role in state sovereignty and collective identity, 97–99; role of confabulations, 96–97
nation-state: challenges posed by regional identities, 104; historical evolution from Peace of Westphalia, 97–98; relevance in the global era, 108–9; state power and cultural identity, 101–2
natural disasters: management and perception, 35
neoliberalism, 10, 24, 46, 74–75, 88–89; critique through vampire metaphor, 88–89; impact on Western societies, 8–9; relationship with authoritarianism, 88–89; resilience of, 57, 66–67; as a structural condition in crisis politics, 71–72. *See also* Global Financial Crisis
neoliberal reforms: connection to economic insecurity and apprehension, 10–11; impact of Reaganite and Thatcherite policies, 10
neo-Marxism, 41
network propaganda: definition of, 135; influence of media on political discourse, 135–36; strategic use by Trump and his allies, 135
new nihilism, 137–38
new normal, 19, 31; concept in relation to crisis cultures, 15–17; critique by Foucault, 15
New World Disorder, 3
Nietzsche, Friedrich, 25, 31–32; focus on future aspirations, 32; opportunities for transformation in modernity, 37; will to power, 31
nihilism, 48
normality: role in crisis cultures, 73–74
normalization: crisis as part of everyday life, 42; role in crisis cultures, 15–16; Vigh's problematization of "normal" in chronic crisis, 19, 41
Nussbaum, Martha: crisis in humanities, 50; love for homeland, 110

Paine, Thomas, 40
pandemic measures: critique by Agamben, 85–87; state of exception and biosecurity, 85–87. *See also*

Agamben; COVID-19; state of exception

Papanikolaou, Dimitris: concept of Archive Trouble, 77–78; role in Greek cultural responses to crisis, 78

patriotism, 130; connection to Trump's support, 130–31

Peace of Westphalia, 19, 97

pedagogy of listening, 187–88

Pegida, 124

Petersen, Anne Helen, 23–24

Peterson, Jordan: critique of "wokeness" and identity politics, 48; critique of postmodernism, 47; cultural neo-Marxism critique, 48

phantasmatic space: concept by Agamben, 37

pharmakon: concept by Han, 64

philoxenia (φιλοξενία): Greek tradition of hospitality, 143–44; interaction with the concept of community, 144–45

Pickering, Michael: horizon as metaphor for experience, 34; temporal disjunction, 25, 28–29

Piketty, Thomas: *Capital in the Twenty-First Century*, critique of neoliberal regimes, 46; comparison with Pinker's view on modernity, 46

Pinker, Steven: defense of Enlightenment achievements, 46–47

poetry: Badiou on the unsaid, 80; Doukas and Erinakis, 80–81; Exploring crisis ambientality, 79–81; Kalfopoulou's themes of belonging, 79–80; Seferis and Greek symbolic imagery, 81. *See also* Doukas, Yiannis; Erinakis, Nikos; Greek Weird Wave; Kalfopoulou, Adrianne; Seferis, George

polarization, 12; as characteristic of crisis cultures, 71; LGBT+, 20, 170–81; as political theatre, 57; role in rise of SYRIZA and Golden Dawn, 72

political theater: crisis as spectacle, 57; role of polarization, 57

polycrisis, 3

populism: anti-elite rhetoric, 94, 129–30; emergence in crisis conditions, 71–73, 179; global examples (Trump, Bolsonaro, Milei, Meloni), 94; Make America Great Again, 11

Postcolonial theory, 106

postmodern(ism): crisis as a response to its conditions, 45–46, 49; crisis of grand narratives, 44; critique by Peterson, 47; critique by Tomaselli, 51; critique by Žižek, 12; critique of its influence on identity and ideology, 47; distinction from crisis cultures, 45–46; as an inherent crisis within modernism, 44; scholarship of, 11–12

post-truth era: influence on confabulation, 125

potentiality, Agamben's concept, 50

power: definition (Berardi), 15; information regime, 59–60

precarity, 42

pride parades: Žižek's critique, 159–61

progress, 29; skepticism towards linear progression, 46

protests: catalysts for political transformation, 57; Indian farmers, 57; motivations of young Catalans, 55; psychopolitics, concept by Han, 59; response to Catalan leaders' sentencing, 54

Przeworski, Adam: analysis of democratic stressors, 57, 64–66; commentary on polarization, 57

Puar, Jasbi K.; concept of homonationalism, 20, 173–77; homonationalism and identity politics, 153–54

QAnon, 13, 123

queer(ing): crisis, 20; identity, 144–49, 159–61; influence in crisis cultures,

150–54, 178–82; politics in contemporary Spain, 154, 170–82; as second skin, 150–51. *See also* homonationalism; identity politics; Puar

rage: Han's concept of, 127–28; role in historical and contemporary contexts, 127–28

Rancière, Jacques: normalization and politics of consensus, 15

referendum: Catalonia's 2017 referendum and consequences, 54; voice to parliament (Australia), 111–12

Renan, Ernest: national identity and selective memory, 100–101, 112–13, 118–19

Republican Party: influence of Donald Trump's rhetoric, 129–30, 135; responses to the Capitol insurrection, 134–35

retrotopias, 14

risk society, 8

Risorgimento (Italy), 103

Roitman, Janet: crisis as a "historico-philosophical concept," 14; crisis as a narrative device, 43; crisis as a persistent state, 5; critique of crisis as a "super concept," 42; critique of generalized usage of crisis, 41; questioning "what went wrong?" in crisis narratives, 11–12

Roma (people), 10

Rose, Jacqueline, 110

Rousseau, Jean-Jacques, 18, 26; *Emile* critique of society, 39; influence on American revolutionary thought, 40; nostalgic view of crisis, 40; notion of a chronic crisis condition, 39

Rumsfeld, Donald, 123–24

Russia: invasion of Ukraine, 7; protests against invasion of Ukraine, 57

Salade Grecque (Greek Salad), TV series, 76

same-sex marriage, 170, 172–73, 175

Sandel, Michael: critique of meritocracy, 40; meritocracy and post-war prosperity, 10

Sartre, Jean-Paul, 149

security: economic, 8, 10

Seferis, George, 81 *See also* crisis ambientality; poetry

self-alienation: Rousseau's perspective, 39

September 11 attacks, 10, 109

smartphones: mediation of crisis experiences, 58; role in crisis ambientality, 18–19, 58, 60–67. *See also* crisis ambientality; digital; virtualization of crisis

social acceleration, 25–26, 28, 30

Socialism: crisis as trigger for revolutionary change, 40

social media, 6; impact on national identity construction, 119–21, 133–34; role in commemorating historical events, 119

society of the spectacle: Debord's concept in relation to crisis ambientality, 60–61

sovereignty: evolution through historical crises, 97–99

space of experience, 33; definition of, 28–29; past and present interaction, 28–29; young Catalans' negotiation of future, 55

Spain, 2, 170–75; Catalan independence, 13, 104, 171, 174; Francoist suppression of regional identities, 104; LGBT+ activism, 169–78; polarization, 20; response to austerity measures, 56; Supreme Court verdict on Catalan leaders, 54

Spivak, Gayatri Chakravorty, 106

spread of conspiracy theories, 120; War on Terror, 10

state of exception: Agamben's concept, 70, 85–87; application during COVID-19 pandemic, 85–87. *See also* Agamben; COVID-19; pandemic measures

student experiences: impact of economic crises on student social interactions, 53
Surplus Rage, 3
surveillance, 23; role in everyday life under the information regime, 60. *See also* information regime; psychopolitics; smartphones
Sykes, Wanda, 15
SYRIZA, 57, 70–73, 81; anti-austerity stance, 70; ideological challenges and capitulation to austerity, 68–69; narrative struggle within Greek crisis, 81. *See also* austerity; Greece; polarization

technology: transformation, 25
temporality, 9, 18, 21, 25–26; in crisis cultures, 27–34; crisis reshaping temporal experience, 50–52 ; fragmentation, 28–29; history and futurity, 9, 14–16, 25; impact on narrative, 28; reconstruction of, 34; role in crisis cultures, 2, 25, 34. *See also* crisis cultures; experience; Koselleck; narrative(s)
tensions in crisis cultures, 21; history and futurity (temporality), 9, 14–16; hope and apprehension (emotion), 9–11; utopia and dystopia (narrative), 9, 11–14
theoxenia (θεοξενία): divine hospitality in Greek culture, 143
There is No Alternative (TINA), 10
time: acceleration of, 25; how crises change our experience of time, 52
time-space compression, 30
Tomaselli, Keyan G., 51
tradition(s): undermining of, 8
Trans-Exclusionary Radical Feminists (TERFs), 162
traveling concept, 26
Troika: role in Greek financial crisis, 69–70
Trump, Donald, 15; anti-establishment rhetoric, 129–31; challenge to 2020 election results, 133–35; engagement with conspiracy theories, 134; influence on Republican Party's ideological shift, 135; as symbol of anti-establishment, 94; use of digital platforms, 129–30

Ukraine, 7
United States: African Americans, 10; Capitol Hill insurrection, 7, 19, 96–97; September 11 attacks, 10, 109; Trump, Donald, 15; Unite the Right Rally, 120
Unite the Right rally, 120
utopias, 9, 11–14; Koselleck's interpretation, 39; role in motivating protest movements, 57; staging of, 188–89; utopian narratives as objects of hope, 12–13. *See also* crisis cultures; dystopia; modernity

Varoufakis, Yanis, 70
Vigh, Henrik: chronic crisis and its normalization, 41–42; concept of "crisis as context," 5, 41
violence: escalation in Catalan protests, 55; as a response to perceived injustices, 55
virtualization of crisis: shift from physical to digital, 59–61. *See also* digital; media; smartphones
virtue signaling, 157–58
Voltaire: catastrophe as norm, 32; interpretation of *Candide*, 32
Vox (political party), 174–78

War on Terror, 10
Weimar Republic, 101
welfare state, 7, 9. *See also* economic crisis; neoliberalism
Western modernity: crisis as a defining feature, 1, 7–8, 28; critique by classical and contemporary thinkers, 49
Wodak, Ruth, 15
wokeness, 48

working class: lived experience, 24
world values survey, 9
World War I, 6
World War II, 9

youth: economic instability and lack of opportunities, 56

Žižek, Slavoj: critique of postmodernism, 12; critique of pride parades, 159–61, 181; interpretation of "unknown knowns," 124; view on capitalism and crisis, 66. *See also* capitalism; identity politics; postmodernism

About the Author

Nicholas Manganas is a senior lecturer in International Studies and Global Societies at the University of Technology Sydney, where he also serves as the deputy head of the School of International Studies and Education. His first book *Las dos Españas: Terror and Crisis in Contemporary Spain* was published in 2016.

Milton Keynes UK
Ingram Content Group UK Ltd.
UKHW030046261024
450197UK00005B/20